Pro Git

■ ■ ■

Scott Chacon

Apress®

Pro Git

Copyright © 2009 by Scott Chacon

ISBN-13 (pbk): 978-1-4302-1833-3

ISBN-13 (electronic): 978-1-4302-1834-0

Printed and bound in the United States of America 9 8 7 6 5 4 3 2 1

Lead Editor: Duncan Parkes
Technical Reviewer: Shawn Pearce
Editorial Board: Clay Andres, Steve Anglin, Mark Beckner, Ewan Buckingham, Tony Campbell,
    Gary Cornell, Jonathan Gennick, Michelle Lowman, Matthew Moodie, Jeffrey Pepper,
    Frank Pohlmann, Ben Renow-Clarke, Dominic Shakeshaft, Matt Wade, Tom Welsh
Project Managers: Beth Christmas, Candace English
Copy Editor: Tiffany Taylor
Associate Production Director: Kari Brooks-Copony
Production Editor: Liz Berry
Compositor: Diana Van Winkle
Proofreader: Dan Shaw
Indexer: Julie Grady
Cover Designer: Anna Ishchenko
Manufacturing Director: Tom Debolski

Distributed to the book trade worldwide by Springer-Verlag New York, Inc., 233 Spring Street, 6th Floor, New York, NY 10013. Phone 1-800-SPRINGER, fax 201-348-4505, e-mail orders-ny@springer-sbm.com, or visit http://www.springeronline.com.

For information on translations, please contact Apress directly at 233 Spring Street, New York, New York, 10013, e-mail info@apress.com, or visit http://www.apress.com.

Apress and friends of ED books may be purchased in bulk for academic, corporate, or promotional use. eBook versions and licenses are also available for most titles. For more information, reference our Special Bulk Sales–eBook Licensing web page at http://www.apress.com/info/bulksales.

The source code for this book is available to readers at http://www.apress.com.

I would like to dedicate this, my first print book, to my little girl, Josephine, whose release date was nearly the same as this book's.

Contents at a Glance

Contents

Foreword

In April 2005, Linus Torvalds published the very first version of Git, the distributed version control system that is the topic of this book, and started managing the Linux kernel project with it.

Countless online pages have been written about Git by third parties since then, but many of them are unfortunately obsolete—not in the sense that the procedures they teach no longer work, but in the sense that there are better ways to do the same things more effectively with more modern versions of Git. The rate at which Git has undergone vast improvements both in capability and usability has been simply too rapid for those pages to keep up.

For a long time, the user manual and the documentation that came with Git were the only up-to-date and accurate sources of information, but they were primarily written by the people who built Git. The Git community sorely lacked good introductory material written from the perspective of the end user.

Enter Scott Chacon, the author of this book, who is also behind git-scm.com, the popular online resource that has become the default home site for Git documentation. In this latest book, Scott makes effective use of graphics to explain the key concepts and writes in plain and clear language to give a readable overview of how to work with Git.

After you gain a solid understanding from this book, I hope you will find yourself being more productive and using Git more effectively.

And, more important, I hope you will enjoy using Git.

Junio C Hamano
Git Project Leader

About the Author

SCOTT CHACON is a Git evangelist and Ruby developer employed at Logical Awesome, working on GitHub.com, the largest Git hosting web site. He is the author of the *Git Internals* Peepcode PDF in addition to maintaining the Git home page (git-scm.com) and the Git Community Book (book.git-scm.com). Scott has presented at conferences such as RailsConf, RubyConf, RubyKaigi, Scotland on Rails, and OSCon, as well as for companies such as Google, Yahoo, and Digg. Scott occasionally talks about Git for a number of local groups and has done corporate training on Git across the country.

About the Technical Reviewer

SHAWN PEARCE is the second in command of the Git project. He has been actively involved in the project since early 2006, contributing more than 1,300 changes in three years. Shawn is the author of git-gui, a Tk based graphical interface shipped with Git; and git-fast-import, a stream-based import system often used for converting projects to Git. In addition, Shawn's opinion, backed by his code, has influenced many key design decisions that form the modern Git implementation.

In early 2006, Shawn founded the JGit project, creating a 100% pure Java reimplementation of the Git version control system. The JGit library can often be found in Java-based products that interact with Git, including Git plug-ins for the popular Eclipse and NetBeans IDEs; the Hudson CI server; Apache Maven; and Gerrit Code Review, a peer code-review system specially designed for Git. Today he continues to develop and maintain JGit, EGit (the Eclipse plug-in based on top of it), and Gerrit Code Review.

Acknowledgments

First, I would like to thank the entire Git development community for giving us such a great tool. I dislike working in C and so have contributed little actual code to the Git project, opting instead to try to teach, document, and evangelize it, which I tend to be a lot better at. However, without the guys that wrote and maintain Git, I would still be living in the sad and hopeless version-controlled world that is Subversion.

I would also very much like to thank Shawn Pearce, who, aside from being one of the more prolific developers on the Git project, is also the technical editor for this book. Shawn has saved me from making countless horrible technical mistakes in this book and has done so on numerous other occasions as well. I always enjoy working with him; I tend to give my best guess at something, and then he teaches me what the right answer is. I have learned a ton from him, which I often get to teach to hundreds of others (who then give me credit).

I want to thank my good friend Nick Hengeveld, who has contributed a lot of work to Git and, more important for me, introduced me to the tool and taught me how to use it back in the pre-1.0 days. There is probably no way I would be doing all this if he had not brought Git to my attention and introduced it to the environment in which we both worked.

Further thanks go to Chris Wanstrath, Tom Preston-Werner, and PJ Hyett for inviting me to join them in working on GitHub very early on, allowing me to spend basically all my time thinking about and working on Git-related projects. It's difficult to imagine a better group of people to work with or a better job to have.

Last, I want to thank my wife, Jessica, who kept me continually working at this. Writing a book of this scope is a heck of a process, and when I stalled out from time to time, she made sure I got back on track. Thanks, Magoo.

Introduction

You're about to spend several hours of your life reading about Git. Let's take a minute to explain what we have in store for you. Here is a quick summary of this book's nine chapters:

In **Chapter 1**, you'll cover Version Control Systems (VCSs) and Git basics—no technical stuff, just what Git is, why it came about in a land full of VCSs, what sets it apart, and why so many people are using it. Then, you'll learn how to download Git and set it up for the first time if you don't already have it on your system.

In **Chapter 2**, you'll go over basic Git usage—how to use Git in the 80% of cases you'll encounter most often. After reading this chapter, you should be able to clone a repository, see what has happened in the history of the project, modify files, and contribute changes. If the book spontaneously combusts at this point, you should already be pretty useful wielding Git in the time it takes you to go pick up another copy.

Chapter 3 is about the branching model in Git, often described as Git's killer feature. Here, you'll learn what truly sets Git apart from the pack. When you're done, you may feel the need to spend a quiet moment pondering how you lived before Git branching was part of your life.

Chapter 4 will cover Git on the server. This chapter is for those of you who want to set up Git inside your organization or on your personal server for collaboration. You'll also explore various hosted options if you prefer to let someone else handle that for you.

Chapter 5 will go over in full detail various distributed workflows and how to accomplish them with Git. When you're done with this chapter, you should be able to work expertly with multiple remote repositories, use Git over e-mail, and deftly juggle numerous remote branches and contributed patches.

Chapter 6 is about advanced Git commands. You'll learn about topics like binary searching to identify bugs, editing history, revision selection in detail, and a lot more. This chapter will round out your knowledge of Git so that you're truly a master.

Chapter 7 is about configuring your custom Git environment. This includes setting up hook scripts to enforce or encourage customized policies and using environment configuration settings so you can work the way you want to. You'll also cover building your own set of scripts to enforce a custom committing policy.

Chapter 8 deals with Git and other VCSs. This includes using Git in a Subversion (SVN) world and converting projects from other VCSs to Git. A lot of organizations still use SVN and aren't about to change, but by this point you'll have learned the incredible power of Git—and this chapter will show you how to cope if you still have to use a SVN server. You'll also cover how to import projects from several different systems in case you do convince everyone to make the plunge.

Now that you know all about Git and can wield it with power and grace, you can move on to **Chapter 9**, which delves into the murky yet beautiful depths of Git internals. Here you'll learn how Git stores its objects, what the object model is, details of packfiles and server protocols, and more. Throughout, the book refers to sections of this chapter in case you feel like looking deeper at that point; but if you're like me and want to dive right into the technical details, you may want to read Chapter 9 first. I leave that up to you.

Let's get started.

■■■

## CHAPTER 1

Getting Started

This chapter is about getting started with Git. We'll begin at the beginning by presenting some background about n version-control tools, then move on to how you get Git running on your system, and finally explain how to set it up so you can start working with Git. At the end of this chapter, you should understand why Git exists and why you should use it, and you should be ready to do so.

About Version Control

What is version control, and why should you care? *Version control* is a system that records changes to a file or set of files over time so that you can recall specific versions later. For the examples in this book, you will use software source code as the files being version controlled, though in reality you can do this with nearly any type of file on a computer.

If you are a graphic or web designer and want to keep every version of an image or layout (which you would most certainly want to), a Version Control System (VCS) is a very wise thing to use. It allows you to revert files back to a previous state, revert the entire project back to a previous state, compare changes over time, see who last modified something that might be causing a problem, who introduced an issue and when, and more. Using a VCS also generally means that if you screw things up or lose files, you can easily recover. In addition, you get all this for very little overhead.

Local Version Control Systems

Many people's version-control method of choice is to copy files into another directory (perhaps a time-stamped directory, if they're clever). This approach is very common because it's so simple, but it's also incredibly error prone. It's easy to forget which directory you're in and accidentally write to the wrong file or copy over files when you don't mean to.

To deal with this issue, programmers long ago developed local VCSs that had a simple database that kept all the changes to files under revision control (see Figure 1-1).

One of the more popular VCS tools was a system called rcs, which is still distributed with many computers today. Even the popular Mac OS X operating system includes the rcs command when you install the Developer Tools. This tool basically works by keeping *patch sets* (that is, the differences between files) from one change to another in a special format on disk; it can then re-create what any file looked like at any point in time by adding up all the patches.

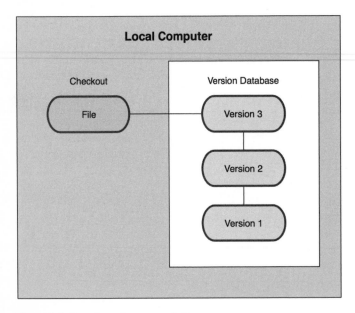

Figure 1-1. *Local version control diagram*

Centralized Version Control Systems

The next major issue that people encounter is that they need to collaborate with developers on other systems. To deal with this problem, Centralized Version Control Systems (CVCSs) were developed. These systems, such as CVS, Subversion, and Perforce, have a single server that contains all the versioned files, and a number of clients that check out files from that central place. For many years, this has been the standard for version control (see Figure 1-2).

This setup offers many advantages, especially over local VCSs. For example, everyone knows to a certain degree what everyone else on the project is doing. Administrators have fine-grained control over who can do what; and it's far easier to administer a CVCS than it is to deal with local databases on every client.

However, this setup also has some serious downsides. The most obvious is the single point of failure that the centralized server represents. If that server goes down for an hour, then during that hour nobody can collaborate at all or save versioned changes to anything they're working on. If the hard disk the central database is on becomes corrupted, and proper backups haven't been kept, you lose absolutely everything—the entire history of the project except whatever single snapshots people happen to have on their local machines. Local VCS systems suffer from this same problem—whenever you have the entire history of the project in a single place, you risk losing everything.

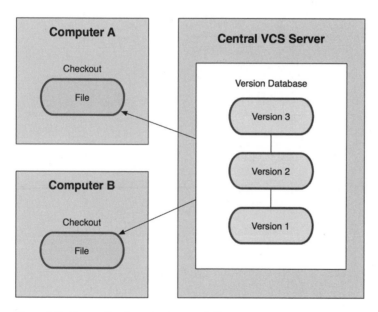

Figure 1-2. *Centralized version control diagram*

Distributed Version Control Systems

This is where Distributed Version Control Systems (DVCSs) step in. In a DVCS (such as Git, Mercurial, Bazaar, or Darcs), clients don't just check out the latest snapshot of the files: they fully mirror the repository. Thus if any server dies, and these systems were collaborating via it, any of the client repositories can be copied back up to the server to restore it. Every *checkout* is really a full backup of all the data (see Figure 1-3).

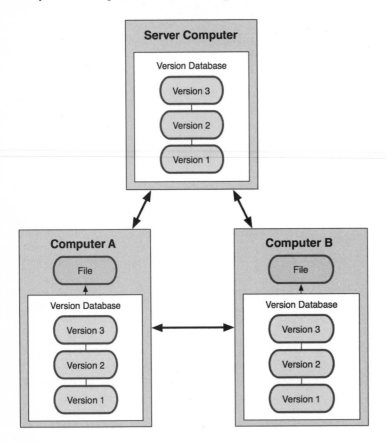

Figure 1-3. *Distributed version control diagram*

Furthermore, many of these systems deal pretty well with having several remote repositories they can work with, so you can collaborate with different groups of people in different ways simultaneously within the same project. This allows you to set up several types of workflows that aren't possible in centralized systems, such as hierarchical models.

A Short History of Git

As with many great things in life, Git began with a bit of creative destruction and fiery controversy. The Linux kernel is an open source software project of fairly large scope. For most of the lifetime of the Linux kernel maintenance (1991–2002), changes to the software were passed around as patches and archived files. In 2002, the Linux kernel project began using a proprietary DVCS system called BitKeeper.

In 2005, the relationship between the community that developed the Linux kernel and the commercial company that developed BitKeeper broke down, and the tool's free-of-charge status was revoked. This prompted the Linux development community (and in particular Linus Torvalds, the creator of Linux) to develop their own tool based on some of the lessons they learned while using BitKeeper. Some of the goals of the new system were as follows:

- Speed

- Simple design

- Strong support for non-linear development (thousands of parallel branches)

- Fully distributed

- Ability to handle large projects like the Linux kernel efficiently (speed and data size)

Since its birth in 2005, Git has evolved and matured to be easy to use and yet retain these initial qualities. It's incredibly fast, it's very efficient with large projects, and it has an incredible branching system for non-linear development (See Chapter 3).

Git Basics

So, what is Git in a nutshell? This is an important section to absorb, because if you understand what Git is and the fundamentals of how it works, then using Git effectively will probably be much easier for you. As you learn Git, try to clear your mind of the things you may know about other VCSs, such as Subversion and Perforce; doing so will help you avoid subtle confusion when using the tool. Git stores and thinks about information much differently than these other systems, even though the user interface is fairly similar; understanding those differences will help prevent you from becoming confused while using it.

Snapshots, Not Differences

The major difference between Git and any other VCS (Subversion and friends included) is the way Git thinks about its data. Conceptually, most other systems store information as a list of file-based changes. These systems (CVS, Subversion, Perforce, Bazaar, and so on) think of the information they keep as a set of files and the changes made to each file over time, as illustrated in Figure 1-4.

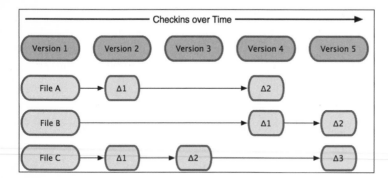

Figure 1-4. *Other systems tend to store data as changes to a base version of each file.*

Git doesn't think of or store its data this way. Instead, Git thinks of its data more like a set of snapshots of a mini filesystem. Every time you *commit*, or save the state of your project in Git, it basically takes a picture of what all your files look like at that moment and stores a reference to that snapshot. To be efficient, if files have not changed, Git doesn't store the file again—just a link to the previous identical file it has already stored. Git thinks about its data more like Figure 1-5.

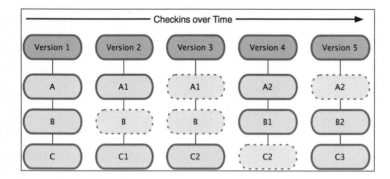

Figure 1-5. *Git stores data as snapshots of the project over time.*

This is an important distinction between Git and nearly all other VCSs. It makes Git reconsider almost every aspect of version control that most other systems copied from the previous generation. This makes Git more like a mini filesystem with some incredibly powerful tools built on top of it, rather than simply a VCS. We'll explore some of the benefits you gain by thinking of your data this way when we cover Git branching in Chapter 3.

Nearly Every Operation Is Local

Most operations in Git only need local files and resources to operate—generally, no information is needed from another computer on your network. If you're used to a CVCS where most operations have that network latency overhead, this aspect of Git will make you think that the gods of speed have blessed Git with unworldly powers. Because you have the entire history of the project right there on your local disk, most operations seem almost instantaneous.

For example, to browse the history of the project, Git doesn't need to go out to the server to get the history and display it for you—it simply reads it directly from your local database. This means you see the project history almost instantly. If you want to see the changes introduced between the current version of a file and the file a month ago, Git can look up the file from a month ago and do a local difference calculation, instead of having to either ask a remote server to do it or pull an older version of the file from the remote server to do it locally.

This also means that there is very little you can't do if you're offline or off VPN. If you get on an airplane or a train and want to do a little work, you can commit happily until you get to a network connection to upload. If you go home and can't get your VPN client working properly, you can still work. In many other systems, doing so is either impossible or painful. In Perforce, for example, you can't do much when you aren't connected to the server; and in Subversion and CVS, you can edit files, but you can't commit changes to your database (because your database is offline). This may not seem like a huge deal, but you may be surprised what a big difference it can make.

Git Has Integrity

Everything in Git is check-summed before it is stored and is then referred to by that checksum. This means it's impossible to change the contents of any file or directory without Git knowing about it. This functionality is built into Git at the lowest levels and is integral to its philosophy. You can't lose information in transit or get file corruption without Git being able to detect it.

The mechanism that Git uses for this check-summing is called a *SHA-1 hash*. This is a 40-character string composed of hexadecimal characters (0–9 and a–f) and calculated based on the contents of a file or directory structure in Git. A SHA-1 hash looks something like this:

```
24b9da6552252987aa493b52f8696cd6d3b00373
```

You'll see these hash values all over the place in Git because it uses them so much. In fact, Git stores everything not by file name but in the Git database addressable by the hash value of its contents.

Git Generally Only Adds Data

When you do actions in Git, nearly all of them only *add* data to the Git database. It is difficult to get the system to do anything that is undoable or to make it erase data. As in any VCS, you can lose or mess up changes you haven't committed yet; but after you commit a snapshot into Git, it is very difficult to lose, especially if you regularly push your database to another repository.

This makes using Git a joy because you know you can experiment without the danger of severely screwing things up. For a more in-depth look at how Git stores its data and how you can recover data that seems lost, see "Under the Covers" in Chapter 9.

The Three States

Now, pay attention. This is the main thing to remember about Git if you want the rest of your learning process to go smoothly. Git has three main states that your files can reside in: *committed*, *modified*, and *staged*. *Committed* means that the data is safely stored in your local database. *Modified* means that you have changed the file but have not committed it to your database yet. *Staged* means that you have marked a modified file in its current version to go into your next commit snapshot.

This leads us to the three main sections of a Git project: the Git *directory*, *the working directory*, and the *staging area* (see Figure 1-6).

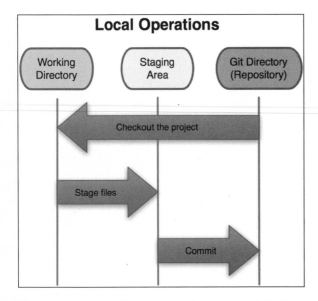

Figure 1-6. *Working directory, staging area, and Git directory*

The Git *directory* is where Git stores the metadata and object database for your project. This is the most important part of Git, and it is what is copied when you clone a repository from another computer.

The *working directory* is a single checkout of one version of the project. These files are pulled out of the compressed database in the Git directory and placed on disk for you to use or modify.

The *staging area* is a simple file, generally contained in your Git directory, that stores information about what will go into your next commit. It's sometimes referred to as the *index*, but it's becoming standard to refer to it as the staging area.

The basic Git workflow goes something like this:

1. You modify files in your working directory.

2. You stage the files, adding snapshots of them to your staging area.

3. You do a commit, which takes the files as they are in the staging area and stores that snapshot permanently to your Git directory.

If a particular version of a file is in the Git directory, it's considered *committed*. If it's modified but has been added to the staging area, it is *staged*. And if it was changed since it was checked out but has not been staged, it is *modified*. In Chapter 2, you'll learn more about these states and how you can either take advantage of them or skip the staged part entirely.

Installing Git

Let's get into using some Git. First things first—you have to install it. You can get it a number of ways; the two major ones are to install it from source or to install an existing package for your platform.

Installing from Source

If you can, it's generally useful to install Git from source, because you'll get the most recent version. Each version of Git tends to include useful UI enhancements, so getting the latest version is often the best route if you feel comfortable compiling software from source. It's also the case that many Linux distributions contain old packages; so unless you're on a very up-to-date distribution or are using backports, installing from source may be the best bet.

To install Git, you need to have the following libraries that Git depends on: curl, zlib, openssl, expat, and libiconv. For example, if you're on a system that has yum (such as Fedora) or apt-get (such as a Debian-based system), you can use one of these commands to install all of the dependencies:

```
$ yum install curl-devel expat-devel gettext-devel \
  openssl-devel zlib-devel

$ apt-get install curl-devel expat-devel gettext-devel \
  openssl-devel zlib-devel
```

When you have all the necessary dependencies, you can go ahead and grab the latest snapshot from the Git web site:

```
http://git-scm.com/download
```

Then, compile and install:

```
$ tar -zxf git-1.6.0.5.tar.gz
$ cd git-1.6.0.5
$ make prefix=/usr/local all
$ sudo make prefix=/usr/local install
```

After this is done, you can also get Git via Git itself for updates:

```
$ git clone git://git.kernel.org/pub/scm/git/git.git
```

Installing on Linux

If you want to install Git on Linux via a binary installer, you can generally do so through the basic package-management tool that comes with your distribution. If you're on Fedora, you can use yum:

```
$ yum install git-core
```

Or if you're on a Debian-based distribution like Ubuntu, try apt-get:

```
$ apt-get install git-core
```

Installing on Mac

There are two easy ways to install Git on a Mac. The easiest is to use the graphical Git installer, which you can download from the Google Code page (see Figure 1-7):

```
http://code.google.com/p/git-osx-installer
```

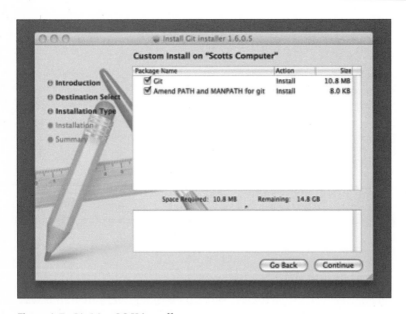

Figure 1-7. *Git Mac OS X installer*

The other major way is to install Git via MacPorts (http://www.macports.org). If you have MacPorts installed, install Git via

```
$ sudo port install git-core +svn +doc +bash_completion +gitweb
```

You don't have to add all the extras, but you'll probably want to include +svn in case you ever have to use Git with Subversion repositories (see Chapter 8).

Installing on Windows

Installing Git on Windows is very easy. The msysGit project has one of the easier installation procedures. Simply download the installer exe file from the Google Code page, and run it:

```
http://code.google.com/p/msysgit
```

After it's installed, you have both a command-line version (including an SSH client that will come in handy later) and the standard GUI.

First-Time Git Setup

Now that you have Git on your system, you'll want to do a few things to customize your Git environment. You should have to do these things only once; they'll stick around between upgrades. You can also change them at any time by running through the commands again.

Git comes with a tool called `git config` that lets you get and set configuration variables that control all aspects of how Git looks and operates. These variables can be stored in three different places:

- `/etc/gitconfig` *file*: Contains values for every user on the system and all their repositories. If you pass the option `--system` to `git config`, it reads and writes from this file specifically.

- `~/.gitconfig` *file*: Specific to your user. You can make Git read and write to this file specifically by passing the `--global` option.

- `config` *file in the* `git` *directory (that is,* `.git/config`) *of whatever repository you're currently using*: Specific to that single repository. Each level overrides values in the previous level, so values in `.git/config` trump those in `/etc/gitconfig`.

On Windows systems, Git looks for the `.gitconfig` file in the `$HOME` directory (`C:\Documents and Settings\$USER` for most people). It also still looks for `/etc/gitconfig`, although it's relative to the `MSys` root, which is wherever you decide to install Git on your Windows system when you run the installer.

Your Identity

The first thing you should do when you install Git is to set your username and e-mail address. This is important because every Git commit uses this information, and it's immutably baked into the commits you pass around:

```
$ git config --global user.name "John Doe"
$ git config --global user.email johndoe@example.com
```

Again, you need to do this only once if you pass the `--global` option, because then Git will always use that information for anything you do on that system. If you want to override this with a different name or e-mail address for specific projects, you can run the command without the `--global` option when you're in that project.

Your Editor

Now that your identity is set up, you can configure the default text editor that will be used when Git needs you to type in a message. By default, Git uses your system's default editor, which is generally Vi or Vim. If you want to use a different text editor, such as Emacs, you can do the following:

```
$ git config --global core.editor emacs
```

Your Diff Tool

Another useful option you may want to configure is the default diff tool to use to resolve merge conflicts. Say you want to use vimdiff:

```
$ git config --global merge.tool vimdiff
```

Git accepts kdiff3, tkdiff, meld, xxdiff, emerge, vimdiff, gvimdiff, ecmerge, and opendiff as valid merge tools. You can also set up a custom tool; see Chapter 7 for more information about doing that.

Checking Your Settings

If you want to check your settings, you can use the `git config --list` command to list all the settings Git can find at that point:

```
$ git config --list
user.name=Scott Chacon
user.email=schacon@gmail.com
color.status=auto
color.branch=auto
color.interactive=auto
color.diff=auto
...
```

You may see keys more than once, because Git reads the same key from different files (/etc/gitconfig and ~/.gitconfig, for example). In this case, Git uses the last value for each unique key it sees.

You can also check what Git thinks a specific key's value is by typing `git config {key}`:

```
$ git config user.name
Scott Chacon
```

Getting Help

If you ever need help while using Git, there are three ways to get the manual page (manpage) help for any of the Git commands:

```
$ git help <verb>
$ git <verb> --help
$ man git-<verb>
```

For example, you can get the manpage help for the config command by running

```
$ git help config
```

These commands are nice because you can access them anywhere, even offline.

If the manpages and this book aren't enough and you need in-person help, you can try the #git or #github channel on the Freenode IRC server (irc.freenode.net). These channels are regularly filled with hundreds of people who are all very knowledgeable about Git and are often willing to help.

Summary

You should now have a basic understanding of what Git is and how it's different from the CVCS you may have been using. You should also now have a working version of Git on your system that's set up with your personal identity. It's now time to learn some Git basics.

CHAPTER 2

■ ■ ■

Git Basics

If you can read only one chapter to get going with Git, this is it. This chapter covers every basic command you need to do the vast majority of the things you'll eventually spend your time doing with Git. By the end of the chapter, you should be able to configure and initialize a repository, begin and stop tracking files, and stage and commit changes. I'll also show you how to set up Git to ignore certain files and file patterns, how to undo mistakes quickly and easily, how to browse the history of your project and view changes between commits, and how to push and pull from remote repositories.

Getting a Git Repository

You can get a Git project using two main approaches. The first takes an existing project or directory and imports it into Git. The second clones an existing Git repository from another server.

Initializing a Repository in an Existing Directory

If you're starting to track an existing project in Git, you need to go to the project's directory and type

```
$ git init
```

This command creates a new subdirectory named .git that contains all of your necessary repository files—a Git repository skeleton. At this point, nothing in your project is tracked yet. (See Chapter 9 for more information about exactly what files are contained in the .git directory you just created.)

If you want to start version-controlling existing files (as opposed to an empty directory), you should probably begin tracking those files and do an initial commit. You can accomplish that with a few git add commands that specify the files you want to track, followed by a commit:

```
$ git add *.c
$ git add README
$ git commit -m 'initial project version'
```

I'll go over what these commands do in just a minute. At this point, you have a Git repository with tracked files and an initial commit.

Cloning an Existing Repository

If you want to get a copy of an existing Git repository—for example, a project you'd like to contribute to—the command you need is git clone. If you're familiar with other VCS systems such as Subversion, you'll notice that the command is clone and not checkout. This is an important distinction—Git receives a copy of nearly all data that the server has. Every version of every file for the history of the project is pulled down when you run git clone. In fact, if your server disk gets corrupted, you can use any of the clones on any client to set the server back to the state it was in when it was cloned (you may lose some server-side hooks and such, but all the versioned data would be there—see Chapter 4 for more details).

You clone a repository with git clone [url]. For example, if you want to clone the Ruby Git library called Grit, you can do so like this:

```
$ git clone git://github.com/schacon/grit.git
```

That creates a directory named grit, initializes a .git directory inside it, pulls down all the data for that repository, and checks out a working copy of the latest version. If you go into the new grit directory, you'll see the project files in there, ready to be worked on or used. If you want to clone the repository into a directory named something other than grit, you can specify that as the next command-line option:

```
$ git clone git://github.com/schacon/grit.git mygrit
```

This command does the same thing as the previous one, but the target directory is called mygrit.

Git has a number of different transfer protocols you can use. The previous example uses the git:// protocol, but you may also see http(s):// or user@server:/path.git, which uses the SSH transfer protocol. Chapter 4 will introduce all of the available options the server can set up to access your Git repository and the pros and cons of each.

Recording Changes to the Repository

You have a bona fide Git repository and a checkout or *working copy* of the files for that project. You need to make some changes and commit snapshots of those changes into your repository each time the project reaches a state you want to record.

Remember that each file in your working directory can be in one of two states: *tracked* or *untracked*. Tracked files are files that were in the last snapshot; they can be unmodified, modified, or staged. Untracked files are everything else—any files in your working directory that weren't in your last snapshot and aren't in your staging area. When you first clone a repository, all of your files will be tracked and unmodified because you just checked them out and haven't edited anything.

As you edit files, Git sees them as modified, because you've changed them since your last commit. You stage these modified files and then commit all your staged changes, and the cycle repeats. This lifecycle is illustrated in Figure 2-1.

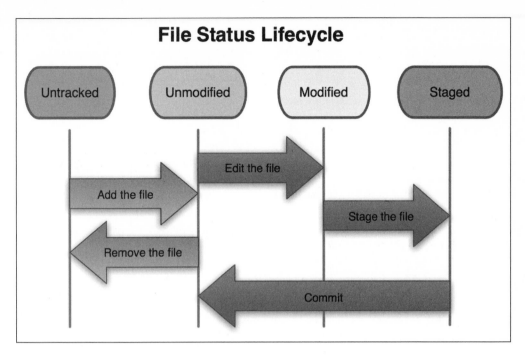

Fig 2-1. *The lifecycle of the status of your files*

Checking the Status of Your Files

The main tool you use to determine which files are in which state is the `git status` command. If you run this command directly after a clone, you should see something like this:

```
$ git status
# On branch master
nothing to commit (working directory clean)
```

This means you have a clean working directory—in other words, there are no tracked and modified files. Git also doesn't see any untracked files, or they would be listed here. Finally, the command tells you which branch you're on. For now, that is always master, which is the default; you won't worry about it here. The next chapter will go over branches and references in detail.

Let's say you add a new file to your project, a simple README file. If the file didn't exist before, and you run `git status`, you see your untracked file like so:

```
$ vim README
$ git status
# On branch master
# Untracked files:
#   (use "git add <file>..." to include in what will be committed)
#
#     README
nothing added to commit but untracked files present (use "git add" to track)
```

You can see that your new README file is untracked, because it's under the "Untracked files" heading in your status output. *Untracked* basically means that Git sees a file you didn't have in the previous snapshot (commit); Git won't start including it in your commit snapshots until you explicitly tell it to do so. It does this so you don't accidentally begin including generated binary files or other files that you didn't mean to include. You do want to start including the README file, so let's start tracking the file.

Tracking New Files

In order to begin tracking a new file, you use the command git add. To begin tracking the README file, you can run this:

```
$ git add README
```

If you run the status command again, you can see that your README file is now tracked and staged:

```
$ git status
# On branch master
# Changes to be committed:
#   (use "git reset HEAD <file>..." to unstage)
#
#      new file:   README
#
```

You can tell that it's staged because it's under the "Changes to be committed" heading. If you commit at this point, the version of the file at the time you ran git add is what will be in the historical snapshot. You may recall that when you ran git init earlier, you then ran git add (files)—that was to begin tracking files in your directory. The git add command takes a path name for either a file or a directory; if it's a directory, the command adds all the files in that directory recursively.

Staging Modified Files

Let's change a file that was already tracked. If you change a previously tracked file called benchmarks.rb and then run the status command again, you get something that looks like this:

```
$ git status
# On branch master
# Changes to be committed:
#   (use "git reset HEAD <file>..." to unstage)
#
#      new file:   README
#
# Changed but not updated:
#   (use "git add <file>..." to update what will be committed)
#
#      modified:   benchmarks.rb
#
```

The `benchmarks.rb` file appears under a section named "Changed but not updated"—which means that a file that is tracked has been modified in the working directory but not yet staged. To stage it, you run the `git add` command (it's a multipurpose command—you use it to begin tracking new files, to stage files, and to do other things like marking merge-conflicted files as resolved). Let's run `git add` now to stage the `benchmarks.rb` file, and then run `git status` again:

```
$ git add benchmarks.rb
$ git status
# On branch master
# Changes to be committed:
#   (use "git reset HEAD <file>..." to unstage)
#
#     new file:   README
#     modified:   benchmarks.rb
#
```

Both files are staged and will go into your next commit. At this point, suppose you remember one little change that you want to make in `benchmarks.rb` before you commit it. You open it again and make that change, and you're ready to commit. However, let's run `git status` one more time:

```
$ vim benchmarks.rb
$ git status
# On branch master
# Changes to be committed:
#   (use "git reset HEAD <file>..." to unstage)
#
#     new file:   README
#     modified:   benchmarks.rb
#
# Changed but not updated:
#   (use "git add <file>..." to update what will be committed)
#
#     modified:   benchmarks.rb
#
```

What the heck? Now `benchmarks.rb` is listed as both staged and unstaged. How is that possible? It turns out that Git stages a file exactly as it is when you run the `git add` command. If you commit now, the version of `benchmarks.rb` as it was when you last ran the `git add` command is how it will go into the commit, not the version of the file as it looks in your working directory when you run `git commit`. If you modify a file after you run `git add`, you have to run `git add` again to stage the latest version of the file:

```
$ git add benchmarks.rb
$ git status
# On branch master
# Changes to be committed:
#   (use "git reset HEAD <file>..." to unstage)
#
```

```
#       new file:   README
#       modified:   benchmarks.rb
#
```

Ignoring Files

Often, you'll have a class of files that you don't want Git to automatically add or even show you as being untracked. These are generally automatically generated files such as log files or files produced by your build system. In such cases, you can create a file named .gitignore listing patterns to match them. Here is an example .gitignore file:

```
$ cat .gitignore
*.[oa]
*~
```

The first line tells Git to ignore any files ending in .o or .a—object and archive files that may be the product of building your code. The second line tells Git to ignore all files that end with a tilde (~), which is used by many text editors, such as Emacs, to mark temporary files. You may also include a log, tmp, or pid directory; automatically generated documentation; and so on. Setting up a .gitignore file before you get going is generally a good idea so you don't accidentally commit files that you really don't want in your Git repository.

The rules for the patterns you can put in the .gitignore file are as follows:

- Blank lines or lines starting with # are ignored.

- Standard glob patterns work.

- You can end patterns with a forward slash (/) to specify a directory.

- You can negate a pattern by starting it with an exclamation point (!).

Glob patterns are like simplified regular expressions that shells use. An asterisk (*) matches zero or more characters; [abc] matches any character inside the brackets (in this case *a*, *b*, or *c*); a question mark (?) matches a single character; and brackets enclosing characters separated by a hyphen ([0-9]) matches any character between them (in this case, 0 through 9).

Here is another example .gitignore file:

```
# a comment - this is ignored
*.a        # no .a files
!lib.a     # but do track lib.a, even though you're ignoring .a files above
/TODO      # only ignore the root TODO file, not subdir/TODO
build/     # ignore all files in the build/ directory
doc/*.txt  # ignore doc/notes.txt, but not doc/server/arch.txt
```

Viewing Your Staged and Unstaged Changes

If the git status command is too vague for you—you want to know exactly what you changed, not just which files were changed—you can use the git diff command. I'll cover git diff in more detail later; but you'll probably use it most often to answer these two questions: What have you changed but not yet staged? And what have you staged that you are about to commit? Although git status answers those questions very generally, git diff shows you the exact lines added and removed—the patch, as it were.

Let's say you edit and stage the README file again and then edit the benchmarks.rb file without staging it. If you run your status command, you once again see something like this:

```
$ git status
# On branch master
# Changes to be committed:
#   (use "git reset HEAD <file>..." to unstage)
#
#       new file:   README
#
# Changed but not updated:
#   (use "git add <file>..." to update what will be committed)
#
#       modified:   benchmarks.rb
#
```

To see what you've changed but not yet staged, type git diff with no other arguments:

```
$ git diff
diff --git a/benchmarks.rb b/benchmarks.rb
index 3cb747f..da65585 100644
--- a/benchmarks.rb
+++ b/benchmarks.rb
@@ -36,6 +36,10 @@ def main
            @commit.parents[0].parents[0].parents[0]
          end

+          run_code(x, 'commits 1') do
+            git.commits.size
+          end
+
          run_code(x, 'commits 2') do
            log = git.commits('master', 15)
            log.size
```

That command compares what is in your working directory with what is in your staging area. The result tells you the changes you've made that you haven't yet staged.

If you want to see what you've staged that will go into your next commit, you can use git diff --cached. (In Git versions 1.6.1 and later, you can also use git diff --staged, which may be easier to remember.) This command compares your staged changes to your last commit:

```
$ git diff --cached
diff --git a/README b/README
new file mode 100644
index 0000000..03902a1
--- /dev/null
+++ b/README2
@@ -0,0 +1,5 @@
+grit
+ by Tom Preston-Werner, Chris Wanstrath
```

```
+ http://github.com/mojombo/grit
+
+Grit is a Ruby library for extracting information from a Git repository
```

It's important to note that git diff by itself doesn't show all changes made since your last commit—only changes that are still unstaged. This can be confusing, because if you've staged all of your changes, git diff gives you no output.

For another example, if you stage the benchmarks.rb file and then edit it, you can use git diff to see the changes in the file that are staged and the changes that are unstaged:

```
$ git add benchmarks.rb
$ echo '# test line' >> benchmarks.rb
$ git status
# On branch master
#
# Changes to be committed:
#
#       modified:   benchmarks.rb
#
# Changed but not updated:
#
#       modified:   benchmarks.rb
#
```

Now you can use git diff to see what is still unstaged:

```
$ git diff
diff --git a/benchmarks.rb b/benchmarks.rb
index e445e28..86b2f7c 100644
--- a/benchmarks.rb
+++ b/benchmarks.rb
@@ -127,3 +127,4 @@ end
 main()

 ##pp Grit::GitRuby.cache_client.stats
+# test line
```

You can use git diff --cached to see what you've staged so far:

```
$ git diff --cached
diff --git a/benchmarks.rb b/benchmarks.rb
index 3cb747f..e445e28 100644
--- a/benchmarks.rb
+++ b/benchmarks.rb
@@ -36,6 +36,10 @@ def main
          @commit.parents[0].parents[0].parents[0]
        end

+        run_code(x, 'commits 1') do
+          git.commits.size
```

```
+        end
+
         run_code(x, 'commits 2') do
           log = git.commits('master', 15)
           log.size
```

Committing Your Changes

Now that your staging area is set up the way you want it, you can commit your changes. Remember that anything that is still unstaged—any files you have created or modified that you haven't run git add on since you edited them—won't go into this commit. They will stay as modified files on your disk.

In this case, the last time you ran git status, you saw that everything was staged, so you're ready to commit your changes. The simplest way to commit is to type git commit:

```
$ git commit
```

Doing so launches your editor of choice. (This is set by your shell's $EDITOR environment variable—usually vim or emacs, although you can configure it with whatever you want using the git config --global core.editor command, as you saw in Chapter 1.)

The editor displays the following text (this example is a Vim screen):

```
# Please enter the commit message for your changes. Lines starting
# with '#' will be ignored, and an empty message aborts the commit.
# On branch master
# Changes to be committed:
#   (use "git reset HEAD <file>..." to unstage)
#
#       new file:   README
#       modified:   benchmarks.rb
~
~
~
".git/COMMIT_EDITMSG" 10L, 283C
```

You can see that the default commit message contains the latest output of the git status command commented out and one empty line on top. You can remove these comments and type your commit message, or you can leave them there to help you remember what you're committing. (For an even more explicit reminder of what you've modified, you can pass the -v option to git commit. Doing so also puts the diff of your change in the editor so you can see exactly what you did.) When you exit the editor, Git creates your commit with that commit message (with the comments and diff stripped out).

Alternatively, you can type your commit message inline with the commit command by specifying it after a -m flag, like this:

```
$ git commit -m "Story 182: Fix benchmarks for speed"
[master]: created 463dc4f: "Fix benchmarks for speed"
 2 files changed, 3 insertions(+), 0 deletions(-)
 create mode 100644 README
```

Now you've created your first commit! The commit has given you some output about itself: which branch you committed to (master), what SHA-1 checksum the commit has (463dc4f), how many files were changed, and statistics about lines added and removed in the commit.

Remember that the commit records the snapshot you set up in your staging area. Anything you didn't stage is still sitting there modified; you can do another commit to add it to your history. Every time you perform a commit, you're recording a snapshot of your project that you can revert to or compare to later.

Skipping the Staging Area

Although it can be amazingly useful for crafting commits exactly how you want them, the staging area is sometimes a bit more complex than you need in your workflow. If you want to skip the staging area, Git provides a simple shortcut. Providing the -a option to the git commit command makes Git automatically stage every file that is already tracked before doing the commit, letting you skip the git add part:

```
$ git status
# On branch master
#
# Changed but not updated:
#
#     modified:   benchmarks.rb
#
$ git commit -a -m 'added new benchmarks'
[master 83e38c7] added new benchmarks
 1 files changed, 5 insertions(+), 0 deletions(-)
```

Notice how you don't have to run git add on the benchmarks.rb file in this case before you commit.

Removing Files

To remove a file from Git, you have to remove it from your tracked files (more accurately, remove it from your staging area) and then commit. The git rm command does that and also removes the file from your working directory so you don't see it as an untracked file next time around.

If you simply remove the file from your working directory, it shows up under the "Changed but not updated" (that is, unstaged) area of your git status output:

```
$ rm grit.gemspec
$ git status
# On branch master
#
# Changed but not updated:
#   (use "git add/rm <file>..." to update what will be committed)
#
#     deleted:    grit.gemspec
#
```

Then, if you run git rm, it stages the file's removal:

```
$ git rm grit.gemspec
rm 'grit.gemspec'
$ git status
# On branch master
#
# Changes to be committed:
#   (use "git reset HEAD <file>..." to unstage)
#
#       deleted:    grit.gemspec
#
```

The next time you commit, the file will be gone and no longer tracked. If you modified the file and added it to the index already, you must force the removal with the -f option. This is a safety feature to prevent accidental removal of data that hasn't yet been recorded in a snapshot and that can't be recovered from Git.

Another useful thing you may want to do is to keep the file in your working tree but remove it from your staging area. In other words, you may want to keep the file on your hard drive but not have Git track it anymore. This is particularly useful if you forgot to add something to your .gitignore file and accidentally added it, like a large log file or a bunch of .a compiled files. To do this, use the --cached option:

```
$ git rm --cached readme.txt
```

You can pass files, directories, and file-glob patterns to the git rm command. That means you can do things such as

```
$ git rm log/\*.log
```

Note the backslash (\) in front of the *. This is necessary because Git does its own filename expansion in addition to your shell's filename expansion. This command removes all files that have the .log extension in the log/ directory. Or, you can do something like this:

```
$ git rm \*~
```

This command removes all files that end with ~.

Moving Files

Unlike many other VCS systems, Git doesn't explicitly track file movement. If you rename a file in Git, no metadata is stored in Git that tells it you renamed the file. However, Git is pretty smart about figuring that out after the fact—you'll deal with detecting file movement a bit later.

Thus it's a bit confusing that Git has a mv command. If you want to rename a file in Git, you can run something like

```
$ git mv file_from file_to
```

and it works fine. In fact, if you run something like this and look at the status, you'll see that Git considers it a renamed file:

```
$ git mv README.txt README
$ git status
# On branch master
# Your branch is ahead of 'origin/master' by 1 commit.
#
# Changes to be committed:
#   (use "git reset HEAD <file>..." to unstage)
#
#       renamed:    README.txt -> README
#
```

However, this is equivalent to running something like this:

```
$ mv README.txt README
$ git rm README.txt
$ git add README
```

Git figures out that it's a rename implicitly, so it doesn't matter if you rename a file that way or with the mv command. The only real difference is that mv is one command instead of three—it's a convenience function. More important, you can use any tool you like to rename a file, and address the add/rm later, before you commit.

Viewing the Commit History

After you have created several commits, or if you have cloned a repository with an existing commit history, you'll probably want to look back to see what has happened. The most basic and powerful tool to do this is the git log command.

These examples use a very simple project called simplegit that I often use for demonstrations. To get the project, run

```
git clone git://github.com/schacon/simplegit-progit.git
```

When you run git log in this project, you should get output that looks something like this:

```
$ git log
commit ca82a6dff817ec66f44342007202690a93763949
Author: Scott Chacon <schacon@gee-mail.com>
Date:   Mon Mar 17 21:52:11 2008 -0700

    changed the version number

commit 085bb3bcb608e1e8451d4b2432f8ecbe6306e7e7
Author: Scott Chacon <schacon@gee-mail.com>
Date:   Sat Mar 15 16:40:33 2008 -0700

    removed unnecessary test code
```

```
commit a11bef06a3f659402fe7563abf99ad00de2209e6
Author: Scott Chacon <schacon@gee-mail.com>
Date:    Sat Mar 15 10:31:28 2008 -0700

    first commit
```

By default, with no arguments, git log lists the commits made in that repository in reverse chronological order. That is, the most recent commits show up first. As you can see, this command lists each commit with its SHA-1 checksum, the author's name and e-mail, the date written, and the commit message.

A huge number and variety of options to the git log command are available to show you exactly what you're looking for. Here, I'll show you some of the most-used options.

One of the more helpful options is -p, which shows the diff introduced in each commit. You can also use -2, which limits the output to only the last two entries:

```
$ git log -p -2
commit ca82a6dff817ec66f44342007202690a93763949
Author: Scott Chacon <schacon@gee-mail.com>
Date:    Mon Mar 17 21:52:11 2008 -0700

    changed the version number

diff --git a/Rakefile b/Rakefile
index a874b73..8f94139 100644
--- a/Rakefile
+++ b/Rakefile
@@ -5,7 +5,7 @@ require 'rake/gempackagetask'
 spec = Gem::Specification.new do |s|
-    s.version     =    "0.1.0"
+    s.version     =    "0.1.1"
     s.author      =    "Scott Chacon"

commit 085bb3bcb608e1e8451d4b2432f8ecbe6306e7e7
Author: Scott Chacon <schacon@gee-mail.com>
Date:    Sat Mar 15 16:40:33 2008 -0700

    removed unnecessary test code

diff --git a/lib/simplegit.rb b/lib/simplegit.rb
index a0a60ae..47c6340 100644
--- a/lib/simplegit.rb
+++ b/lib/simplegit.rb
@@ -18,8 +18,3 @@ class SimpleGit
     end

 end
-
-if $0 == __FILE__
```

```
-  git = SimpleGit.new
-  puts git.show
-end
\ No newline at end of file
```

This option displays the same information but with a diff directly following each entry. This is very helpful for code review or to quickly browse what happened during a series of commits that a collaborator has added.

You can also use a series of summarizing options with git log. For example, if you want to see some abbreviated stats for each commit, you can use the --stat option:

```
$ git log --stat
commit ca82a6dff817ec66f44342007202690a93763949
Author: Scott Chacon <schacon@gee-mail.com>
Date:   Mon Mar 17 21:52:11 2008 -0700

    changed the version number

 Rakefile |    2 +-
 1 files changed, 1 insertions(+), 1 deletions(-)

commit 085bb3bcb608e1e8451d4b2432f8ecbe6306e7e7
Author: Scott Chacon <schacon@gee-mail.com>
Date:   Sat Mar 15 16:40:33 2008 -0700

    removed unnecessary test code

 lib/simplegit.rb |    5 -----
 1 files changed, 0 insertions(+), 5 deletions(-)

commit a11bef06a3f659402fe7563abf99ad00de2209e6
Author: Scott Chacon <schacon@gee-mail.com>
Date:   Sat Mar 15 10:31:28 2008 -0700

    first commit

 README          |    6 ++++++
 Rakefile        |   23 +++++++++++++++++++++++
 lib/simplegit.rb |   25 +++++++++++++++++++++++++
 3 files changed, 54 insertions(+), 0 deletions(-)
```

As you can see, the --stat option prints below each commit entry a list of modified files, how many files were changed, and how many lines in those files were added and removed. It also puts a summary of the information at the end.

Another really useful option is --pretty. This option changes the log output to formats other than the default. A few prebuilt options are available for you to use. The oneline option prints each commit on a single line, which is useful if you're looking at a lot of commits. In addition, the short, full, and fuller options show the output in roughly the same format but with less or more information, respectively:

```
$ git log --pretty=oneline
ca82a6dff817ec66f44342007202690a93763949 changed the version number
085bb3bcb608e1e8451d4b2432f8ecbe6306e7e7 removed unnecessary test code
a11bef06a3f659402fe7563abf99ad00de2209e6 first commit
```

The most interesting option is format, which allows you to specify your own log output format. This is especially useful when you're generating output for machine parsing—because you specify the format explicitly, you know it won't change with updates to Git:

```
$ git log --pretty=format:"%h - %an, %ar : %s"
ca82a6d - Scott Chacon, 11 months ago : changed the version number
085bb3b - Scott Chacon, 11 months ago : removed unnecessary test code
a11bef0 - Scott Chacon, 11 months ago : first commit
```

Table 2-1 lists some of the more useful options that format takes.

Table 2-1. *Formatting Options for the* git log pretty *Output*

Option	Description of Output
%H	Commit hash
%h	Abbreviated commit hash
%T	Tree hash
%t	Abbreviated tree hash
%P	Parent hashes
%p	Abbreviated parent hashes
%an	Author name
%ae	Author e-mail
%ad	Author date (format respects the –date= option)
%ar	Author date, relative
%cn	Committer name
%ce	Committer e-mail
%cd	Committer date
%cr	Committer date, relative
%s	Subject

■**Note** You may be wondering what the difference is between author and committer. The *author* is the person who originally wrote the work, whereas the *committer* is the person who last applied the work. So, if you send in a patch to a project and one of the core members applies the patch, both of you get credit—you as the author and the core member as the committer. I'll cover this distinction a bit more in Chapter 5.

The `oneline` and `format` options are particularly useful with another log option called `--graph`. This option adds a nice little ASCII graph showing your branch and merge history, in which you can see your copy of the Grit project repository:

```
$ git log --pretty=format:"%h %s" --graph
* 2d3acf9 ignore errors from SIGCHLD on trap
*   5e3ee11 Merge branch 'master' of git://github.com/dustin/grit
|\
| * 420eac9 Added a method for getting the current branch.
* | 30e367c timeout code and tests
* | 5a09431 add timeout protection to grit
* | e1193f8 support for heads with slashes in them
|/
* d6016bc require time for xmlschema
*   11d191e Merge branch 'defunkt' into local
```

Those are only some simple output-formatting options to `git log`—there are many more. Table 2-2 lists the options I've covered so far and some other common formatting options that may be useful, along with how they change the output of the `log` command.

Table 2-2. *Common `git log` Output Formatting Options*

Option	Description
-p	Show the patch introduced with each commit.
--stat	Show statistics for files modified in each commit.
--shortstat	Display only the changed/insertions/deletions line from the --stat command.
--name-only	Show the list of files modified after the commit information.
--name-status	Show the list of files affected with added/modified/deleted information as well.
--abbrev-commit	Show only the first few characters of the SHA-1 checksum instead of all 40.
--relative-date	Display the date in a relative format (for example, "2 weeks ago") instead of using the full date format.
--graph	Display an ASCII graph of the branch and merge history beside the log output.
--pretty	Show commits in an alternate format. Options include oneline, short, full, fuller, and format (where you specify your own format).

Limiting Log Output

In addition to output-formatting options, `git log` takes a number of useful limiting options—that is, options that let you show only a subset of commits. You've seen one such option already—the `-2` option, which show only the last two commits. In fact, you can do `-<n>`, where n is any integer to show the last n commits. In reality, you're unlikely to use that often, because Git by default pipes all output through a pager so you see only one page of log output at a time.

However, the time-limiting options such as `--since` and `--until` are very useful. For example, this command gets the list of commits made in the last two weeks:

```
$ git log --since=2.weeks
```

This command works with lots of formats—you can specify a specific date ("2008-01-15") or a relative date such as "2 years 1 day 3 minutes ago".

You can also filter the list to commits that match some search criteria. The `--author` option allows you to filter on a specific author, and the `--grep` option lets you search for keywords in the commit messages. (Note that if you want to specify both author and grep options, you have to add `--all-match` or the command will match commits with either.)

The last really useful option to pass to `git log` as a filter is a path. If you specify a directory or file name, you can limit the log output to commits that introduced a change to those files. This is always the last option and is generally preceded by double dashes (`--`) to separate the paths from the options.

In Table 2-3, I list these and a few other common options for your reference.

Table 2-3. *Common `git log` Filtering Options*

Option	Description
`-(n)`	Show only the last n commits.
`--since, --after`	Limit the commits to those made after the specified date.
`--until, --before`	Limit the commits to those made before the specified date.
`--author`	Only show commits in which the author entry matches the specified string.
`--committer`	Only show commits in which the committer entry matches the specified string.

For example, if you want to see which commits in the Git source code history were committed by Junio Hamano and were not merges in the month of October 2008, you can run something like this:

```
$ git log --pretty="%h:%s" --author=gitster --since="2008-10-01" \
   --before="2008-11-01" --no-merges -- t/
5610e3b - Fix testcase failure when extended attribute
acd3b9e - Enhance hold_lock_file_for_{update,append}()
f563754 - demonstrate breakage of detached checkout wi
d1a43f2 - reset --hard/read-tree --reset -u: remove un
51a94af - Fix "checkout --track -b newbranch" on detac
b0ad11e - pull: allow "git pull origin $something:$cur
```

Of the nearly 20,000 commits in the Git source code history, this command shows the 6 that match those criteria.

Using a GUI to Visualize History

If you like to use a more graphical tool to visualize your commit history, you may want to take a look at a Tcl/Tk program called gitk that is distributed with Git. gitk is basically a visual git log tool, and it accepts nearly all the filtering options that git log does. If you type gitk on the command line in your project, you should see something like Figure 2-2.

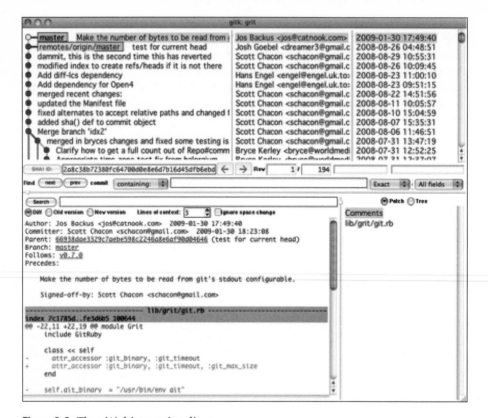

Figure 2-2. *The* gitk *history visualizer*

You can see the commit history in the top half of the window along with a nice ancestry graph. The diff viewer in the bottom half of the window shows you the changes introduced at any commit you click.

Undoing Things

At any stage, you may want to undo something. Here, I'll review a few basic tools for undoing changes that you've made. Be careful, because you can't always undo some of these undos. This is one of the few areas in Git where you may lose some work if you do it wrong.

Changing Your Last Commit

One of the common undos takes place when you commit too early and possibly forget to add some files, or you mess up your commit message. If you want to try that commit again, you can run commit with the --amend option:

```
$ git commit --amend
```

This command takes your staging area and uses it for the commit. If you have made no changes since your last commit (for instance, you run this command it immediately after your previous commit), then your snapshot will look exactly the same and all you'll change is your commit message.

The same commit-message editor fires up, but it already contains the message of your previous commit. You can edit the message the same as always, but it overwrites your previous commit.

As an example, if you commit and then realize you forgot to stage the changes in a file you wanted to add to this commit, you can do something like this:

```
$ git commit -m 'initial commit'
$ git add forgotten_file
$ git commit --amend
```

All three of these commands end up with a single commit—the second command replaces the results of the first.

Unstaging a Staged File

The next two sections demonstrate how to wrangle your staging area and working directory changes. The nice part is that the command you use to determine the state of those two areas also reminds you how to undo changes to them. For example, let's say you've changed two files and want to commit them as two separate changes, but you accidentally type git add * and stage them both. How can you unstage one of the two? The git status command reminds you:

```
$ git add .
$ git status
# On branch master
# Changes to be committed:
#   (use "git reset HEAD <file>..." to unstage)
#
#       modified:   README.txt
#       modified:   benchmarks.rb
#
```

Right below the "Changes to be committed" text, it says use "git reset HEAD <file>..." to unstage. So, let's use that advice to unstage the benchmarks.rb file:

```
$ git reset HEAD benchmarks.rb
benchmarks.rb: locally modified
$ git status
# On branch master
# Changes to be committed:
#   (use "git reset HEAD <file>..." to unstage)
#
#       modified:   README.txt
#
# Changed but not updated:
#   (use "git add <file>..." to update what will be committed)
```

```
#   (use "git checkout -- <file>..." to discard changes in working directory)
#
#       modified:   benchmarks.rb
#
```

The command is a bit strange, but it works. The benchmarks.rb file is modified but once again unstaged.

Unmodifying a Modified File

What if you realize that you don't want to keep your changes to the benchmarks.rb file? How can you easily unmodify it—revert it back to what it looked like when you last committed (or initially cloned, or however you got it into your working directory)? Luckily, git status tells you how to do that, too. In the last example output, the unstaged area looks like this:

```
# Changed but not updated:
#   (use "git add <file>..." to update what will be committed)
#   (use "git checkout -- <file>..." to discard changes in working directory)
#
#       modified:   benchmarks.rb
#
```

It tells you pretty explicitly how to discard the changes you've made (at least, the newer versions of Git, 1.6.1 and later, do this—if you have an older version, I highly recommend upgrading it to get some of these nicer usability features). Let's do what it says:

```
$ git checkout -- benchmarks.rb
$ git status
# On branch master
# Changes to be committed:
#   (use "git reset HEAD <file>..." to unstage)
#
#       modified:   README.txt
#
```

You can see that the changes have been reverted. You should also realize that this is a dangerous command: any changes you made to that file are gone—you just copied another file over it. Don't ever use this command unless you absolutely know that you don't want the file. If you just need to get it out of the way, I'll go over stashing and branching in the next chapter; these are generally better ways to go.

Remember, anything that is committed in Git can almost always be recovered. Even commits that were on branches that were deleted or commits that were overwritten with an --amend commit can be recovered (see Chapter 9 for data recovery). However, anything you lose that was *never* committed is likely never to be seen again.

Working with Remotes

To be able to collaborate on any Git project, you need to know how to manage your remote repositories. *Remote repositories* are versions of your project that are hosted on the Internet or network somewhere. You can have several of them, each of which generally is either read-only or read/write for you. Collaborating with others involves managing these remote repositories and pushing and pulling data to and from them when you need to share work.

Managing remote repositories includes knowing how to add remote repositories, remove remotes that are no longer valid, manage various remote branches and define them as being tracked or not, and more. In this section, I'll cover these remote-management skills.

Showing Your Remotes

To see which remote servers you have configured, you can run the `git remote` command. It lists the shortnames of each remote handle you've specified. If you've cloned your repository, you should at least see origin—that is the default name Git gives to the server you cloned from:

```
$ git clone git://github.com/schacon/ticgit.git
Initialized empty Git repository in /private/tmp/ticgit/.git/
remote: Counting objects: 595, done.
remote: Compressing objects: 100% (269/269), done.
remote: Total 595 (delta 255), reused 589 (delta 253)
Receiving objects: 100% (595/595), 73.31 KiB | 1 KiB/s, done.
Resolving deltas: 100% (255/255), done.
$ cd ticgit
$ git remote
origin
```

You can also specify -v, which shows you the URL that Git has stored for the shortname to be expanded to:

```
$ git remote -v
origin    git://github.com/schacon/ticgit.git
```

If you have more than one remote, the command lists them all. For example, my Grit repository looks something like this.

```
$ cd grit
$ git remote -v
bakkdoor  git://github.com/bakkdoor/grit.git
cho45     git://github.com/cho45/grit.git
defunkt   git://github.com/defunkt/grit.git
koke      git://github.com/koke/grit.git
origin    git@github.com:mojombo/grit.git
```

This means I can pull contributions from any of these users pretty easily. But notice that only the origin remote is an SSH URL, so it's the only one I can push to (I'll cover why this is in Chapter 4).

Adding Remote Repositories

I've mentioned and given some demonstrations of adding remote repositories in previous sections, but here is how to do it explicitly. To add a new remote Git repository as a short-name you can reference easily, run git remote add [*shortname*] [*url*]:

```
$ git remote
origin
$ git remote add pb git://github.com/paulboone/ticgit.git
$ git remote -v
origin      git://github.com/schacon/ticgit.git
pb      git://github.com/paulboone/ticgit.git
```

Now you can use the string pb on the command line in lieu of the whole URL. For example, if you want to fetch all the information that Paul has but that you don't yet have in your repository, you can run git fetch pb:

```
$ git fetch pb
remote: Counting objects: 58, done.
remote: Compressing objects: 100% (41/41), done.
remote: Total 44 (delta 24), reused 1 (delta 0)
Unpacking objects: 100% (44/44), done.
From git://github.com/paulboone/ticgit
 * [new branch]      master     -> pb/master
 * [new branch]      ticgit     -> pb/ticgit
```

Paul's master branch is accessible locally as pb/master—you can merge it into one of your branches, or you can check out a local branch at that point if you want to inspect it.

Fetching and Pulling from Your Remotes

As you just saw, to get data from your remote projects, you can run

```
$ git fetch [remote-name]
```

The command goes out to that remote project and pulls down all the data from that remote project that you don't have yet. After you do this, you should have references to all the branches from that remote, which you can merge in or inspect at any time. (I'll go over what branches are and how to use them in much more detail in Chapter 3.)

If you cloned a repository, the command automatically adds that remote repository under the name origin. So, git fetch origin fetches any new work that has been pushed to that server since you cloned (or last fetched from) it. It's important to note that the fetch command pulls the data to your local repository—it doesn't automatically merge it with any of your work or modify what you're currently working on. You have to merge it manually into your work when you're ready.

If you have a branch set up to track a remote branch (see the next section and Chapter 3 for more information), you can use the git pull command to automatically fetch and then merge a remote branch into your current branch. This may be an easier or more comfortable workflow for you; and by default, the git clone command automatically sets up your local master branch to track the remote master branch on the server you cloned from (assuming the remote has a master branch). Running git pull generally fetches data from the server you originally cloned from and automatically tries to merge it into the code you're currently working on.

Pushing to Your Remotes

When you have your project at a point that you want to share, you have to push it upstream. The command for this is simple: git push [*remote-na*me] [*branch-na*me]. If you want to push your master branch to your origin server (again, cloning generally sets up both of those names for you automatically), then you can run this to push your work back up to the server:

```
$ git push origin master
```

This command works only if you cloned from a server to which you have write access and if nobody has pushed in the meantime. If you and someone else clone at the same time and they push upstream and then you push upstream, your push will rightly be rejected. You'll have to pull down their work first and incorporate it into yours before you'll be allowed to push. See Chapter 3 for more detailed information on how to push to remote servers.

Inspecting a Remote

If you want to see more information about a particular remote, you can use the git remote show [remote-name] command. If you run this command with a particular shortname, such as origin, you get something like this:

```
$ git remote show origin
* remote origin
  URL: git://github.com/schacon/ticgit.git
  Remote branch merged with 'git pull' while on branch master
    master
  Tracked remote branches
    master
    ticgit
```

It lists the URL for the remote repository as well as the tracking branch information. The command helpfully tells you that if you're on the master branch and you run git pull, it will automatically merge in the master branch on the remote after it fetches all the remote references. It also lists all the remote references it has pulled down.

That is a simple example you're likely to encounter. When you're using Git more heavily, however, you may see much more information from git remote show:

```
$ git remote show origin
* remote origin
  URL: git@github.com:defunkt/github.git
  Remote branch merged with 'git pull' while on branch issues
    issues
  Remote branch merged with 'git pull' while on branch master
    master
  New remote branches (next fetch will store in remotes/origin)
    caching
```

```
  Stale tracking branches (use 'git remote prune')
    libwalker
    walker2
Tracked remote branches
    acl
    apiv2
    dashboard2
    issues
    master
    postgres
Local branch pushed with 'git push'
    master:master
```

This command shows which branch is automatically pushed when you run git push on certain branches. It also shows you which remote branches on the server you don't yet have, which remote branches you have that have been removed from the server, and multiple branches that are automatically merged when you run git pull.

Removing and Renaming Remotes

If you want to rename a reference, in newer versions of Git you can run git remote rename to change a remote's shortname. For instance, if you want to rename pb to paul, you can do so with git remote rename:

```
$ git remote rename pb paul
$ git remote
origin
paul
```

It's worth mentioning that this changes your remote branch names, too. What used to be referenced at pb/master is now at paul/master.

If you want to remove a reference for some reason—you've moved the server or are no longer using a particular mirror, or perhaps a contributor isn't contributing anymore—you can use git rm:

```
$ git remote rm paul
$ git remote
origin
```

Tagging

Like most VCSs, Git has the ability to tag specific points in history as being important. Generally, people use this functionality to mark release points (v1.0, and so on). In this section, you'll learn how to list the available tags, how to create new tags, and what the different types of tags are.

Listing Your Tags

Listing the available tags in Git is straightforward. Just type `git tag`:

```
$ git tag
v0.1
v1.3
```

This command lists the tags in alphabetical order; the order in which they appear has no real importance.

You can also search for tags with a particular pattern. The Git source repo, for instance, contains more than 240 tags. If you're only interested in looking at the 1.4.2 series, you can run this:

```
$ git tag -l v1.4.2.*
v1.4.2.1
v1.4.2.2
v1.4.2.3
v1.4.2.4
```

Creating Tags

Git uses two main types of tags: lightweight and annotated. A *lightweight tag* is very much like a branch that doesn't change—it's just a pointer to a specific commit. *Annotated tags*, however, are stored as full objects in the Git database. They're check-summed; contain the tagger name, e-mail, and date; have a tagging message; and can be signed and verified with GNU Privacy Guard (GPG). It's generally recommended that you create annotated tags so you can have all this information; but if you want a temporary tag or for some reason don't want to keep the other information, lightweight tags are available too.

Annotated Tags

Creating an annotated tag in Git is simple. The easiest way is to specify `-a` when you run the tag command:

```
$ git tag -a v1.4 -m 'my version 1.4'
$ git tag
v0.1
v1.3
v1.4
```

The `-m` specifies a tagging message, which is stored with the tag. If you don't specify a message for an annotated tag, Git launches your editor so you can type it in.

You can see the tag data along with the commit that was tagged by using the `git show` command:

```
$ git show v1.4
tag v1.4
Tagger: Scott Chacon <schacon@gee-mail.com>
Date:   Mon Feb 9 14:45:11 2009 -0800
```

```
my version 1.4
commit 15027957951b64cf874c3557a0f3547bd83b3ff6
Merge: 4a447f7... a6b4c97...
Author: Scott Chacon <schacon@gee-mail.com>
Date:    Sun Feb 8 19:02:46 2009 -0800

    Merge branch 'experiment'
```

That shows the tagger information, the date the commit was tagged, and the annotation message before showing the commit information.

Signed Tags

You can also sign your tags with GPG, assuming you have a private key. All you have to do is use -s instead of -a:

```
$ git tag -s v1.5 -m 'my signed 1.5 tag'
You need a passphrase to unlock the secret key for
user: "Scott Chacon <schacon@gee-mail.com>"
1024-bit DSA key, ID F721C45A, created 2009-02-09
```

If you run git show on that tag, you can see your GPG signature attached to it:

```
$ git show v1.5
tag v1.5
Tagger: Scott Chacon <schacon@gee-mail.com>
Date:    Mon Feb 9 15:22:20 2009 -0800

my signed 1.5 tag
-----BEGIN PGP SIGNATURE-----
Version: GnuPG v1.4.8 (Darwin)

iEYEABECAAYFAkmQurIACgkQON3DxfchxFr5cACeIMN+ZxLKggJQfOQYiQBwgySN
KiOAn2JeAVUCAiJ7Ox6ZEtK+NvZAj82/
=WryJ
-----END PGP SIGNATURE-----
commit 15027957951b64cf874c3557a0f3547bd83b3ff6
Merge: 4a447f7... a6b4c97...
Author: Scott Chacon <schacon@gee-mail.com>
Date:    Sun Feb 8 19:02:46 2009 -0800

    Merge branch 'experiment'
```

A bit later, you'll learn how to verify signed tags.

Lightweight Tags

Another way to tag commits is with a lightweight tag. This is basically the commit checksum stored in a file—no other information is kept. To create a lightweight tag, don't supply the -a, -s, or -m option:

```
$ git tag v1.4-lw
$ git tag
v0.1
v1.3
v1.4
v1.4-lw
v1.5
```

This time, if you run git show on the tag, you don't see the extra tag information. The command just shows the commit:

```
$ git show v1.4-lw
commit 15027957951b64cf874c3557a0f3547bd83b3ff6
Merge: 4a447f7... a6b4c97...
Author: Scott Chacon <schacon@gee-mail.com>
Date:   Sun Feb 8 19:02:46 2009 -0800

    Merge branch 'experiment'
```

Verifying Tags

To verify a signed tag, you use git tag -v [tag-name]. This command uses GPG to verify the signature. You need the signer's public key in your keyring for this to work properly:

```
$ git tag -v v1.4.2.1
object 883653babd8ee7ea23e6a5c392bb739348b1eb61
type commit
tag v1.4.2.1
tagger Junio C Hamano <junkio@cox.net> 1158138501 -0700

GIT 1.4.2.1

Minor fixes since 1.4.2, including git-mv and git-http with alternates.
gpg: Signature made Wed Sep 13 02:08:25 2006 PDT using DSA key ID F3119B9A
gpg: Good signature from "Junio C Hamano <junkio@cox.net>"
gpg:                 aka "[jpeg image of size 1513]"
Primary key fingerprint: 3565 2A26 2040 E066 C9A7  4A7D C0C6 D9A4 F311 9B9A
```

If you don't have the signer's public key, you get something like this instead:

```
gpg: Signature made Wed Sep 13 02:08:25 2006 PDT using DSA key ID F3119B9A
gpg: Can't check signature: public key not found
error: could not verify the tag 'v1.4.2.1'
```

Tagging Later

You can also tag commits after you've moved past them. Suppose your commit history looks like this:

```
$ git log --pretty=oneline
15027957951b64cf874c3557a0f3547bd83b3ff6 Merge branch 'experiment'
a6b4c97498bd301d84096da251c98a07c7723e65 beginning write support
0d52aaab4479697da7686c15f77a3d64d9165190 one more thing
6d52a271eda8725415634dd79daabbc4d9b6008e Merge branch 'experiment'
0b7434d86859cc7b8c3d5e1dddfed66ff742fcbc added a commit function
4682c3261057305bdd616e23b64b0857d832627b added a todo file
166ae0c4d3f420721acbb115cc33848dfcc2121a started write support
9fceb02d0ae598e95dc970b74767f19372d61af8 updated rakefile
964f16d36dfccde844893cac5b347e7b3d44abbc commit the todo
8a5cbc430f1a9c3d00faaeffd07798508422908a updated readme
```

Now, suppose you forgot to tag the project at v1.2, which was at the updated rakefile commit. You can add it after the fact. To tag that commit, you specify the commit checksum (or part of it) at the end of the command:

```
$ git tag -a v1.2 9fceb02
```

You can see that you've tagged the commit:

```
$ git tag
v0.1
v1.2
v1.3
v1.4
v1.4-lw
v1.5

$ git show v1.2
tag v1.2
Tagger: Scott Chacon <schacon@gee-mail.com>
Date:   Mon Feb 9 15:32:16 2009 -0800

version 1.2
commit 9fceb02d0ae598e95dc970b74767f19372d61af8
Author: Magnus Chacon <mchacon@gee-mail.com>
Date:   Sun Apr 27 20:43:35 2008 -0700

    updated rakefile
...
```

Sharing Tags

By default, the `git push` command doesn't transfer tags to remote servers. You have to explicitly push tags to a shared server after you create them. This process is just like sharing remote branches—you can run `git push origin [`*`tagname`*`]`:

```
$ git push origin v1.5
Counting objects: 50, done.
Compressing objects: 100% (38/38), done.
Writing objects: 100% (44/44), 4.56 KiB, done.
Total 44 (delta 18), reused 8 (delta 1)
To git@github.com:schacon/simplegit.git
* [new tag]         v1.5 -> v1.5
```

If you have a lot of tags that you want to push up at once, you can also use the `--tags` option to the `git push` command. This transfers to the remote server all of your tags that aren't already there:

```
$ git push origin --tags
Counting objects: 50, done.
Compressing objects: 100% (38/38), done.
Writing objects: 100% (44/44), 4.56 KiB, done.
Total 44 (delta 18), reused 8 (delta 1)
To git@github.com:schacon/simplegit.git
 * [new tag]         v0.1 -> v0.1
 * [new tag]         v1.2 -> v1.2
 * [new tag]         v1.4 -> v1.4
 * [new tag]         v1.4-lw -> v1.4-lw
 * [new tag]         v1.5 -> v1.5
```

Now, when someone else clones or pulls from your repository, they will get all your tags as well.

Tips and Tricks

Before I finish this chapter on basic Git, a few little tips and tricks may make your Git experience a bit simpler, easier, or more familiar. Many people use Git without using any of these tips, and I won't refer to them or assume you've used them later in the book; but you should probably know how to do them.

Auto-Completion

If you use the Bash shell, Git comes with a nice auto-completion script you can enable. Download the Git source code, and look in the `contrib/completion` directory; there should be a file called `git-completion.bash`. Copy this file to your home directory, and add this to your `.bashrc` file:

```
source ~/.git-completion.bash
```

If you want to set up Git to automatically have Bash shell completion for all users, copy this script to the `/opt/local/etc/bash_completion.d` directory on Mac systems or to the `/etc/bash_completion.d/` directory on Linux systems. This is a directory of scripts that Bash will automatically load to provide shell completions.

If you're using Windows with Git Bash, which is the default when installing Git on Windows with msysGit, auto-completion should be preconfigured.

Press the Tab key when you're writing a Git command, and it should return a set of suggestions for you to pick from:

```
$ git co<tab><tab>
commit config
```

In this case, typing **git co** and then pressing the Tab key twice suggests `commit` and `config`. Adding **m<tab>** completes `git commit` automatically.

This also works with options, which is probably more useful. For instance, if you're running a `git log` command and can't remember one of the options, you can start typing it and press Tab to see what matches:

```
$ git log --s<tab>
--shortstat  --since=  --src-prefix=  --stat   --summary
```

That's a pretty nice trick and may save you some time and documentation reading.

Git Aliases

Git doesn't infer your command if you type it in partially. If you don't want to type the entire text of each of the Git commands, you can easily set up an alias for each command using `git config`. Here are a couple of examples you may want to set up:

```
$ git config --global alias.co checkout
$ git config --global alias.br branch
$ git config --global alias.ci commit
$ git config --global alias.st status
```

This means that, for example, instead of typing **git commit**, you just need to type **git ci**. As you go on using Git, you'll probably use other commands frequently as well; in this case, don't hesitate to create new aliases.

This technique can also be very useful in creating commands that you think should exist. For example, to correct the usability problem you encountered with unstaging a file, you can add your own `unstage` alias to Git:

```
$ git config --global alias.unstage 'reset HEAD --'
```

This makes the following two commands equivalent:

```
$ git unstage fileA
$ git reset HEAD fileA
```

This seems a bit clearer. It's also common to add a `last` command, like this:

```
$ git config --global alias.last 'log -1 HEAD'
```

This way, you can see the last commit easily:

```
$ git last
commit 66938dae3329c7aebe598c2246a8e6af90d04646
Author: Josh Goebel <dreamer3@gee-mail.com>
Date:   Tue Aug 26 19:48:51 2008 +0800

    test for current head

    Signed-off-by: Scott Chacon <schacon@gee-mail.com>
```

As you can tell, Git simply replaces the new command with whatever you alias it for. However, maybe you want to run an external command, rather than a Git subcommand. In that case, you start the command with a ! character. This is useful if you write your own tools that work with a Git repository. I can demonstrate by aliasing `git visual` to run `gitk`:

```
$ git config --global alias.visual "!gitk"
```

Summary

At this point, you can do all the basic local Git operations—creating or cloning a repository, making changes, staging and committing those changes, and viewing the history of all the changes the repository has been through. Next, I'll cover Git's killer feature: its branching model.

CHAPTER 3

■■■

Git Branching

Nearly every VCS has some form of branching support. *Branching* means you diverge from the main line of development and continue to do work without messing with that main line. In many VCS tools, this is a somewhat expensive process, often requiring you to create a new copy of your source code directory, which can take a long time for large projects.

Some people refer to the branching model in Git as its "killer feature," and it certainly sets Git apart in the VCS community. Why is it so special? The way Git branches is incredibly lightweight, making branching operations nearly instantaneous and switching back and forth between branches generally just as fast. Unlike many other VCSs, Git encourages a workflow that branches and merges often, even multiple times in a day. Understanding and mastering this feature gives you a powerful and unique tool and can literally change the way that you develop.

What a Branch Is

To really understand the way Git does branching, you need to take a step back and examine how Git stores its data. As you may remember from Chapter 1, Git doesn't store data as a series of changesets or deltas, but instead as a series of snapshots.

When you commit in Git, Git stores a commit object that contains a pointer to the snapshot of the content you staged, the author and message metadata, and zero or more pointers to the commit or commits that were the direct parents of this commit: zero parents for the first commit, one parent for a normal commit, and multiple parents for a commit that results from a merge of two or more branches.

To visualize this, let's assume that you have a directory containing three files, and you stage them all and commit. Staging the files checksums each one (the SHA-1 hash I mentioned in Chapter 1), stores that version of the file in the Git repository (Git refers to them as *blobs*), and adds that checksum to the staging area:

```
$ git add README test.rb LICENSE2
$ git commit -m 'initial commit of my project'
```

When you create the commit by running git commit, Git checksums each subdirectory (in this case, just the root project directory) and stores those tree objects in the Git repository. Git then creates a commit object that has the metadata and a pointer to the root project tree so it can re-create that snapshot when needed.

Your Git repository now contains five objects: one blob for the contents of each of your three files, one tree that lists the contents of the directory and specifies which file names are stored as which blobs, and one commit with the pointer to that root tree and all the commit metadata. Conceptually, the data in your Git repository looks something like Figure 3-1.

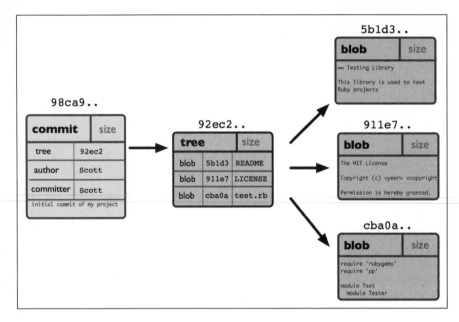

Figure 3-1. *Single-commit repository data*

If you make some changes and commit again, the next commit stores a pointer to the commit that came immediately before it. After two more commits, your history might look something like Figure 3-2.

A *branch* in Git is simply a lightweight movable pointer to one of these commits. The default branch name in Git is master. As you initially make commits, you're given a master branch that points to the last commit you made. Every time you commit, it moves forward automatically.

What happens if you create a new branch? Well, doing so creates a new pointer for you to move around. Let's say you create a new branch called testing. You do this with the git branch command:

```
$ git branch testing
```

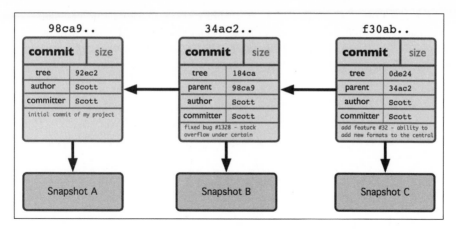

Figure 3-2. *Git object data for multiple commits*

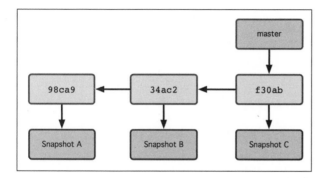

Figure 3-3. *Branch pointing into the commit data's history*

This creates a new pointer at the same commit you're currently on (see Figure 3-4).

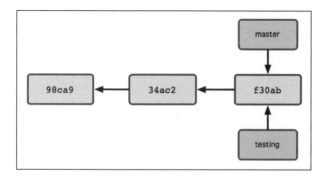

Figure 3-4. *Multiple branches pointing into the commit's data history*

How does Git know what branch you're currently on? It keeps a special pointer called HEAD. Note that this is a lot different than the concept of HEAD in other VCSs you may be used to, such as Subversion or CVS. In Git, this is a pointer to the local branch you're currently on. In this case, you're still on master. The git branch command only created a new branch—it didn't switch to that branch (see Figure 3-5).

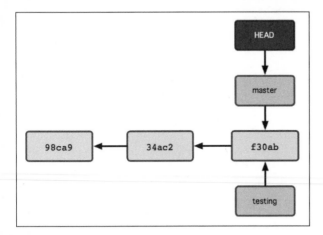

Figure 3-5. *HEAD file pointing to the branch you're on*

To switch to an existing branch, you run the git checkout command. Let's switch to the new testing branch:

```
$ git checkout testing
```

This moves HEAD to point to the testing branch (see Figure 3-6).

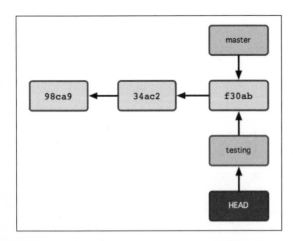

Figure 3-6. *HEAD points to another branch when you switch branches.*

What is the significance of that? Well, do another commit:

```
$ vim test.rb
$ git commit -a -m 'made a change'
```

Figure 3-7 illustrates the result.

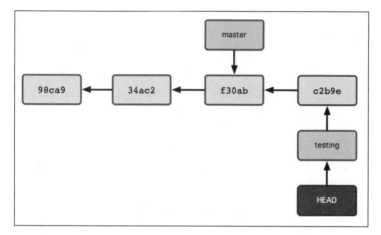

Figure 3-7. *The branch that HEAD points to moves forward with each commit.*

This is interesting, because now your testing branch has moved forward, but your master branch still points to the commit you were on when you ran git checkout to switch branches. Let's switch back to the master branch:

```
$ git checkout master
```

Figure 3-8 shows the result.

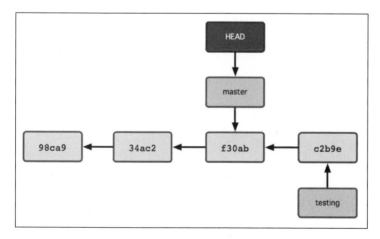

Figure 3-8. *HEAD moves to another branch on a checkout.*

That command did two things. It moved the HEAD pointer back to point to the master branch, and it reverted the files in your working directory back to the snapshot that master points to. This also means the changes you make from this point forward will diverge from an older version of the project. It essentially rewinds the work you've done in your testing branch temporarily so you can go in a different direction.

Let's make a few changes and commit again:

```
$ vim test.rb
$ git commit -a -m 'made other changes'
```

Now your project history has diverged (see Figure 3-9). You created and switched to a branch, did some work on it, and then switched back to your main branch and did other work. Both of those changes are isolated in separate branches: you can switch back and forth between the branches and merge them together when you're ready. And you did all that with simple branch and checkout commands.

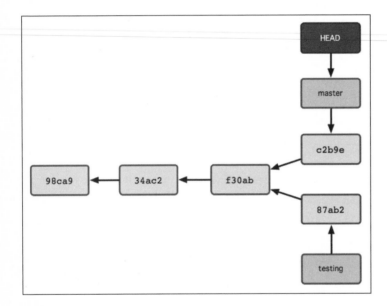

Figure 3-9. *The branch histories have diverged.*

Because a branch in Git is in actuality a simple file that contains the 40-character SHA-1 checksum of the commit it points to, branches are cheap to create and destroy. Creating a new branch is as quick and simple as writing 41 bytes to a file (40 characters and a newline).

This is in sharp contrast to the way most VCS tools branch, which involves copying all of the project's files into a second directory. This can take several seconds or even minutes, depending on the size of the project, whereas in Git the process is always instantaneous. Also, because you're recording the parents when you commit, finding a proper merge base for merging is automatically done for you and is generally very easy. These features help encourage developers to create and use branches often.

Let's see why you should do so.

Basic Branching and Merging

Let's go through a simple example of branching and merging with a workflow that you might use in the real world. You'll follow these steps:

1. Do work on a web site.

2. Create a branch for a new story you're working on.

3. Do some work in that branch.

At this stage, you'll receive a call that another issue is critical and you need a hotfix. You'll do the following:

1. Revert back to your production branch.

2. Create a branch to add the hotfix.

3. After it's tested, merge the hotfix branch, and push to production.

4. Switch back to your original story, and continue working.

Basic Branching

First, let's say you're working on your project and have a couple of commits already (see Figure 3-10).

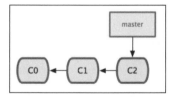

Figure 3-10. *A short and simple commit history*

You've decided that you're going to work on issue #53 in whatever issue-tracking system your company uses. To be clear, Git isn't tied into any particular issue-tracking system; but because #53 is a focused topic that you want to work on, you'll create a new branch in which to work. To create a branch and switch to it at the same time, you can run the git checkout command with the -b switch:

```
$ git checkout -b iss53
Switched to a new branch "iss53"
```

This is shorthand for

```
$ git branch iss53
$ git checkout iss53
```

Figure 3-11 illustrates the result.

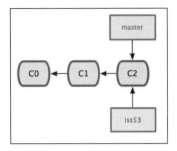

Figure 3-11. *Creating a new branch pointer*

You work on your web site and do some commits. Doing so moves the iss53 branch forward, because you have it checked out (that is, your HEAD is pointing to it; see Figure 3-12):

```
$ vim index.html
$ git commit -a -m 'added a new footer [issue 53]'
```

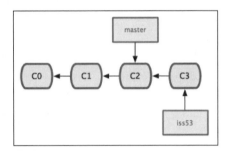

Figure 3-12. *The iss53 branch has moved forward with your work.*

Now you get the call that there is an issue with the web site, and you need to fix it immediately. With Git, you don't have to deploy your fix along with the iss53 changes you've made, and you don't have to put a lot of effort into reverting those changes before you can work on applying your fix to what is in production. All you have to do is switch back to your master branch.

However, before you do that, note that if your working directory or staging area has uncommitted changes that conflict with the branch you're checking out, Git won't let you switch branches. It's best to have a clean working state when you switch branches. There are ways to get around this (namely, stashing and commit amending) that I'll cover later. For now, you've committed all your changes, so you can switch back to your master branch:

```
$ git checkout master
Switched to branch "master"
```

At this point, your project working directory is exactly the way it was before you started working on issue #53, and you can concentrate on your hotfix. This is an important point to remember: Git resets your working directory to look like the snapshot of the commit that the branch you check out points to. It adds, removes, and modifies files automatically to make sure your working copy is what the branch looked like on your last commit to it.

Next, you have a hotfix to make. You create a hotfix branch on which to work until it's completed (see Figure 3-13):

```
$ git checkout -b 'hotfix'
Switched to a new branch "hotfix"
$ vim index.html
$ git commit -a -m 'fixed the broken email address'
[hotfix]: created 3a0874c: "fixed the broken email address"
 1 files changed, 0 insertions(+), 1 deletions(-)
```

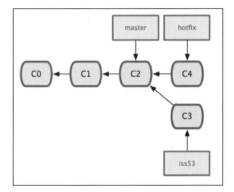

Figure 3-13. *hotfix branch based back at your master branch point*

You can run your tests, make sure the hotfix is what you want, and merge it back into your master branch to deploy to production. You do this with the git merge command:

```
$ git checkout master
$ git merge hotfix
Updating f42c576..3a0874c
Fast forward
 README |    1 -
 1 files changed, 0 insertions(+), 1 deletions(-)
```

You'll notice the phrase *Fast forward* in that merge. Because the commit pointed to by the branch you merged in was directly upstream of the commit you're on, Git moves the pointer forward. To phrase that another way, when you try to merge one commit with a commit that can be reached by following the first commit's history, Git simplifies things by moving the pointer forward because there is no divergent work to merge together—this is called a *fast forward*.

Your change is now in the snapshot of the commit pointed to by the master branch, and you can deploy your change (see Figure 3-14).

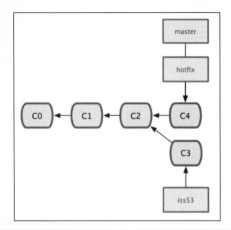

Figure 3-14. *Your master branch points to the same place as your hotfix branch after the merge.*

After your super-important fix is deployed, you're ready to switch back to the work you were doing before you were interrupted. However, first you'll delete the hotfix branch, because you no longer need it—the master branch points at the same place. You can delete it with the -d option to git branch:

```
$ git branch -d hotfix
Deleted branch hotfix (3a0874c).
```

Now you can switch back to your work-in-progress branch on issue #53 and continue working on it (see Figure 3-15):

```
$ git checkout iss53
Switched to branch "iss53"
$ vim index.html
$ git commit -a -m 'finished the new footer [issue 53]'
[iss53]: created ad82d7a: "finished the new footer [issue 53]"
 1 files changed, 1 insertions(+), 0 deletions(-)
```

It's worth noting here that the work you did in your hotfix branch is *not* contained in the files in your iss53 branch. If you need to pull it in, you can merge your master branch into your iss53 branch by running git merge master, or you can wait to integrate those changes until you decide to pull the iss53 branch back into master later.

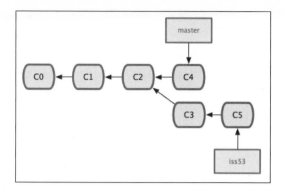

Figure 3-15. *Your iss53 branch can move forward independently.*

Basic Merging

Suppose you've decided that your issue #53 work is complete and ready to be merged into your master branch. In order to do that, you'll merge in your iss53 branch, much like you merged in your hotfix branch earlier. All you have to do is check out the branch you wish to merge into and then run the git merge command:

```
$ git checkout master
$ git merge iss53
Merge made by recursive.
 README |    1 +
 1 files changed, 1 insertions(+), 0 deletions(-)
```

This looks a bit different than the hotfix merge you did earlier. In this case, your development history has diverged from some older point. Because the commit on the branch you're on isn't a direct ancestor of the branch you're merging in, Git has to do some work. In this case, Git does a simple three-way merge, using the two snapshots pointed to by the branch tips and the common ancestor of the two. Figure 3-16 highlights the three snapshots that Git uses to do its merge in this case.

Instead of just moving the branch pointer forward, Git creates a new snapshot that results from this three-way merge and automatically creates a new commit that points to it (see Figure 3-17). This is referred to as a *merge commit* and is special in that it has more than one parent.

It's worth pointing out that Git determines the best common ancestor to use for its merge base; this is different than CVS or Subversion (before version 1.5), where the developer doing the merge has to figure out the best merge base for themselves. This makes merging a heck of a lot easier in Git than in these other systems.

Now that your work is merged in, you have no further need for the iss53 branch. You can delete it and then manually close the ticket in your ticket-tracking system:

```
$ git branch -d iss53
```

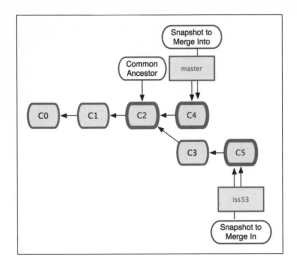

Figure 3-16. *Git automatically identifies the best common-ancestor merge base for branch merging.*

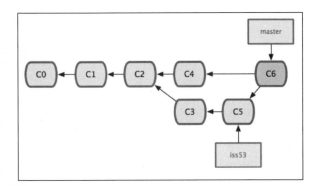

Figure 3-17. *Git automatically creates a new commit object that contains the merged work.*

Basic Merge Conflicts

Occasionally, this process doesn't go smoothly. If you changed the same part of the same file differently in the two branches you're merging together, Git won't be able to merge them cleanly. If your fix for issue #53 modified the same part of a file as the hotfix, you get a merge conflict that looks something like this:

```
$ git merge iss53
Auto-merging index.html
CONFLICT (content): Merge conflict in index.html
Automatic merge failed; fix conflicts and then commit the result.
```

Git hasn't automatically created a new merge commit. It has paused the process while you resolve the conflict. If you want to see which files are unmerged at any point after a merge conflict, you can run git status:

```
[master*]$ git status
index.html: needs merge
# On branch master
# Changed but not updated:
#   (use "git add <file>..." to update what will be committed)
#   (use "git checkout -- <file>..." to discard changes in working directory)
#
#     unmerged:   index.html
#
```

Anything that has merge conflicts and hasn't been resolved is listed as unmerged. Git adds standard conflict-resolution markers to the files that have conflicts, so you can open them manually and resolve those conflicts. Your file contains a section that looks something like this:

```
<<<<<<< HEAD:index.html
<div id="footer">contact : email.support@github.com</div>
=======
<div id="footer">
  please contact us at support@github.com
</div>
>>>>>>> iss53:index.html
```

This means the version in HEAD (your master branch, because that was what you had checked out when you ran your merge command) is the top part of that block (everything above the =======), whereas the version in your iss53 branch looks like everything in the bottom part. In order to resolve the conflict, you have to either choose one side or the other or merge the contents yourself. For instance, you might resolve this conflict by replacing the entire block with this:

```
<div id="footer">
please contact us at email.support@github.com
</div>
```

This resolution has a little of each section, and I've fully removed the <<<<<<<, =======, and >>>>>>> lines. After you've resolved each of these sections in each conflicted file, run git add on each file to mark it as resolved. Staging the file marks it as resolved in Git.

If you want to use a graphical tool to resolve these issues, you can run git mergetool, which fires up an appropriate visual merge tool and walks you through the conflicts:

```
$ git mergetool
merge tool candidates: kdiff3 tkdiff xxdiff meld gvimdiff opendiff emerge vimdiff
Merging the files: index.html

Normal merge conflict for 'index.html':
  {local}: modified
  {remote}: modified
Hit return to start merge resolution tool (opendiff):
```

If you want to use a merge tool other than the default (Git chose `opendiff` for me in this case because I ran the command on a Mac), you can see all the supported tools listed at the top after "merge tool candidates". Type the name of the tool you'd rather use. In Chapter 7, I'll discuss how you can change this default value for your environment.

After you exit the merge tool, Git asks you if the merge was successful. If you tell the script that it was, it stages the file to mark it as resolved for you.

You can run `git status` again to verify that all conflicts have been resolved:

```
$ git status
# On branch master
# Changes to be committed:
#    (use "git reset HEAD <file>..." to unstage)
#
#     modified:   index.html
#
```

If you're happy with that, and you verify that everything that had conflicts has been staged, you can type `git commit` to finalize the merge commit. The commit message by default looks something like this:

```
Merge branch 'iss53'

Conflicts:
  index.html
#
# It looks like you may be committing a MERGE.
# If this is not correct, please remove the file
# .git/MERGE_HEAD
# and try again.
#
```

You can modify that message with details about how you resolved the merge if you think it would be helpful to others looking at this merge in the future—why you did what you did, if it's not obvious.

Branch Management

Now that you've created, merged, and deleted some branches, let's look at some branch-management tools that will come in handy when you begin using branches all the time.

The `git branch` command does more than just create and delete branches. If you run it with no arguments, you get a simple listing of your current branches:

```
$ git branch
  iss53
* master
  testing
```

Notice the * character that prefixes the `master` branch: it indicates the branch that you currently have checked out. This means that if you commit at this point, the `master` branch will be moved forward with your new work. To see the last commit on each branch, you can run `git branch -v`:

```
$ git branch -v
  iss53   93b412c fix javascript issue
* master  7a98805 Merge branch 'iss53'
  testing 782fd34 add scott to the author list in the readmes
```

Another useful option to figure out what state your branches are in is to filter this list to branches that you have or have not yet merged into the branch you're currently on. The useful `--merged` and `--no-merged` options have been available in Git since version 1.5.6 for this purpose. To see which branches are already merged into the branch you're on, you can run `git branch --merged`:

```
$ git branch --merged
  iss53
* master
```

Because you already merged in `iss53` earlier, you see it in your list. Branches on this list without the * in front of them are generally fine to delete with `git branch -d`; you've already incorporated their work into another branch, so you're not going to lose anything.

To see all the branches that contain work you haven't yet merged in, you can run `git branch --no-merged`:

```
$ git branch --no-merged
  testing
```

This shows your other branch. Because it contains work that isn't merged in yet, trying to delete it with `git branch -d` will fail:

```
$ git branch -d testing
error: The branch 'testing' is not an ancestor of your current HEAD.
If you are sure you want to delete it, run 'git branch -D testing'.
```

If you really do want to delete the branch and lose that work, you can force it with `-D`, as the helpful message points out.

Branching Workflows

Now that you have the basics of branching and merging down, what can or should you do with them? In this section, I'll cover some common workflows that this lightweight branching makes possible, so you can decide if you would like to incorporate it into your own development cycle.

Long-Running Branches

Because Git uses a simple three-way merge, merging from one branch into another multiple times over a long period is generally easy to do. This means you can have several branches that are always open and that you use for different stages of your development cycle; you can merge regularly from some of them into others.

Many Git developers have a workflow that embraces this approach, such as having only code that is entirely stable in their master branch—possibly only code that has been or will be released. They have another parallel branch named develop or next that they work from or use to test stability—it isn't necessarily always stable, but whenever it gets to a stable state, it can be merged into master. It's used to pull in topic branches (short-lived branches, like your earlier iss53 branch) when they're ready, to make sure they pass all the tests and don't introduce bugs.

In reality, I'm talking about pointers moving up the line of commits you're making. The stable branches are farther down the line in your commit history, and the bleeding-edge branches are farther up the history (see Figure 3-18).

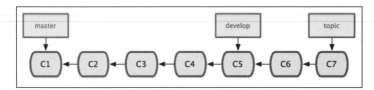

Figure 3-18. *More stable branches are generally farther down the commit history.*

It's generally easier to think about them as work silos, where sets of commits graduate to a more stable silo when they're fully tested (see Figure 3-19).

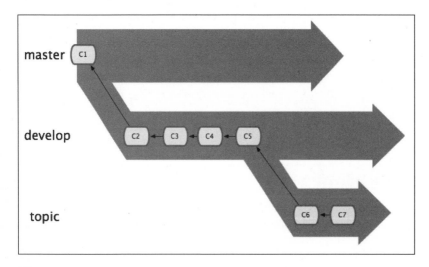

Figure 3-19. *It may be helpful to think of your branches as silos.*

You can keep doing this for several levels of stability. Some larger projects also have a `proposed` or `pu` (proposed updates) branch that has integrated branches that may not be ready to go into the next or `master` branch. The idea is that your branches are at various levels of stability; when they reach a more stable level, they're merged into the branch above them.

Again, having multiple long-running branches isn't necessary, but it's often helpful, especially when you're dealing with very large or complex projects.

Topic Branches

Topic branches, however, are useful in projects of any size. A *topic branch* is a short-lived branch that you create and use for a single particular feature or related work. This is something you've likely never done with a VCS before because it's generally too expensive to create and merge branches. But in Git it's common to create, work on, merge, and delete branches several times a day.

You saw this in the last section with the `iss53` and `hotfix` branches you created. You did a few commits on them and deleted them directly after merging them into your main branch. This technique allows you to context-switch quickly and completely—because your work is separated into silos where all the changes in that branch have to do with that topic, it's easier to see what has happened during code review and such. You can keep the changes there for minutes, days, or months, and merge them in when they're ready, regardless of the order in which they were created or worked on.

Consider an example of doing some work (on `master`), branching off for an issue (`iss91`), working on it for a bit, branching off the second branch to try another way of handling the same thing (`iss91v2`), going back to your `master` branch and working there for a while, and then branching off there to do some work that you're not sure is a good idea (`dumbidea` branch). Your commit history looks something like Figure 3-20.

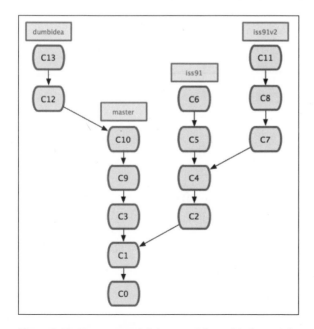

Figure 3-20. *Your commit history with multiple topic branches*

Now, let's say you decide you like the second solution to your issue best (iss91v2). You showed the dumbidea branch to your coworkers, and it turns out to be genius. You can throw away the original iss91 branch (losing commits C5 and C6) and merge in the other two. Your history then looks like Figure 3-21.

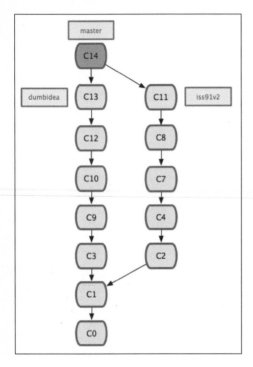

Figure 3-21. *Your history after merging in dumbidea and* iss91v2

It's important to remember when you're doing all this that these branches are completely local. When you're branching and merging, everything is being done only in your Git repository—no server communication is happening.

Remote Branches

Remote branches are references to the state of branches on your remote repositories. They're local branches that you can't move; they're moved automatically whenever you do any network communication. Remote branches act as bookmarks to remind you where the branches on your remote repositories were the last time you connected to them.

They take the form (*remote*)/(*branch*). For instance, if you wanted to see what the master branch on your origin remote looked like as of the last time you communicated with it, you would check the origin/master branch. If you were working on an issue with a partner and they pushed up an iss53 branch, you might have your own local iss53 branch; but the branch on the server would point to the commit at origin/iss53.

This may be a bit confusing, so let's look at an example. Let's say you have a Git server on your network at git.ourcompany.com. If you clone from this, Git automatically names it origin for you, pulls down all its data, creates a pointer to where its master branch is, and names it origin/master locally; and you can't move it. Git also gives you your own master branch starting at the same place as origin's master branch, so you have something to work from (see Figure 3-22).

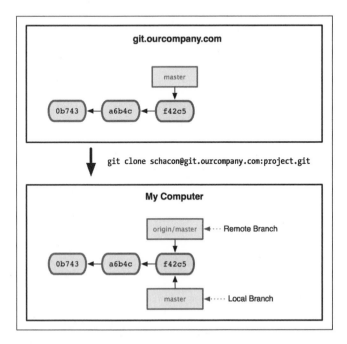

Figure 3-22. *A Git clone gives you your own master branch and origin/master pointing to origin's master branch.*

If you do some work on your local master branch and, in the meantime, someone else pushes to git.ourcompany.com and updates its master branch, then your histories move forward differently. Also, as long as you stay out of contact with your origin server, your origin/master pointer doesn't move (see Figure 3-23).

To synchronize your work, you run a git fetch origin command. This command looks up which server origin is (in this case, it's git.ourcompany.com), fetches any data from it that you don't yet have, and updates your local database, moving your origin/master pointer to its new, more up-to-date position (see Figure 3-24).

To demonstrate having multiple remote servers and what remote branches for those remote projects look like, let's assume you have another internal Git server that is used only for development by one of your sprint teams. This server is at git.team1.ourcompany.com. You can add it as a new remote reference to the project you're currently working on by running the git remote add command as I covered in Chapter 2. Name this remote teamone, which will be your shortname for that whole URL (see Figure 3-25).

Now, you can run git fetch teamone to fetch everything the server has that you don't have yet. Because that server is a subset of the data your origin server has right now, Git fetches no data but sets a branch called teamone/master to point to the commit that teamone has as its master branch (see Figure 3-26).

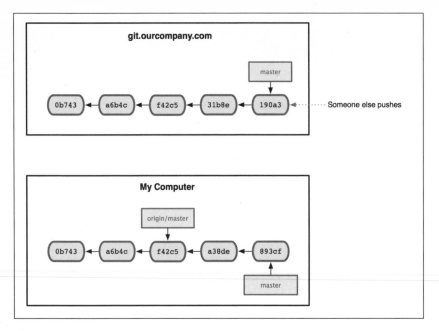

Figure 3-23. *Working locally and having someone push to your remote server makes each history move forward differently.*

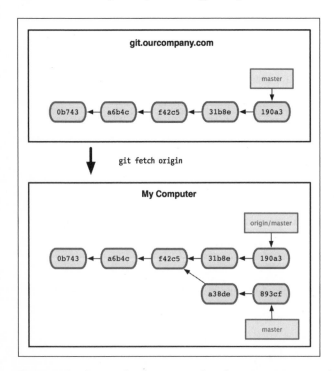

Figure 3-24. *The* git fetch *command updates your remote references.*

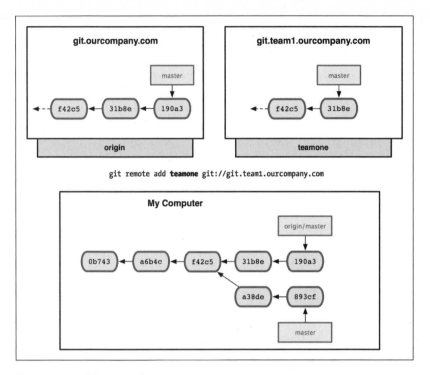

Figure 3-25. *Adding another server as a remote*

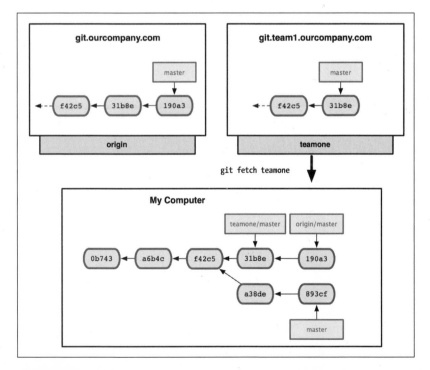

Figure 3-26. *You get a reference to teamone's master branch position locally.*

Pushing

When you want to share a branch with the world, you need to push it up to a remote that you have write access to. Your local branches aren't automatically synchronized to the remotes you write to—you have to explicitly push the branches you want to share. That way, you can use private branches to do work you don't want to share, and push up only the topic branches you want to collaborate on.

If you have a branch named serverfix that you want to work on with others, you can push it up the same way you pushed your first branch. Run git push (remote) (branch):

```
$ git push origin serverfix
Counting objects: 20, done.
Compressing objects: 100% (14/14), done.
Writing objects: 100% (15/15), 1.74 KiB, done.
Total 15 (delta 5), reused 0 (delta 0)
To git@github.com:schacon/simplegit.git
 * [new branch]      serverfix -> serverfix
```

This is a bit of a shortcut. Git automatically expands the serverfix branch name out to refs/heads/serverfix:refs/heads/serverfix, which means, "Take my serverfix local branch and push it to update the remote's serverfix branch." I'll go over the refs/heads/ part in detail in Chapter 9, but you can generally leave it off. You can also do git push origin serverfix:serverfix, which does the same thing—it says, "Take my serverfix and make it the remote's serverfix." You can use this format to push a local branch into a remote branch that is named differently. If you didn't want it to be called serverfix on the remote, you could instead run git push origin serverfix:awesomebranch to push your serverfix branch to the awesomebranch branch on the remote project.

The next time one of your collaborators fetches from the server, they will get a reference to where the server's version of serverfix is under the remote branch origin/serverfix:

```
$ git fetch origin
remote: Counting objects: 20, done.
remote: Compressing objects: 100% (14/14), done.
remote: Total 15 (delta 5), reused 0 (delta 0)
Unpacking objects: 100% (15/15), done.
From git@github.com:schacon/simplegit
 * [new branch]      serverfix    -> origin/serverfix
```

It's important to note that when you do a fetch that brings down new remote branches, you don't automatically have local, editable copies of them. In other words, in this case, you don't have a new serverfix branch—you only have an origin/serverfix pointer that you can't modify.

To merge this work into your current working branch, you can run git merge origin/serverfix. If you want your own serverfix branch that you can work on, you can base it off your remote branch:

```
$ git checkout -b serverfix origin/serverfix
Branch serverfix set up to track remote branch refs/remotes/origin/serverfix.
Switched to a new branch "serverfix"
```

This gives you a local branch that you can work on that starts where `origin/serverfix` is.

Tracking Branches

Checking out a local branch from a remote branch automatically creates what is called a *tracking branch*. Tracking branches are local branches that have a direct relationship to a remote branch. If you're on a tracking branch and type `git push`, Git automatically knows which server and branch to push to. Also, running `git pull` while on one of these branches fetches all the remote references and then automatically merges in the corresponding remote branch.

When you clone a repository, it generally automatically creates a `master` branch that tracks `origin/master`. That's why `git push` and `git pull` work out of the box with no other arguments. However, you can set up other tracking branches if you wish—ones that don't track branches on `origin` and don't track the `master` branch. The simple case is the example you just saw, running `git checkout -b [branch] [remotename]/[branch]`. If you have Git version 1.6.2 or later, you can also use the `--track` shorthand:

```
$ git checkout --track origin/serverfix
Branch serverfix set up to track remote branch refs/remotes/origin/serverfix.
Switched to a new branch "serverfix"
```

To set up a local branch with a different name than the remote branch, you can easily use the first version with a different local branch name:

```
$ git checkout -b sf origin/serverfix
Branch sf set up to track remote branch refs/remotes/origin/serverfix.
Switched to a new branch "sf"
```

Now, your local branch `sf` will automatically push to and pull from `origin/serverfix`.

Deleting Remote Branches

Suppose you're done with a remote branch—say, you and your collaborators are finished with a feature and have merged it into your remote's `master` branch (or whatever branch your stable codeline is in). You can delete a remote branch using the rather obtuse syntax `git push [remotename] :[branch]`. If you want to delete your `serverfix` branch from the server, you run the following:

```
$ git push origin :serverfix
To git@github.com:schacon/simplegit.git
 - [deleted]         serverfix
```

Boom. No more branch on your server. You may want to dog-ear this page, because you'll need that command, and you'll likely forget the syntax. A way to remember this command is by recalling the `git push [remotename] [localbranch]:[remotebranch]` syntax that I went over a bit earlier. If you leave off the `[localbranch]` portion, then you're basically saying, "Take nothing on my side and make it be `[remotebranch]`."

Rebasing

In Git, there are two main ways to integrate changes from one branch into another: the *merge* and the *rebase*. In this section you'll learn what rebasing is, how to do it, why it's a pretty amazing tool, and in what cases you won't want to use it.

The Basic Rebase

If you go back to an earlier example from the "Basic Branching and Merging" section (see Figure 3-27), you can see that you diverged your work and made commits on two different branches.

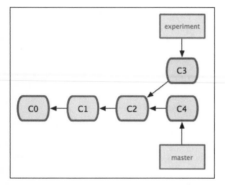

Figure 3-27. *Your initial diverged commit history*

The easiest way to integrate the branches, as I've already covered, is the merge command. It performs a three-way merge between the two latest branch snapshots (C3 and C4) and the most recent common ancestor of the two (C2), creating a new snapshot (and commit), as shown in Figure 3-28.

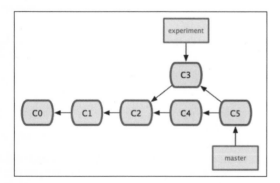

Figure 3-28. *Merging a branch to integrate the diverged work history*

However, there is another way: you can take the patch of the change that was introduced in C3 and reapply it on top of C4. In Git, this is called *rebasing*. With the rebase command, you can take all the changes that were committed on one branch and replay them on another one.

In this example, you'd run the following:

```
$ git checkout experiment
$ git rebase master
First, rewinding head to replay your work on top of it...
Applying: added staged command
```

It works by going to the common ancestor of the two branches (the one you're on and the one you're rebasing onto), getting the diff introduced by each commit of the branch you're on, saving those diffs to temporary files, resetting the current branch to the same commit as the branch you are rebasing onto, and finally applying each change in turn. Figure 3-29 illustrates this process.

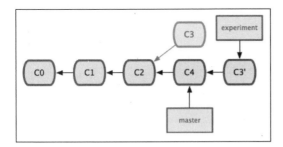

Figure 3-29. *Rebasing the change introduced in C3 onto C4*

At this point, you can go back to the master branch and do a fast-forward merge (see Figure 3-30).

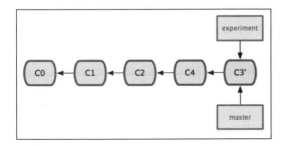

Figure 3-30. *Fast-forwarding the master branch*

Now, the snapshot pointed to by C3 is exactly the same as the one that was pointed to by C5 in the merge example. There is no difference in the end product of the integration, but rebasing makes for a cleaner history. If you examine the log of a rebased branch, it looks like a linear history: it appears that all the work happened in series, even when it originally happened in parallel.

Often, you'll do this to make sure your commits apply cleanly on a remote branch—perhaps in a project to which you're trying to contribute but that you don't maintain. In this case, you'd do your work in a branch and then rebase your work onto `origin/master` when you were ready to submit your patches to the main project. That way, the maintainer doesn't have to do any integration work—just a fast-forward or a clean apply.

Note that the snapshot pointed to by the final commit you end up with, whether it's the last of the rebased commits for a rebase or the final merge commit after a merge, is the same snapshot—it's the history that is different. Rebasing replays changes from one line of work onto another in the order they were introduced, whereas merging takes the endpoints and merges them together.

More Interesting Rebases

You can also have your rebase replay on something other than the rebase branch. Take a history like Figure 3-31, for example. You branched a topic branch (`server`) to add some server-side functionality to your project, and made a commit. Then, you branched off that to make the client-side changes (`client`) and committed a few times. Finally, you went back to your `server` branch and did a few more commits.

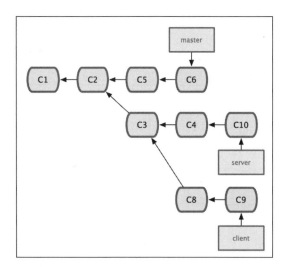

Figure 3-31. *A history with a topic branch off another topic branch*

Suppose you decide that you want to merge your client-side changes into your mainline for a release, but you want to hold off on the server-side changes until it's tested further. You can take the changes on `client` that aren't on `server` (C8 and C9) and replay them on your `master` branch by using the `--onto` option of `git rebase`:

```
$ git rebase --onto master server client
```

This basically says, "Check out the `client` branch, figure out the patches from the common ancestor of the `client` and `server` branches, and then replay them onto `master`." It's a bit complex; but the result, shown in Figure 3-32, is pretty cool.

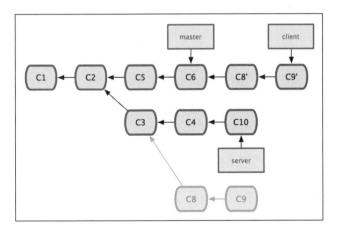

Figure 3-32. *Rebasing a topic branch off another topic branch*

Now you can fast-forward your `master` branch (see Figure 3-33):

```
$ git checkout master
$ git merge client
```

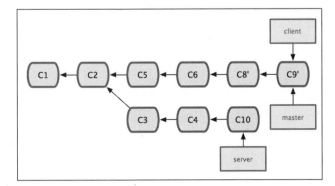

Figure 3-33. *Fast-forwarding your master branch to include the client branch changes*

Let's say you decide to pull in your `server` branch as well. You can rebase the `server` branch onto the `master` branch without having to check it out first by running `git rebase` [*basebranch*] [*topicbranch*]—which checks out the topic branch (in this case, `server`) for you and replays it onto the base branch (`master`):

```
$ git rebase master server
```

This replays your server work on top of your master work, as shown in Figure 3-34.

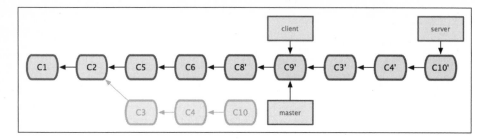

Figure 3-34. *Rebasing your server branch on top of your master branch*

Then, you can fast-forward the base branch (master):

```
$ git checkout master
$ git merge server
```

You can remove the client and server branches because all the work is integrated and you don't need them anymore, leaving your history for this entire process looking like Figure 3-35:

```
$ git branch -d client
$ git branch -d server
```

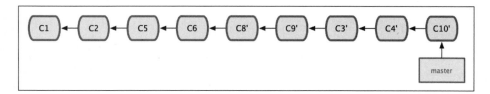

Figure 3-35. *Final commit history*

The Perils of Rebasing

Ahh, but the bliss of rebasing isn't without its drawbacks, which can be summed up in a single line:

> *Do not rebase commits that you have pushed to a public repository.*

If you follow that guideline, you'll be fine. If you don't, people will hate you, and you'll be scorned by friends and family.

When you rebase stuff, you're abandoning existing commits and creating new ones that are similar but different. If you push commits somewhere and others pull them down and base work on them, and then you rewrite those commits with git rebase and push them up again, your collaborators will have to re-merge their work and things will get messy when you try to pull their work back into yours.

Let's look at an example of how rebasing work that you've made public can cause problems. Suppose you clone from a central server and then do some work off that. Your commit history looks like Figure 3-36.

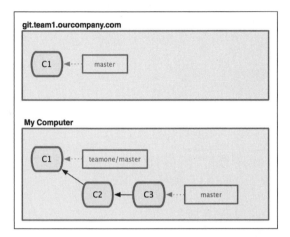

Figure 3-36. *Clone a repository, and base some work on it.*

Now, someone else does more work that includes a merge, and pushes that work to the central server. You fetch them and merge the new remote branch into your work, making your history look something like Figure 3-37.

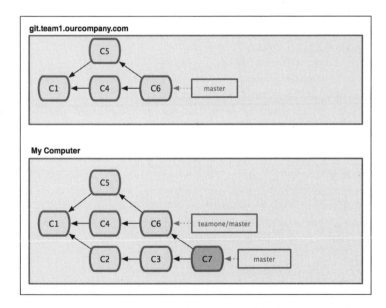

Figure 3-37. *Fetch more commits, and merge them into your work.*

Next, the person who pushed the merged work decides to go back and rebase their work instead; they do a `git push --force` to overwrite the history on the server. You then fetch from that server, bringing down the new commits (see Figure 3-38).

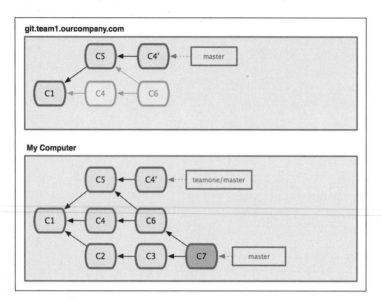

Figure 3-38. *Someone pushes rebased commits, abandoning commits you've based your work on.*

At this point, you have to merge this work in again, even though you've already done so. Rebasing changes the SHA-1 hashes of these commits so to Git they look like new commits, when in fact you already have the C4 work in your history (see Figure 3-39).

You have to merge that work in at some point so you can keep up with the other developer in the future. After you do that, your commit history will contain both the C4 and C4' commits, which have different SHA-1 hashes but introduce the same work and have the same commit message. If you run a `git log` when your history looks like this, you'll see two commits that have the same author date and message, which will be confusing. Furthermore, if you push this history back up to the server, you'll reintroduce all those rebased commits to the central server, which can further confuse people.

If you treat rebasing as a way to clean up and work with commits before you push them, and if you only rebase commits that have never been available publicly, then you'll be fine. If you rebase commits that have already been pushed publicly, and people may have based work on those commits, then you may be in for some frustrating trouble.

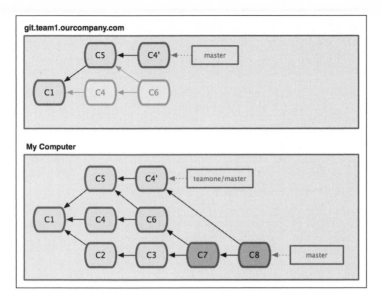

Figure 3-39. *You merge in the same work again into a new merge commit.*

Summary

I've covered basic branching and merging in Git. You should feel comfortable creating and switching to new branches, switching between branches, and merging local branches together. You should also be able to share your branches by pushing them to a shared server, working with others on shared branches and rebasing your branches before they're shared.

■■■

## CHAPTER 4

Git on the Server

At this point, you should be able to do most of the day-to-day tasks for which you'll be using Git. However, in order to do any collaboration in Git, you'll need to have a remote Git repository. Although you can technically push change to and pull changes from individuals' repositories, doing so is discouraged because you can fairly easily confuse what they're working on if you're not careful. Furthermore, you want your collaborators to be able to access the repository even if your computer is offline—having a more reliable common repository is often useful. Therefore, the preferred method for collaborating with someone is to set up an intermediate repository that you both have access to, and push to and pull from that. I'll refer to this repository as a *Git server*; but you'll notice that it generally takes a tiny amount of resources to host a Git repo, so you'll rarely need to use an entire server for it.

Running a Git server is simple. First, you choose which protocols you want your server to communicate with. The first section of this chapter will cover the available protocols and the pros and cons of each. The next sections will explain some typical setups using those protocols and how to get your server running with them. Last, I'll go over a few hosted options, if you don't mind hosting your code on someone else's server and don't want to go through the hassle of setting up and maintaining your own server.

If you have no interest in running your own server, you can skip to the last section of the chapter to see some options for setting up a hosted account and then move on to the next chapter, where I discuss the various ins and outs of working in a distributed source control environment.

A remote repository is generally a *bare repository*—a Git repository that has no working directory. Because the repository is only used as a collaboration point, there is no reason to have a snapshot checked out on disk; it's just the Git data. In the simplest terms, a bare repository is the contents of your project's `.git` directory and nothing else.

The Protocols

Git can use four major network protocols to transfer data: Local, Secure Shell (SSH), Git, and HTTP. Here I'll discuss what they are and in what basic circumstances you would want (or not want) to use them.

It's important to note that with the exception of the HTTP protocols, all of these require Git to be installed and working on the server.

Local Protocol

The most basic is the Local protocol, in which the remote repository is in another directory on disk. This is often used if everyone on your team has access to a shared filesystem such as an NFS mount, or in the less likely case that everyone logs in to the same computer. The latter wouldn't be ideal, because all your code repository instances would reside on the same computer, making a catastrophic loss much more likely.

If you have a shared mounted filesystem, then you can clone, push to, and pull from a local file-based repository. To clone a repository like this or to add one as a remote to an existing project, use the path to the repository as the URL. For example, to clone a local repository, you can run something like this:

```
$ git clone /opt/git/project.git
```

Or you can do this:

```
$ git clone file:///opt/git/project.git
```

Git operates slightly differently if you explicitly specify file:// at the beginning of the URL. If you just specify the path, Git tries to use hardlinks or directly copy the files it needs. If you specify file://, Git fires up the processes that it normally uses to transfer data over a network, which is generally a lot less efficient method of transferring the data. The main reason to specify the file:// prefix is if you want a clean copy of the repository with extraneous references or objects left out—generally after an import from another version-control system or something similar (see Chapter 9 for maintenance tasks). You'll use the normal path here because doing so is almost always faster.

To add a local repository to an existing Git project, you can run something like this:

```
$ git remote add local_proj /opt/git/project.git
```

Then, you can push to and pull from that remote as though you were doing so over a network.

The Pros

The pros of file-based repositories are that they're simple and they use existing file permissions and network access. If you already have a shared filesystem to which your whole team has access, setting up a repository is very easy. You stick the bare repository copy somewhere everyone has shared access to and set the read/write permissions as you would for any other shared directory. I'll discuss how to export a bare repository copy for this purpose in the next section, "Getting Git on a Server."

This is also a nice option for quickly grabbing work from someone else's working repository. If you and a co-worker are working on the same project and they want you to check something out, running a command like git pull /home/john/project is often easier than them pushing to a remote server and you pulling down.

The Cons

The cons of this method are that shared access is generally more difficult to set up and reach from multiple locations than basic network access. If you want to push from your laptop when you're at home, you have to mount the remote disk, which can be difficult and slow compared to network-based access.

It's also important to mention that this isn't necessarily the fastest option if you're using a shared mount of some kind. A local repository is fast only if you have fast access to the data. A repository on NFS is often slower than the repository over SSH on the same server, allowing Git to run off local disks on each system.

The SSH Protocol

Probably the most common transport protocol for Git is SSH. This is because SSH access to servers is already set up in most places—and if it isn't, it's easy to do. SSH is also the only network-based protocol that you can easily read from and write to. The other two network protocols (HTTP and Git) are generally read-only, so even if you have them available for the unwashed masses, you still need SSH for your own write commands. SSH is also an authenticated network protocol; and because it's ubiquitous, it's generally easy to set up and use.

To clone a Git repository over SSH, you can specify `ssh://` URL like this:

```
$ git clone ssh://user@server:project.git
```

Or you can not specify a protocol—Git assumes SSH if you aren't explicit:

```
$ git clone user@server:project.git
```

You can also not specify a user, and Git assumes the user you're currently logged in as.

The Pros

The pros of using SSH are many. First, you basically have to use it if you want authenticated write access to your repository over a network. Second, SSH is relatively easy to set up—SSH daemons are commonplace, many network admins have experience with them, and many OS distributions are set up with them or have tools to manage them. Next, access over SSH is secure—all data transfer is encrypted and authenticated. Last, like the Git and Local protocols, SSH is efficient, making the data as compact as possible before transferring it.

The Cons

The negative aspect of SSH is that you can't serve anonymous access of your repository over it. People must have access to your machine over SSH to access it, even in a read-only capacity, which doesn't make SSH access conducive to open source projects. If you're using it only within your corporate network, SSH may be the only protocol you need to deal with. If you want to allow anonymous read-only access to your projects, you'll have to set up SSH for you to push over but something else for others to pull over.

The Git Protocol

Next is the Git protocol. This is a special daemon that comes packaged with Git; it listens on a dedicated port (9418) that provides a service similar to the SSH protocol, but with absolutely no authentication. In order for a repository to be served over the Git protocol, you must create the `git-export-daemon-ok` file—the daemon won't serve a repository without that file in it—but other than that there is no security. Either the Git repository is available for everyone to clone or it isn't. This means that there is generally no pushing over this protocol. You can enable push access; but given the lack of authentication, if you turn on push access, anyone on the Internet who finds your project's URL could push to your project. Suffice it to say that this is rare.

The Pros

The Git protocol is the fastest transfer protocol available. If you're serving a lot of traffic for a public project or serving a very large project that doesn't require user authentication for read access, it's likely that you'll want to set up a Git daemon to serve your project. It uses the same data-transfer mechanism as the SSH protocol but without the encryption and authentication overhead.

The Cons

The downside of the Git protocol is the lack of authentication. It's generally undesirable for the Git protocol to be the only access to your project. Generally, you'll pair it with SSH access for the few developers who have push (write) access and have everyone else use git:// for read-only access.

It's also probably the most difficult protocol to set up. It must run its own daemon, which is custom—you'll look at setting one up in the "Gitosis" section of this chapter—and it requires xinetd configuration or the like, which isn't always a walk in the park. It also requires firewall access to port 9418, which isn't a standard port that corporate firewalls always allow. Behind big corporate firewalls, this obscure port is commonly blocked.

The HTTP/S Protocol

Last you have the HTTP protocol. The beauty of the HTTP or HTTPS protocol is the simplicity of setting it up. Basically, all you have to do is put the bare Git repository under your HTTP document root and set up a specific post-receive hook, and you're done (See Chapter 7 for details on Git hooks). At that point, anyone who can access the web server under which you put the repository can also clone your repository. To allow read access to your repository over HTTP, do something like this:

```
$ cd /var/www/htdocs/
$ git clone --bare /path/to/git_project gitproject.git
$ cd gitproject.git
$ mv hooks/post-update.sample hooks/post-update
$ chmod a+x hooks/post-update
```

That's all. The post-update hook that comes with Git by default runs the appropriate command (git update-server-info) to make HTTP fetching and cloning work properly. This command is run when you push to this repository over SSH; then, other people can clone via something like

```
$ git clone http://example.com/gitproject.git
```

In this particular case, you're using the /var/www/htdocs path that is common for Apache setups, but you can use any static web server—just put the bare repository in its path. The Git data is served as basic static files (see Chapter 9 for details about exactly how it's served).

It's possible to make Git push over HTTP as well, although that technique isn't as widely used and requires you to set up complex WebDAV requirements. Because it's rarely used, I won't cover it in this book. If you're interested in using the HTTP-push protocols, you can read about preparing a repository for this purpose at `http://www.kernel.org/pub/software/scm/git/docs/howto/setup-git-server-over-http.txt`. One nice thing about making Git push over HTTP is that you can use any WebDAV server, without specific Git features; so, you can use this functionality if your web-hosting provider supports WebDAV for writing updates to your web site.

The Pros

The upside of using the HTTP protocol is that it's easy to set up. Running the handful of required commands gives you a simple way to give the world read access to your Git repository. It takes only a few minutes to do. The HTTP protocol also isn't very resource intensive on your server. Because it generally uses a static HTTP server to serve all the data, a normal Apache server can serve thousands of files per second on average—it's difficult to overload even a small server.

You can also serve your repositories read-only over HTTPS, which means you can encrypt the content transfer; or you can go so far as to make the clients use specific signed SSL certificates. Generally, if you're going to these lengths, it's easier to use SSH public keys; but it may be a better solution in your specific case to use signed SSL certificates or other HTTP-based authentication methods for read-only access over HTTPS.

Another nice thing is that HTTP is such a commonly used protocol that corporate firewalls are often set up to allow traffic through this port.

The Cons

The downside of serving your repository over HTTP is that it's relatively inefficient for the client. It generally takes a lot longer to clone or fetch from the repository, and you often have a lot more network overhead and transfer volume over HTTP than with any of the other network protocols. Because it's not as intelligent about transferring only the data you need— there is no dynamic work on the part of the server in these transactions—the HTTP protocol is often referred to as a *dumb* protocol. For more information about the differences in efficiency between the HTTP protocol and the other protocols, see Chapter 9.

Getting Git on a Server

In order to initially set up any Git server, you have to export an existing repository into a new *bare* repository—a repository that doesn't contain a working directory. This is generally straightforward to do.

In order to clone your repository to create a new bare repository, you run the `clone` command with the `--bare` option. By convention, bare repository directories end in `.git`, like so:

```
$ git clone --bare my_project my_project.git
Initialized empty Git repository in /opt/projects/my_project.git/
```

The output for this command is a little confusing. Because `clone` is basically a `git init` and then a `git fetch`, you see some output from the `git init` part, which creates an empty directory. The actual object transfer gives no output, but it does happen. You should now have a copy of the Git directory data in your `my_project.git` directory.

This is roughly equivalent to something like

```
$ cp -Rf my_project/.git my_project.git
```

There are a couple of minor differences in the configuration file; but for your purpose, this is close to the same thing. It takes the Git repository by itself, without a working directory, and creates a directory specifically for it alone.

Putting the Bare Repository on a Server

Now that you have a bare copy of your repository, all you need to do is put it on a server and set up your protocols. Let's say you've set up a server called `git.example.com` that you have SSH access to, and you want to store all your Git repositories under the `/opt/git` directory. You can set up your new repository by copying your bare repository over:

```
$ scp -r my_project.git user@git.example.com:/opt/git
```

At this point, other users who have SSH access to the same server, which has read access to the `/opt/git` directory, can clone your repository by running

```
$ git clone user@git.example.com:/opt/git/my_project.git
```

If a user SSHs into a server and has write access to the `/opt/git/my_project.git` directory, they also automatically have push access. Git automatically adds group write permissions to a repository properly if you run the `git init` command with the `--shared` option:

```
$ ssh user@git.example.com
$ cd /opt/git/my_project.git
$ git init --bare --shared
```

You see how easy it is to take a Git repository, create a bare version, and place it on a server to which you and your collaborators have SSH access. Now you're ready to collaborate on the same project.

It's important to note that this is literally all you need to do to run a useful Git server to which several people have access—just add SSH-able accounts on a server, and stick a bare repository somewhere that all those users have read and write access to. You're ready to go—nothing else is needed.

In the next few sections, you'll see how to expand to more sophisticated setups. This discussion will include not having to create user accounts for each user, adding public read access to repositories, setting up web UIs, using the Gitosis tool, and more. However, keep in mind that to collaborate with a couple of people on a private project, all you need is an SSH server and a bare repository.

Small Setups

If you're a small outfit or are just trying out Git in your organization and have only a few developers, things can be simple for you. One of the most complicated aspects of setting up a Git server is user management. If you want some repositories to be read-only to certain users and read/write to others, access and permissions can be a bit difficult to arrange.

SSH Access

If you already have a server to which all your developers have SSH access, it's generally easiest to set up your first repository there, because you have to do almost no work (as I covered in the last section). If you want more complex access control type permissions on your repositories, you can handle them with the normal filesystem permissions of the operating system your server runs.

If you want to place your repositories on a server that doesn't have accounts for everyone on your team whom you want to have write access, then you must set up SSH access for them. I assume that if you have a server with which to do this, you already have an SSH server installed, and that's how you're accessing the server.

There are a few ways you can give access to everyone on your team. The first is to set up accounts for everybody, which is straightforward but can be cumbersome. You may not want to run adduser and set temporary passwords for every user.

A second method is to create a single "git" user on the machine, ask every user who is to have write access to send you an SSH public key, and add that key to the ~/.ssh/authorized_keys file of your new "git" user. At that point, everyone will be able to access that machine via the "git" user. This doesn't affect the commit data in any way—the SSH user you connect as doesn't affect the commits you've recorded.

Another way to do it is to have your SSH server authenticate from an LDAP server or some other centralized authentication source that you may already have set up. As long as each user can get shell access on the machine, any SSH authentication mechanism you can think of should work.

Generating Your SSH Public Key

That being said, many Git servers authenticate using SSH public keys. In order to provide a public key, each user in your system must generate one if they don't already have one. This process is similar across all operating systems.

First, you should check to make sure you don't already have a key. By default, a user's SSH keys are stored in that user's ~/.ssh directory. You can easily check to see if you have a key already by going to that directory and listing the contents:

```
$ cd ~/.ssh
$ ls
authorized_keys2  id_dsa       known_hosts
config            id_dsa.pub
```

You're looking for a pair of files named *something* and *something*.pub, where the *something* is usually id_dsa or id_rsa. The .pub file is your public key, and the other file is your private key. If you don't have these files (or you don't even have a .ssh directory), you can create them by running a program called ssh-keygen, which is provided with the SSH package on Linux/Mac systems and comes with the MSysGit package on Windows:

```
$ ssh-keygen
Generating public/private rsa key pair.
Enter file in which to save the key (/Users/schacon/.ssh/id_rsa):
Enter passphrase (empty for no passphrase):
Enter same passphrase again:
Your identification has been saved in /Users/schacon/.ssh/id_rsa.
Your public key has been saved in /Users/schacon/.ssh/id_rsa.pub.
The key fingerprint is:
43:c5:5b:5f:b1:f1:50:43:ad:20:a6:92:6a:1f:9a:3a schacon@agadorlaptop.local
```

First it confirms where you want to save the key (.ssh/id_rsa), and then it asks twice for a passphrase, which you can leave empty if you don't want to type a password when you use the key.

Now, each user that does this has to send their public key to you or whoever is administrating the Git server (assuming you're using an SSH server setup that requires public keys). All they have to do is copy the contents of the .pub file and e-mail it. The public keys look something like this:

```
$ cat ~/.ssh/id_rsa.pub
ssh-rsa AAAAB3NzaC1yc2EAAAABIwAAAQEAklOUpkDHrfHY17SbrmTIpNLTGK9Tjom/BWDSU
GPl+nafzlHDTYW7hdI4yZ5ew18JH4JW9jbhUFrviQzM7xlELEVf4h9lFX5QVkbPppSwgOcda3
Pbv7kOdJ/MTyBlWXFCR+HAo3FXRitBqxiX1nKhXpHAZsMciLq8V6RjsNAQwdsdMFvSlVK/7XA
t3FaoJoAsncM1Q9x5+3VOWw68/eIFmb1zuUFljQJKprrX88XypNDvjYNby6vw/PbOrwert/En
mZ+AW4OZPnTPI89ZPmVMLuayrD2cE86Z/il8b+gw3r3+1nKatmIkjn2so1dO1QraTlMqVSsbx
NrRFi9wrf+M7Q== schacon@agadorlaptop.local
```

For a more in-depth tutorial on creating an SSH key on multiple operating systems, see the GitHub guide on SSH keys at http://github.com/guides/providing-your-ssh-key.

Setting Up the Server

Let's walk through setting up SSH access on the server side. In this example, you'll use the authorized_keys method for authenticating your users. I also assume you're running a standard Linux distribution like Ubuntu. First, you create a "git" user and a .ssh directory for that user:

```
$ sudo adduser git
$ su git
$ cd
$ mkdir .ssh
```

Next, you need to add some developer SSH public keys to the authorized_keys file for that user. Let's assume you've received a few keys by e-mail and saved them to temporary files. Again, the public keys look something like this:

```
$ cat /tmp/id_rsa.john.pub
ssh-rsa AAAAB3NzaC1yc2EAAAADAQABAAABAQCBOO7n/ww+ouN4gSLKssMxXnBOvf9LGt4L
ojG6rs6hPBO9j9R/T17/x4lhJAOF3FR1rP6kYBRsWj2aThGw6HXLm9/5zytK6Ztg3RPKK+4k
Yjh6541NYsnEAZuXzOjTTyAUfrtU3Z5EOO3C4oxOj6HOrfIF1kKI9MAQLMdpGW1GYEIgS9Ez
Sdfd8AcCIicTDWbqLAcU4UpkaX8KyGlLwsNuuGztobF8m72ALC/nLF6JLtPofwFBlgc+myiv
O7TCUSBdLQlgMVOFq1I2uPWQOkOWQAHukEOmfjy2jctxSDBQ22OymjaNsHT4kgtZg2AYYgPq
dAv8JggJICUvax2T9va5 gsg-keypair
```

You append them to your authorized_keys file:

```
$ cat /tmp/id_rsa.john.pub >> ~/.ssh/authorized_keys
$ cat /tmp/id_rsa.josie.pub >> ~/.ssh/authorized_keys
$ cat /tmp/id_rsa.jessica.pub >> ~/.ssh/authorized_keys
```

Now, you can set up an empty repository for them by running git init with the --bare option, which initializes the repository without a working directory:

```
$ cd /opt/git
$ mkdir project.git
$ cd project.git
$ git --bare init
```

Then, John, Josie, or Jessica can push the first version of their project into that repository by adding it as a remote and pushing up a branch. Note that someone must shell onto the machine and create a bare repository every time you want to add a project. Let's use gitserver as the hostname of the server on which you've set up your "git" user and repository. If you're running it internally, and you set up DNS for gitserver to point to that server, then you can use the commands pretty much as is:

```
# on Johns computer
$ cd myproject
$ git init
$ git add .
$ git commit -m 'initial commit'
$ git remote add origin git@gitserver:/opt/git/project.git
$ git push origin master
```

At this point, the others can clone it down and push changes back up just as easily:

```
$ git clone git@gitserver:/opt/git/project.git
$ vim README
$ git commit -am 'fix for the README file'
$ git push origin master
```

With this method, you can quickly get a read/write Git server up and running for a hand-ful of developers.

As an extra precaution, you can easily restrict the "git" user to only doing Git activities with a limited shell tool called `git-shell` that comes with Git. If you set this as your "git" user's login shell, then the "git" user can't have normal shell access to your server. To use this, specify `git-shell` instead of `bash` or `csh` for your user's login shell. To do so, you'll likely have to edit your `/etc/passwd` file:

```
$ sudo vim /etc/passwd
```

At the bottom, you should find a line that looks something like this:

```
git:x:1000:1000::/home/git:/bin/sh
```

Change `/bin/sh` to `/usr/bin/git-shell` (or run `which git-shell` to see where it's installed). The line should look something like this:

```
git:x:1000:1000::/home/git:/usr/bin/git-shell
```

Now, the "git" user can only use the SSH connection to push and pull Git repositories and can't shell onto the machine. If you try, you'll see a login rejection:

```
$ ssh git@gitserver
fatal: What do you think I am? A shell?
Connection to gitserver closed.
```

Public Access

What if you want anonymous read access to your project? Perhaps instead of hosting an inter-nal private project, you want to host an open source project. Or maybe you have a bunch of automated build servers or continuous integration servers that change a lot, and you don't want to have to generate SSH keys all the time—you just want to add simple anonymous read access.

Probably the simplest way for smaller setups is to run a static web server with its docu-ment root where your Git repositories are, and then enable that post-update hook I mentioned in the first section of this chapter. You'll work from the previous example. Say you have your repositories in the `/opt/git` directory, and an Apache server is running on your machine. Again, you can use any web server for this; but as an example, I'll demonstrate some basic Apache configurations that should give you an idea of what you might need.

First you need to enable the hook:

```
$ cd project.git
$ mv hooks/post-update.sample hooks/post-update
$ chmod a+x hooks/post-update
```

If you're using a version of Git earlier than 1.6, the `mv` command isn't necessary—Git started naming the hooks examples with the `.sample` postfix only recently.

What does this post-update hook do? It looks basically like this:

```
$ cat .git/hooks/post-update
#!/bin/sh
exec git-update-server-info
```

This means that when you push to the server via SSH, Git runs this command to update the files needed for HTTP fetching.

Next, you need to add a VirtualHost entry to your Apache configuration with the document root as the root directory of your Git projects. Here, I'm assuming that you have wildcard DNS set up to send `*.gitserver` to whatever box you're using to run all this:

```
<VirtualHost *:80>
    ServerName git.gitserver
    DocumentRoot /opt/git
    <Directory /opt/git/>
        Order allow, deny
        allow from all
    </Directory>
</VirtualHost>
```

You also need to set the Unix user group of the `/opt/git` directories to `www-data` so your web server can read-access the repositories, because the Apache instance running the CGI script will (by default) be running as that user:

```
$ chgrp -R www-data /opt/git
```

When you restart Apache, you should be able to clone your repositories under that directory by specifying the URL for your project:

```
$ git clone http://git.gitserver/project.git
```

This way, you can set up HTTP-based read access to any of your projects for a fair number of users in a few minutes. Another simple option for public unauthenticated access is to start a Git daemon, although that requires you to daemonize the process—I'll cover this option in the next section, if you prefer that route.

GitWeb

Now that you have basic read/write and read-only access to your project, you may want to set up a simple web-based visualizer. Git comes with a CGI script called GitWeb that is commonly used for this. You can see GitWeb in use at sites like `http://git.kernel.org` (see Figure 4-1).

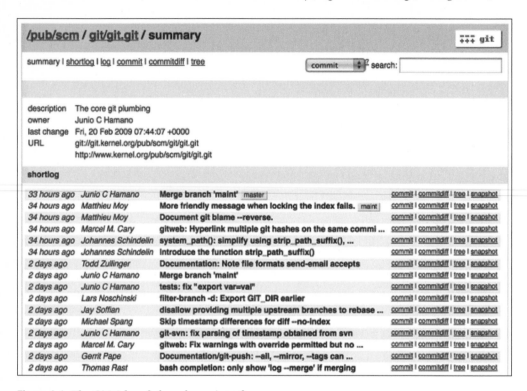

Figure 4-1. *The GitWeb web-based user interface*

If you want to check out what GitWeb would look like for your project, Git comes with a command to fire up a temporary instance if you have a lightweight server on your system like lighttpd or webrick. On Linux machines, lighttpd is often installed, so you may be able to get it to run by typing **git instaweb** in your project directory. If you're running a Mac, Leopard comes preinstalled with Ruby, so webrick may be your best bet. To start `instaweb` with a non-lighttpd handler, you can run it with the `--httpd` option.

```
$ git instaweb --httpd=webrick
[2009-02-21 10:02:21] INFO  WEBrick 1.3.1
[2009-02-21 10:02:21] INFO  ruby 1.8.6 (2008-03-03) [universal-darwin9.0]
```

That starts up an HTTPD server on port 1234 and then automatically starts a web browser that opens on that page. It's pretty easy on your part. When you're done and want to shut down the server, you can run the same command with the `--stop` option:

```
$ git instaweb --httpd=webrick --stop
```

If you want to run the web interface on a server all the time for your team or for an open source project you're hosting, you'll need to set up the CGI script to be served by your normal web server. Some Linux distributions have a `gitweb` package that you may be able to install via apt or yum, so you may want to try that first.

I'll walk through installing GitWeb manually very quickly. First, you need to get the Git source code, which GitWeb comes with, and generate the custom CGI script:

```
$ git clone git://git.kernel.org/pub/scm/git/git.git
$ cd git/
$ make GITWEB_PROJECTROOT="/opt/git" \
       prefix=/usr gitweb/gitweb.cgi
$ sudo cp -Rf gitweb /var/www/
```

Notice that you have to tell the command where to find your Git repositories with the `GITWEB_PROJECTROOT` variable. Now, you need to make Apache use CGI for that script, for which you can add a VirtualHost:

```
<VirtualHost *:80>
    ServerName gitserver
    DocumentRoot /var/www/gitweb
    <Directory /var/www/gitweb>
        Options ExecCGI +FollowSymLinks +SymLinksIfOwnerMatch
        AllowOverride All
        order allow,deny
        Allow from all
        AddHandler cgi-script cgi
        DirectoryIndex gitweb.cgi
</Directory>
</VirtualHost>
```

Again, GitWeb can be served with any CGI-capable web server; if you prefer to use something else, it shouldn't be difficult to set up. At this point, you should be able to visit `http://gitserver/` to view your repositories online, and you can use `http://git.gitserver` to clone and fetch your repositories over HTTP.

Gitosis

Keeping all users' public keys in the `authorized_keys` file for access works well only for a while. When you have hundreds of users, it's much more of a pain to manage that process. You have to shell onto the server each time, and there is no access control—everyone in the file has read and write access to every project.

You may want to turn to a widely used software project called Gitosis. Gitosis is basically a set of scripts that help you manage the `authorized_keys` file as well as implement some simple access controls. The really interesting part is that the UI for this tool for adding people and determining access isn't a web interface but a special Git repository. You set up the information in that project; and when you push it, Gitosis reconfigures the server based on that, which is cool.

Installing Gitosis isn't the simplest task ever, but it's not too difficult. It's easiest to use a Linux server for it—these examples use a stock Ubuntu 8.10 server.

Gitosis requires some Python tools, so first you have to install the Python setuptools package, which Ubuntu provides as python-setuptools:

```
$ apt-get install python-setuptools
```

Next, you clone and install Gitosis from the project's main site:

```
$ git clone git://eagain.net/gitosis.git
$ cd gitosis
$ sudo python setup.py install
```

That installs a couple of executables that Gitosis will use. Next, Gitosis wants to put its repositories under /home/git, which is fine. But you have already set up your repositories in /opt/git, so instead of reconfiguring everything, you create a symlink:

```
$ ln -s /opt/git /home/git/repositories
```

Gitosis is going to manage your keys for you, so you need to remove the current file, re-add the keys later, and let Gitosis control the authorized_keys file automatically. For now, move the authorized_keys file out of the way:

```
$ mv /home/git/.ssh/authorized_keys /home/git/.ssh/ak.bak
```

You need to turn your shell back on for the "git" user, if you changed it to the git-shell command. People still won't be able to log in, but Gitosis will control that for you. So, change this line in your /etc/passwd file

```
git:x:1000:1000::/home/git:/usr/bin/git-shell
```

back to this:

```
git:x:1000:1000::/home/git:/bin/sh
```

Now it's time to initialize Gitosis. You do this by running the gitosis-init command with your personal public key. If your public key isn't on the server, you'll have to copy it there:

```
$ sudo -H -u git gitosis-init < /tmp/id_dsa.pub
Initialized empty Git repository in /opt/git/gitosis-admin.git/
Reinitialized existing Git repository in /opt/git/gitosis-admin.git/
```

This lets the user with that key modify the main Git repository that controls the Gitosis setup. Next, you have to manually set the execute bit on the post-update script for your new control repository.

```
$ sudo chmod 755 /opt/git/gitosis-admin.git/hooks/post-update
```

You're ready to roll. If you're set up correctly, you can try to SSH into your server as the user for which you added the public key to initialize Gitosis. You should see something like this:

```
$ ssh git@gitserver
PTY allocation request failed on channel 0
fatal: unrecognized command 'gitosis-serve schacon@quaternion'
  Connection to gitserver closed.
```

That means Gitosis recognized you but shut you out because you're not trying to do any Git commands. So, do an actual Git command and clone the Gitosis control repository:

```
# on your local computer
$ git clone git@gitserver:gitosis-admin.git
```

Now you have a directory named gitosis-admin, which has two major parts:

```
$ cd gitosis-admin
$ find .
./gitosis.conf
./keydir
./keydir/scott.pub
```

The gitosis.conf file is the control file you use to specify users, repositories, and permissions. The keydir directory is where you store the public keys of all the users who have any sort of access to your repositories—one file per user. The name of the file in keydir (in the previous example, scott.pub) will be different for you—Gitosis takes that name from the description at the end of the public key that was imported with the gitosis-init script.

If you look at the gitosis.conf file, it should only specify information about the gitosis-admin project that you just cloned:

```
$ cat gitosis.conf
[gitosis]

[group gitosis-admin]
writable = gitosis-admin
members = scott
```

It shows you that the "scott" user—the user with whose public key you initialized Gitosis—is the only one who has access to the gitosis-admin project.

Now you can add a new project. You'll add a new section called mobile where you'll list the developers on your mobile team and projects that those developers need access to. Because "scott" is the only user in the system right now, you add him as the only member and create a new project called iphone_project to start on:

```
[group mobile]
writable = iphone_project
members = scott
```

Whenever you make changes to the gitosis-admin project, you have to commit the changes and push them back up to the server in order for them to take effect:

```
$ git commit -am 'add iphone_project and mobile group'
[master]: created 8962da8: "changed name"
 1 files changed, 4 insertions(+), 0 deletions(-)
$ git push
Counting objects: 5, done.
Compressing objects: 100% (2/2), done.
Writing objects: 100% (3/3), 272 bytes, done.
Total 3 (delta 1), reused 0 (delta 0)
```

```
To git@gitserver:/opt/git/gitosis-admin.git
   fb27aec..8962da8  master -> master
```

You can make your first push to the new iphone_project project by adding your server as a remote to your local version of the project and pushing. You no longer have to manually create a bare repository for new projects on the server—Gitosis creates them automatically when it sees the first push:

```
$ git remote add origin git@gitserver:iphone_project.git
$ git push origin master
Initialized empty Git repository in /opt/git/iphone_project.git/
Counting objects: 3, done.
Writing objects: 100% (3/3), 230 bytes, done.
Total 3 (delta 0), reused 0 (delta 0)
To git@gitserver:iphone_project.git
 * [new branch]      master -> master
```

Notice that you don't need to specify the path (in fact, doing so won't work), just a colon and then the name of the project—Gitosis finds it for you.

You want to work on this project with your friends, so you have to re-add their public keys. But instead of appending them manually to the ~/.ssh/authorized_keys file on your server, you'll add them, one key per file, into the keydir directory. How you name the keys determines how you refer to the users in the gitosis.conf file. Re-add the public keys for John, Josie, and Jessica:

```
$ cp /tmp/id_rsa.john.pub keydir/john.pub
$ cp /tmp/id_rsa.josie.pub keydir/josie.pub
$ cp /tmp/id_rsa.jessica.pub keydir/jessica.pub
```

Now you can add them all to your "mobile" team so they have read and write access to iphone_project:

```
[group mobile]
writable = iphone_project
members = scott john josie jessica
```

After you commit and push that change, all four users will be able to read from and write to that project.

Gitosis has simple access controls as well. If you want John to have only read access to this project, you can do this instead:

```
[group mobile]
writable = iphone_project
members = scott josie jessica

[group mobile_ro]
readable = iphone_project
members = john
```

Now John can clone the project and get updates, but Gitosis won't allow him to push back up to the project. You can create as many of these groups as you want, each containing different users and projects. You can also specify another group as one of the members, to inherit all of its members automatically.

If you have any issues, it may be useful to add `loglevel=DEBUG` under the `[gitosis]` section. If you've lost push access by pushing a messed-up configuration, you can manually fix the file on the server under /home/git/.gitosis.conf—the file from which Gitosis reads its info. A push to the project takes the `gitosis.conf` file you just pushed up and sticks it there. If you edit that file manually, it remains like that until the next successful push to the gitosis-admin project.

Git Daemon

For public, unauthenticated read access to your projects, you'll want to move past the HTTP protocol and start using the Git protocol. The main reason is speed. The Git protocol is far more efficient and thus faster than the HTTP protocol, so using it will save your users time.

Again, this is for unauthenticated read-only access. If you're running this on a server outside your firewall, it should only be used for projects that are publicly visible to the world. If the server you're running it on is inside your firewall, you might use it for projects that a large number of people or computers (continuous integration or build servers) have read-only access to, when you don't want to have to add an SSH key for each.

In any case, the Git protocol is relatively easy to set up. Basically, you need to run this command in a daemonized manner:

```
git daemon --reuseaddr --base-path=/opt/git/ /opt/git/
```

`--reuseaddr` allows the server to restart without waiting for old connections to time out, the `--base-path` option allows people to clone projects without specifying the entire path, and the path at the end tells the Git daemon where to look for repositories to export. If you're running a firewall, you also need to punch a hole in it at port 9418 on the box you're setting this up on.

You can daemonize this process a number of ways, depending on the operating system you're running. On an Ubuntu machine, you use an Upstart script. So, in the following file

```
/etc/event.d/local-git-daemon
```

you put this script:

```
start on startup
stop on shutdown
exec /usr/bin/git daemon \
    --user=git --group=git \
    --reuseaddr \
    --base-path=/opt/git/ \
    /opt/git/
respawn
```

For security reasons, you're strongly encouraged to have this daemon run as a user with read-only permissions to the repositories—you can easily do this by creating a new user git-ro and running the daemon as that user. For the sake of simplicity, run it as the same "git" user that Gitosis is running as.

When you restart your machine, your Git daemon starts automatically and respawns if it goes down. To get it running without having to reboot, you can run this:

```
initctl start local-git-daemon
```

On other systems, you may want to use xinetd, a script in your sysvinit system, or something else—as long as you get that command daemonized and watched somehow.

Next, you have to tell your Gitosis server which repositories to allow unauthenticated Git server-based access to. If you add a section for each repository, you can specify the ones from which you want your Git daemon to allow reading. If you want to allow Git protocol access for your iphone project, you add this to the end of the gitosis.conf file:

```
[repo iphone_project]
daemon = yes
```

When that is committed and pushed up, your running daemon should start serving requests for the project to anyone who has access to port 9418 on your server.

If you decide not to use Gitosis, but you want to set up a Git daemon, you have to run this on each project you want the Git daemon to serve:

```
$ cd /path/to/project.git
$ touch git-daemon-export-ok
```

The presence of that file tells Git that it's OK to serve this project without authentication.

Gitosis can also control which projects GitWeb shows. First, you need to add something like the following to the /etc/gitweb.conf file:

```
$projects_list = "/home/git/gitosis/projects.list";
$projectroot = "/home/git/repositories";
$export_ok = "git-daemon-export-ok";
@git_base_url_list = ('git://gitserver');
```

You can control which projects GitWeb lets users browse by adding or removing a gitweb setting in the Gitosis configuration file. For instance, if you want the iphone project to show up on GitWeb, you make the repo setting look like this:

```
[repo iphone_project]
daemon = yes
gitweb = yes
```

Now, if you commit and push the project, GitWeb will automatically start showing your iphone project.

Hosted Git

If you don't want to go through all the work involved in setting up your own Git server, you have several options for hosting your Git projects on an external dedicated hosting site. Doing so offers a number of advantages: a hosting site is generally quick to set up and easy to start projects on, and no server maintenance or monitoring is involved. Even if you set up and run your own server internally, you may still want to use a public hosting site for your open source code—it's generally easier for the open source community to find and help you with.

These days, you have a huge number of hosting options to choose from, each with different advantages and disadvantages. To see an up-to-date list, check out the GitHosting page on the main Git wiki:

http://git.or.cz/gitwiki/GitHosting

Because I can't cover all the hosting sites, and because I happen to work at one of them, I'll use this section to walk through setting up an account and creating a new project at GitHub. This will give you an idea of what is involved.

GitHub is by far the largest open source Git hosting site, and it's also one of the very few that offers both public and private hosting options so you can keep your open source and private commercial code in the same place. In fact, I used GitHub while writing this book.

GitHub

GitHub is slightly different than most code-hosting sites in the way that it namespaces projects. Instead of being primarily based on the project, GitHub is user centric. That means when you host our grit project on GitHub, you won't find it at github.com/grit but instead at github.com/schacon/grit. There is no canonical version of any project, which allows a project to move from one user to another seamlessly if the first author abandons the project.

GitHub is also a commercial company that charges for accounts that maintain private repositories, but anyone can quickly get a free account to host as many open source projects as they want. I'll quickly go over how that is done.

Setting Up a User Account

The first thing you need to do is set up a free user account. If you visit the Pricing and Signup page at http://github.com/plans and click the Sign Up button on the Free account (see Figure 4-2), you're taken to the signup page.

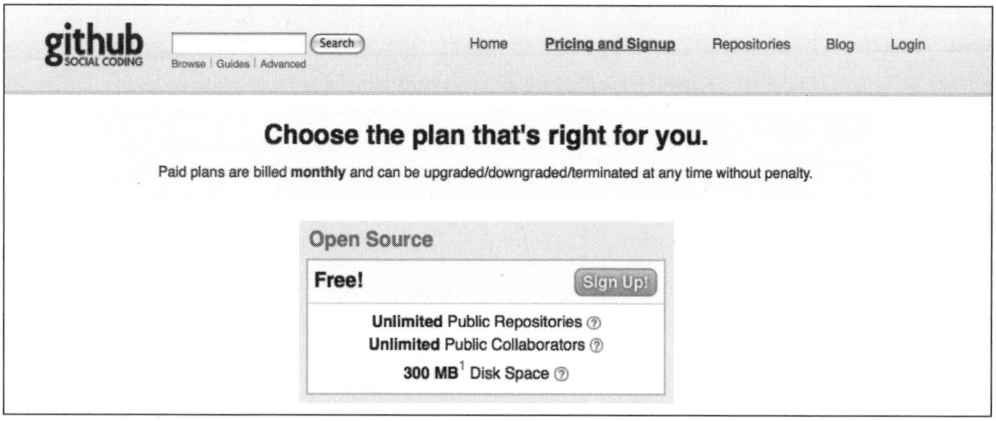

Figure 4-2. *The GitHub plan page*

Here you must choose a username that isn't yet taken in the system and enter an e-mail address that will be associated with the account and a password (see Figure 4-3).

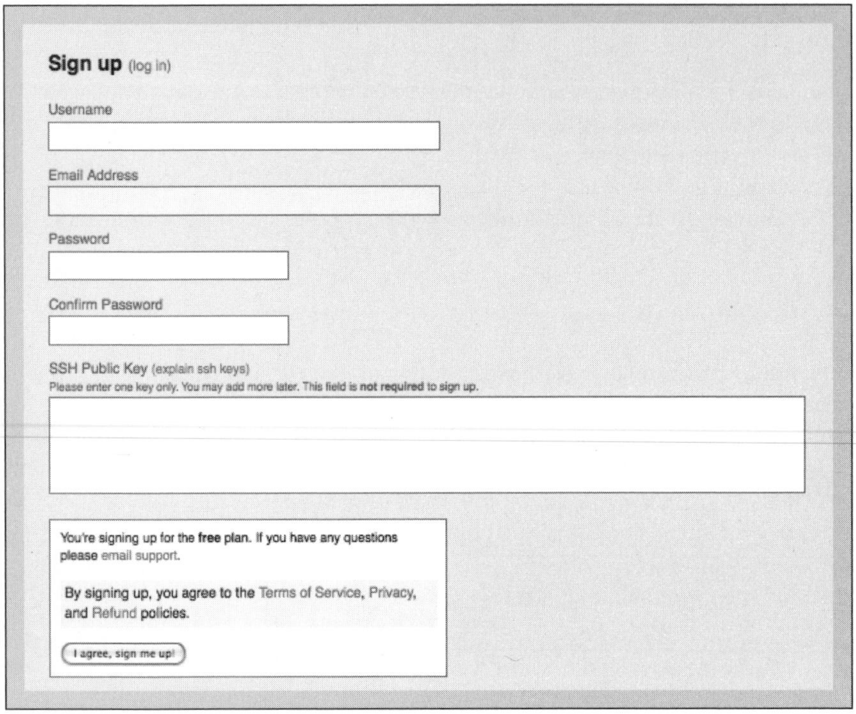

Figure 4-3. *The GitHub user signup form*

If you have it available, this is a good time to add your public SSH key as well. I covered how to generate a new key earlier, in the "Small Setups" section. Take the contents of the public key of that pair, and paste it into the SSH Public Key text box. Clicking the "explain ssh keys" link takes you to detailed instructions on how to do so on all major operating systems.

Clicking the "I agree, sign me up" button takes you to your new user dashboard (see Figure 4-4).

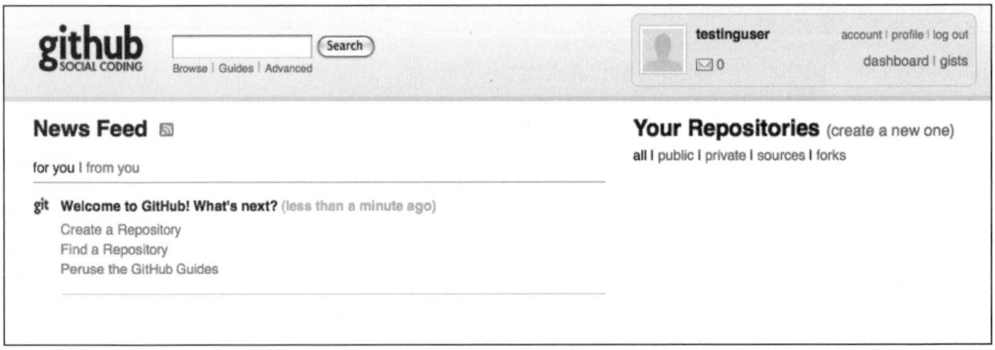

Figure 4-4. *The GitHub user dashboard*

Next, you can create a new repository.

Creating a New Repository

Start by clicking the "create a new one" link next to Your Repositories on the user dashboard. You're taken to the Create a New Repository form (see Figure 4-5).

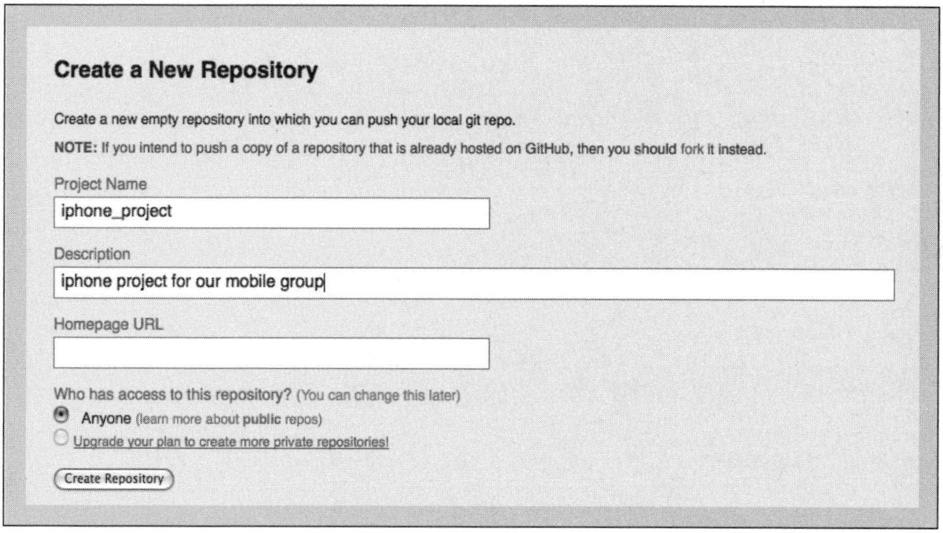

Figure 4-5. *Creating a new repository on GitHub*

All you really have to do is provide a project name, but you can also add a description. When that is done, click the Create Repository button. Now you have a new repository on GitHub (see Figure 4-6).

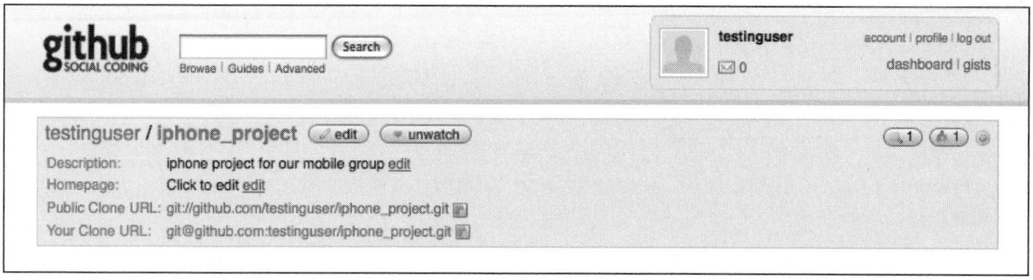

Figure 4-6. *GitHub project header information*

Because you have no code there yet, GitHub shows you instructions for how to create a brand-new project, push up an existing Git project, or import a project from a public Subversion repository (see Figure 4-7).

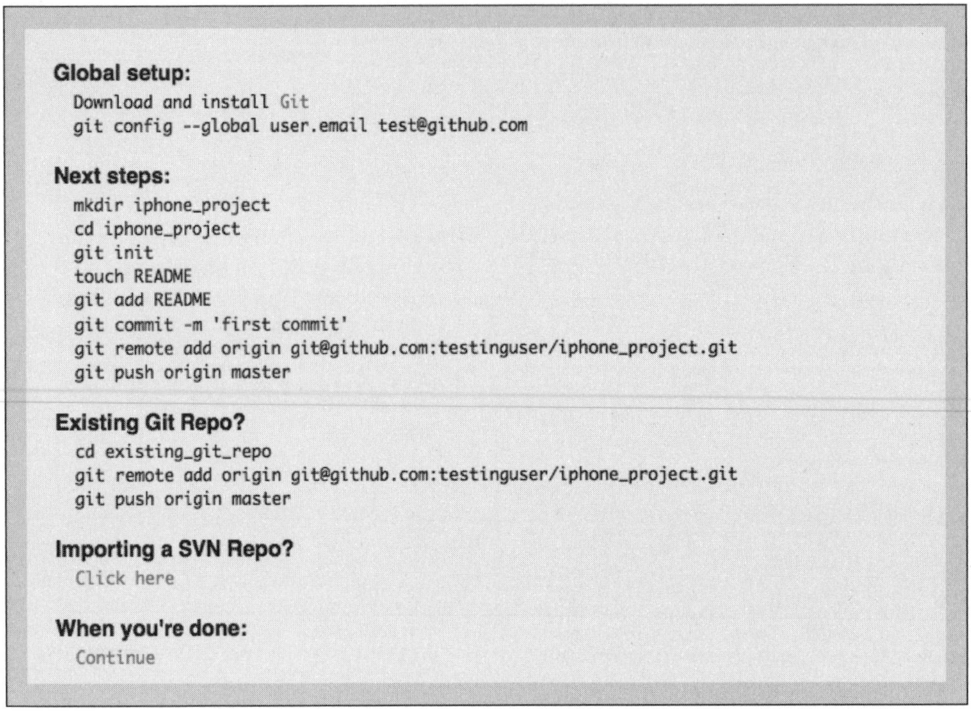

```
Global setup:
  Download and install Git
  git config --global user.email test@github.com

Next steps:
  mkdir iphone_project
  cd iphone_project
  git init
  touch README
  git add README
  git commit -m 'first commit'
  git remote add origin git@github.com:testinguser/iphone_project.git
  git push origin master

Existing Git Repo?
  cd existing_git_repo
  git remote add origin git@github.com:testinguser/iphone_project.git
  git push origin master

Importing a SVN Repo?
  Click here

When you're done:
  Continue
```

Figure 4-7. *Instructions for a new repository*

These instructions are similar to what you've already gone over. To initialize a project if it isn't already a Git project, you use

```
$ git init
$ git add .
$ git commit -m 'initial commit'
```

When you have a Git repository locally, add GitHub as a remote and push up your master branch:

```
$ git remote add origin git@github.com:testinguser/iphone_project.git
$ git push origin master
```

Now your project is hosted on GitHub, and you can give the URL to anyone you want to share your project with. In this case, it's http://github.com/testinguser/iphone_project. You can also see from the header on each of your project's pages that you have two Git URLs (see Figure 4-8).

testinguser / **iphone_project** ✎ edit   ☀ unwatch

Description: iphone project for our mobile group edit
Homepage: Click to edit edit
Public Clone URL: git://github.com/testinguser/iphone_project.git 📋
Your Clone URL: git@github.com:testinguser/iphone_project.git 📋

Figure 4-8. *Project header with a public URL and a private URL*

The Public Clone URL is a public, read-only Git URL over which anyone can clone the project. Feel free to give out that URL and post it on your web site or what have you.

The Your Clone URL is a read/write SSH-based URL that you can read or write over only if you connect with the SSH private key associated with the public key you uploaded for your user. When other users visit this project page, they won't see that URL—only the public one.

Importing from Subversion

If you have an existing public Subversion project that you want to import into Git, GitHub can often do that for you. At the bottom of the instructions page is a link to a Subversion import. If you click it, you see a form with information about the import process and a text box where you can paste in the URL of your public Subversion project (see Figure 4-9).

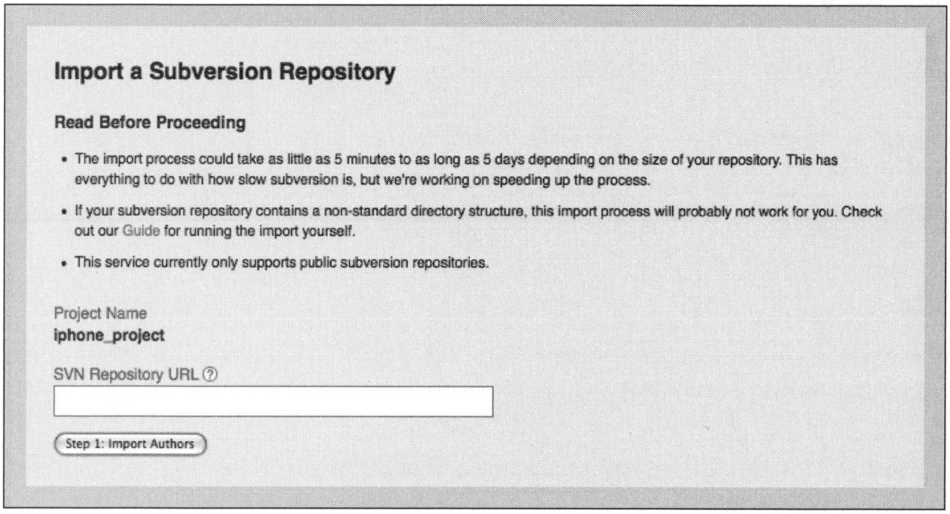

Import a Subversion Repository

Read Before Proceeding

- The import process could take as little as 5 minutes to as long as 5 days depending on the size of your repository. This has everything to do with how slow subversion is, but we're working on speeding up the process.

- If your subversion repository contains a non-standard directory structure, this import process will probably not work for you. Check out our Guide for running the import yourself.

- This service currently only supports public subversion repositories.

Project Name
iphone_project

SVN Repository URL ⑦

[   ]

(Step 1: Import Authors)

Figure 4-9. *Subversion importing interface*

If your project is very large, nonstandard, or private, this process probably won't work for you. In Chapter 7, you'll learn how to do more complicated manual project imports.

Adding Collaborators

You'll now add the rest of the team. If John, Josie, and Jessica all sign up for accounts on GitHub, and you want to give them push access to your repository, you can add them to your project as collaborators. Doing so allows pushes from their public keys to work.

Click the "edit" button in the project header or the Admin tab at the top of the project to reach the Admin page of your GitHub project (see Figure 4-10).

testinguser / **iphone_project**   ⬤1 ⬤1 ⬤

Description:	iphone project for our mobile group edit
Homepage:	Click to edit edit
Public Clone URL:	git://github.com/testinguser/iphone_project.git 📄
Your Clone URL:	git@github.com:testinguser/iphone_project.git 📄
GitHub Page:	Generate Your Project Page
Pull Requests: ⑦	Add auto-responder
RubyGem: ⑦	☐
Donations: ⑦	Inactive edit

Privacy

⬤ This repo is viewable by everyone.

If you upgrade your plan you can make this repository private!

Repository Collaborators

Add another collaborator

Figure 4-10. *GitHub administration page*

To give another user write access to your project, click the "Add another collaborator" link. A new text box appears, into which you can type a username. As you type, a helper pops up, showing you possible username matches. When you find the correct user, click the Add button to add that user as a collaborator on your project (see Figure 4-11).

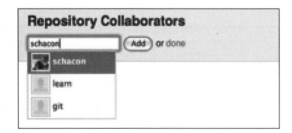

Figure 4-11. *Adding a collaborator to your project*

When you're finished adding collaborators, you should see a list of them in the Repository Collaborators box (see Figure 4-12).

If you need to revoke access to individuals, you can click the "revoke" link, and their push access will be removed. For future projects, you can also copy collaborator groups by copying the permissions of an existing project.

Figure 4-12. *A list of collaborators on your project*

Your Project

After you push your project up or have it imported from Subversion, you have a main project page that looks something like Figure 4-13.

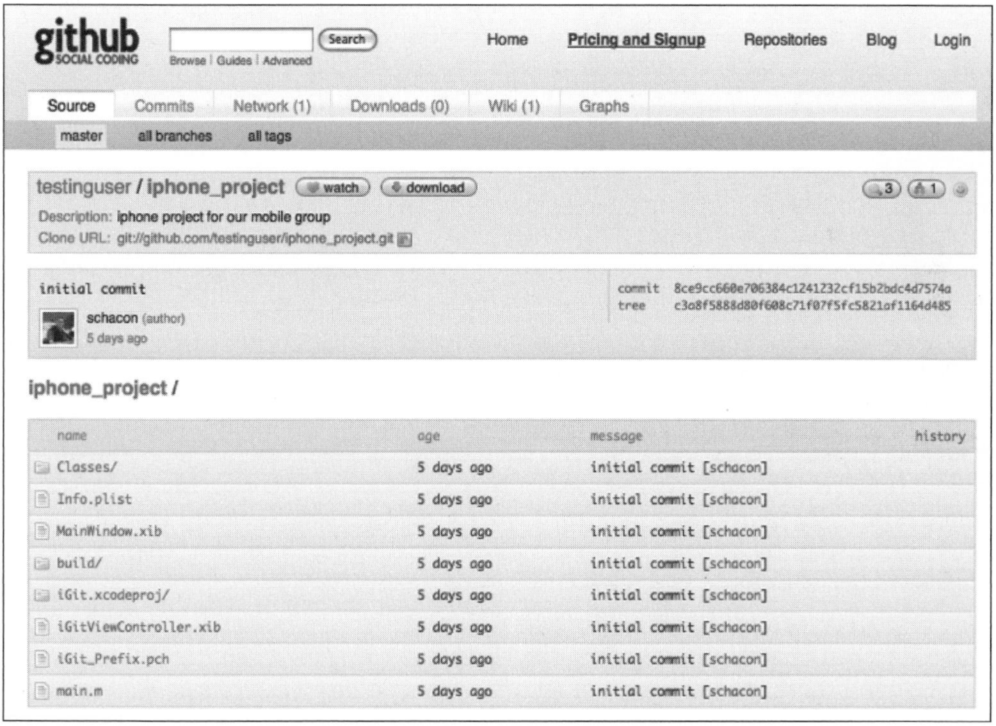

Figure 4-13. *A GitHub main project page*

When people visit your project, they see this page. It contains tabs to different aspects of your projects. The Commits tab shows a list of commits in reverse chronological order, similar to the output of the `git log` command. The Network tab shows all the people who have forked your project and contributed back. The Downloads tab allows you to upload project binaries and link to tarballs and zipped versions of any tagged points in your project. The Wiki tab provides a wiki where you can write documentation or other information about your project. The Graphs tab has some contribution visualizations and statistics about your project. The main Source tab that you land on shows your project's main directory listing and automatically renders the `README` file below it if you have one. This tab also shows a box with the latest commit information.

Forking Projects

If you want to contribute to an existing project to which you don't have push access, GitHub encourages forking the project. When you land on a project page that looks interesting and you want to hack on it a bit, you can click the "fork" button in the project header to have GitHub copy that project to your user so you can push to it.

This way, projects don't have to worry about adding users as collaborators to give them push access. People can fork a project and push to it, and the main project maintainer can pull in those changes by adding them as remotes and merging in their work.

To fork a project, visit the project page (in this case, `mojombo/chronic`) and click the "fork" button in the header (see Figure 4-14).

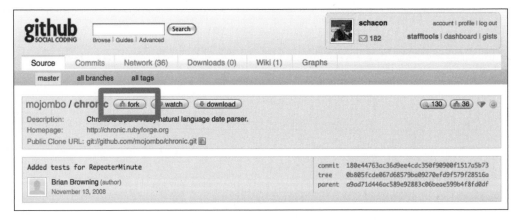

Figure 4-14. *Get a writable copy of any repository by clicking the "fork" button.*

After a few seconds, you're taken to your new project page, which indicates that this project is a fork of another one (see Figure 4-15).

Figure 4-15. *Your fork of a project*

GitHub Summary

That's all I'll cover about GitHub, but it's important to note how quickly you can do all this. You can create an account, add a new project, and push to it in a matter of minutes. If your project is open source, you also get a huge community of developers who now have visibility into your project and may well fork it and help contribute to it. At the very least, this may be a way to get up and running with Git and try it out quickly.

Summary

You have several options to get a remote Git repository up and running so that you can collaborate with others or share your work.

Running your own server gives you a lot of control and allows you to run the server within your own firewall, but such a server generally requires a fair amount of your time to set up and maintain. If you place your data on a hosted server, it's easy to set up and maintain; however, you have to be able to keep your code on someone else's servers, and some organizations don't allow that.

It should be fairly straightforward to determine which solution or combination of solutions is appropriate for you and your organization.

■■■

Distributed Git

Now that you have a remote Git repository set up as a point for all the developers to share their code, and you're familiar with basic Git commands in a local workflow, you'll look at how to utilize some of the distributed workflows that Git affords you.

In this chapter, you'll see how to work with Git in a distributed environment as a contributor and an integrator. That is, you'll learn how to contribute code successfully to a project and make it as easy on you and the project maintainer as possible, and also how to maintain a project successfully with a number of developers contributing.

Distributed Workflows

Unlike Centralized Version Control Systems (CVCSs), the distributed nature of Git allows you to be far more flexible in how developers collaborate on projects. In centralized systems, every developer is a node working more or less equally on a central hub. In Git, however, every developer is potentially both a node and a hub—that is, every developer can both contribute code to other repositories and maintain a public repository on which others can base their work and which they can contribute to. This opens a vast range of workflow possibilities for your project and/or your team, so I'll cover a few common paradigms that take advantage of this flexibility. I'll go over the strengths and possible weaknesses of each design; you can choose a single one to use, or you can mix and match features from each.

Centralized Workflow

In centralized systems, there is generally a single collaboration model—the *centralized workflow*. One central hub, or repository, can accept code, and everyone synchronizes their work to it. A number of developers are nodes—consumers of that hub—and synchronize to that one place (see Figure 5-1).

This means that if two developers clone from the hub and both make changes, the first developer to push their changes back up can do so with no problems. The second developer must merge in the first one's work before pushing changes up, so as not to overwrite the first developer's changes. This concept is true in Git as it is in Subversion (or any CVCS), and this model works perfectly in Git.

If you have a small team or are already comfortable with a centralized workflow in your company or team, you can easily continue using that workflow with Git. Simply set up a single repository, and give everyone on your team push access; Git won't let users overwrite each other. If one developer clones, makes changes, and then tries to push their changes while another developer has pushed in the meantime, the server will reject that developer's changes. They will be told that they're trying to push non-fast-forward changes and that they won't be able to do so until they fetch and merge.

This workflow is attractive to a lot of people because it's a paradigm that many are familiar and comfortable with.

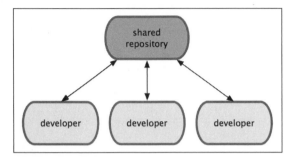

Figure 5-1. *Centralized workflow*

Integration-Manager Workflow

Because Git allows you to have multiple remote repositories, it's possible to have a workflow where each developer has write access to their own public repository and read access to everyone else's. This scenario often includes a canonical repository that represents the "official" project. To contribute to that project, you create your own public clone of the project and push your changes to it. Then, you can send a request to the maintainer of the main project to pull in your changes. They can add your repository as a remote, test your changes locally, merge them into their branch, and push back to their repository. The process works as follows (see Figure 5-2):

1. The project maintainer pushes to their public repository.

2. A contributor clones that repository and makes changes.

3. The contributor pushes to their own public copy.

4. The contributor sends the maintainer an e-mail asking them to pull changes.

5. The maintainer adds the contributor's repo as a remote and merges locally.

6. The maintainer pushes merged changes to the main repository.

This is a very common workflow with sites like GitHub, where it's easy to fork a project and push your changes into your fork for everyone to see. One of the main advantages of this approach is that you can continue to work, and the maintainer of the main repository can pull in your changes at any time. Contributors don't have to wait for the project to incorporate their changes—each party can work at their own pace.

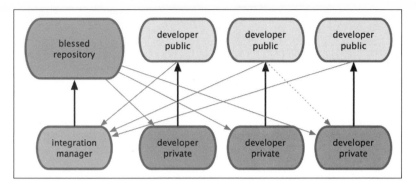

Figure 5-2. *Integration-manager workflow*

Dictator and Lieutenants Workflow

This is a variant of a multiple-repository workflow. It's generally used by huge projects with hundreds of collaborators; one famous example is the Linux kernel. Various integration managers are in charge of certain parts of the repository; they're called *lieutenants*. All the lieutenants have one integration manager known as the *benevolent dictator*. The benevolent dictator's repository serves as the reference repository from which all the collaborators need to pull. The process works like this (see Figure 5-3):

1. Regular developers work on their topic branch and rebase their work on top of master. The master branch is that of the dictator.

2. Lieutenants merge the developers' topic branches into their master branch.

3. The dictator merges the lieutenants' master branches into the dictator's master branch.

4. The dictator pushes their master to the reference repository so the other developers can rebase on it.

This kind of workflow isn't common but can be useful in very big projects or in highly hierarchical environments, because it allows the project leader (the dictator) to delegate much of the work and collect large subsets of code at multiple points before integrating them.

These are some commonly used workflows that are possible with a distributed system like Git, but you can see that many variations are possible to suit your particular real-world workflow. Now that you can (I hope) determine which workflow combination may work for you, I'll cover some more specific examples of how to accomplish the main roles that make up the different flows.

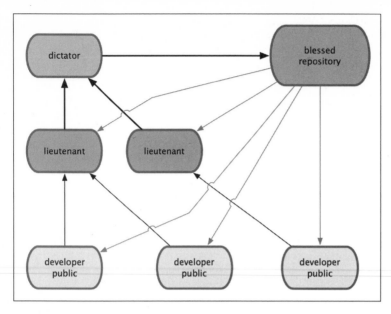

Figure 5-3. *Benevolent dictator workflow*

Contributing to a Project

You know what the different workflows are, and you should have a pretty good grasp of fundamental Git usage. In this section, you'll learn about a few common patterns for contributing to a project.

The main difficulty with describing this process is that there are a huge number of variations on how it's done. Because Git is very flexible, people can and do work together in many ways, and it's problematic to describe how you should contribute to a project—every project is a bit different. Some of the variables involved are active contributor size, chosen workflow, your commit access, and possibly the external contribution method.

The first variable is active contributor size. How many users are actively contributing code to this project, and how often? In many instances, you'll have two or three developers with a few commits a day, or possibly less for somewhat dormant projects. For really large companies or projects, the number of developers could be in the thousands, with dozens or even hundreds of patches coming in each day. This is important because with more and more developers, you run into more issues with making sure your code applies cleanly or can be easily merged. Changes you submit may be rendered obsolete or severely broken by work that is merged in while you were working or while your changes were waiting to be approved or applied. How can you keep your code consistently up to date and your patches valid?

The next variable is the workflow in use for the project. Is it centralized, with each developer having equal write access to the main codeline? Does the project have a maintainer or integration manager who checks all the patches? Are all the patches peer-reviewed and approved? Are you involved in that process? Is a lieutenant system in place, and do you have to submit your work to them first?

The next issue is your commit access. The workflow required in order to contribute to a project is much different if you have write access to the project than if you don't. If you don't have write access, how does the project prefer to accept contributed work? Does it even have a policy? How much work are you contributing at a time? How often do you contribute?

All these questions can affect how you contribute effectively to a project and what workflows are preferred or available to you. I'll cover aspects of each of these in a series of use cases, moving from simple to more complex; you should be able to construct the specific workflows you need in practice from these examples.

Commit Guidelines

Before you start looking at the specific use cases, here's a quick note about commit messages. Having a good guideline for creating commits and sticking to it makes working with Git and collaborating with others a lot easier. The Git project provides a document that lays out a number of good tips for creating commits from which to submit patches—you can read it in the Git source code in the Documentation/SubmittingPatches file.

First, you don't want to submit any whitespace errors. Git provides an easy way to check for this—before you commit, run git diff --check, which identifies possible whitespace errors and lists them for you. Here is an example, where I've replaced a red terminal color with Xs:

```
$ git diff --check
lib/simplegit.rb:5: trailing whitespace.
+    @git_dir = File.expand_path(git_dir)XX
lib/simplegit.rb:7: trailing whitespace.
+ XXXXXXXXXXX
lib/simplegit.rb:26: trailing whitespace.
+    def command(git_cmd)XXXX
```

If you run that command before committing, you can tell if you're about to commit whitespace issues that may annoy other developers.

Next, try to make each commit a logically separate changeset. If you can, try to make your changes digestible—don't code for a whole weekend on five different issues and then submit them all as one massive commit on Monday. Even if you don't commit during the weekend, use the staging area on Monday to split your work into at least one commit per issue, with a useful message per commit. If some of the changes modify the same file, try to use git add --patch to partially stage files (covered in detail in Chapter 6). The project snapshot at the tip of the branch is identical whether you do one commit or five, as long as all the changes are added at some point, so try to make things easier on your fellow developers when they have to review your changes. This approach also makes it easier to pull out or revert one of the changesets if you need to later. Chapter 6 describes a number of useful Git tricks for rewriting history and interactively staging files—you can use these tools to help craft a clean and understandable history.

The last thing to keep in mind is the commit message. Getting in the habit of creating quality commit messages makes using and collaborating with Git a lot easier. As a general rule, your messages should start with a single line that's no more than about 50 characters and that describes the changeset concisely, followed by a blank line, followed by a more detailed explanation. The Git project requires that the more detailed explanation include your motivation for the change and contrast its implementation with previous behavior—this is a good guideline to follow. It's also a good idea to use the imperative present tense in these messages. In other words, use commands. Instead of "I added tests for" or "Adding tests for," use "Add tests for."

Here is a template originally written by Tim Pope at tpope.net:

```
Short (50 chars or less) summary of changes

More detailed explanatory text, if necessary.  Wrap it to about 72
characters or so.  In some contexts, the first line is treated as the
subject of an email and the rest of the text as the body.  The blank
line separating the summary from the body is critical (unless you omit
the body entirely); tools like rebase can get confused if you run the
two together.

Further paragraphs come after blank lines.

 - Bullet points are okay, too

 - Typically a hyphen or asterisk is used for the bullet, preceded by a
   single space, with blank lines in between, but conventions vary here
```

If all your commit messages look like this, things will be a lot easier for you and the developers you work with. The Git project has well-formatted commit messages—I encourage you to run git log --no-merges there to see what a nicely formatted project-commit history looks like.

In the following examples, and throughout most of this book, for the sake of brevity I don't format messages nicely like this; instead, I use the -m option to git commit. Do as I say, not as I do.

Private Small Team

The simplest setup you're likely to encounter is a private project with one or two other developers. By *private*, I mean closed source—not read-accessible to the outside world. You and the other developers all have push access to the repository.

In this environment, you can follow a workflow similar to what you might do when using Subversion or another centralized system. You still get the advantages of things like offline committing and vastly simpler branching and merging, but the workflow can be very similar; the main difference is that merges happen client-side rather than on the server at commit time.

Let's see what it might look like when two developers start to work together with a shared repository. The first developer, John, clones the repository, makes a change, and commits locally. (I'm replacing the protocol messages with … in these examples to shorten them somewhat.)

```
# John's Machine
$ git clone john@githost:simplegit.git
Initialized empty Git repository in /home/john/simplegit/.git/
...
```

```
$ cd simplegit/
$ vim lib/simplegit.rb
$ git commit -am 'removed invalid default value'
[master 738ee87] removed invalid default value
 1 files changed, 1 insertions(+), 1 deletions(-)
```

The second developer, Jessica, does the same thing—clones the repository and commits a change:

```
# Jessica's Machine
$ git clone jessica@githost:simplegit.git
Initialized empty Git repository in /home/jessica/simplegit/.git/
...
$ cd simplegit/
$ vim TODO
$ git commit -am 'add reset task'
[master fbff5bc] add reset task
 1 files changed, 1 insertions(+), 0 deletions(-)
```

Now, Jessica pushes her work up to the server:

```
# Jessica's Machine
$ git push origin master
...
To jessica@githost:simplegit.git
   1edee6b..fbff5bc  master -> master
```

John tries to push his change up, too:

```
# John's Machine
$ git push origin master
To john@githost:simplegit.git
 ! [rejected]        master -> master (non-fast forward)
error: failed to push some refs to 'john@githost:simplegit.git'
```

John isn't allowed to push because Jessica has pushed in the meantime. This is especially important to understand if you're used to Subversion, because you'll notice that the two developers didn't edit the same file. Although Subversion automatically does such a merge on the server if different files are edited, in Git you must merge the commits locally. John has to fetch Jessica's changes and merge them in before he will be allowed to push:

```
$ git fetch origin
...
From john@githost:simplegit
 + 049d078...fbff5bc master     -> origin/master
```

At this point, John's local repository looks something like Figure 5-4.

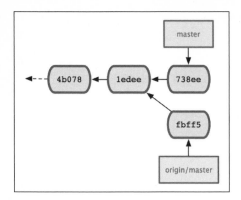

Figure 5-4. *John's initial repository*

John has a reference to the changes Jessica pushed up, but he has to merge them into his own work before he is allowed to push:

```
$ git merge origin/master
Merge made by recursive.
 TODO |    1 +
 1 files changed, 1 insertions(+), 0 deletions(-)
```

The merge goes smoothly—John's commit history now looks like Figure 5-5.

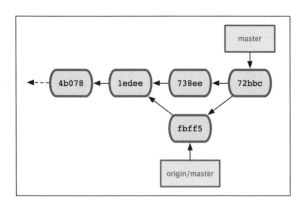

Figure 5-5. *John's repository after merging* origin/master

Now, John can test his code to make sure it still works properly, and then he can push his new merged work up to the server:

```
$ git push origin master
...
To john@githost:simplegit.git
   fbff5bc..72bbc59  master -> master
```

Finally, John's commit history looks like Figure 5-6.

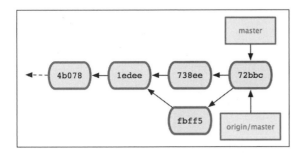

Figure 5-6. *John's history after pushing to the* `origin` *server*

In the meantime, Jessica has been working on a topic branch. She's created a topic branch called `issue54` and done three commits on that branch. She hasn't fetched John's changes yet, so her commit history looks like Figure 5-7.

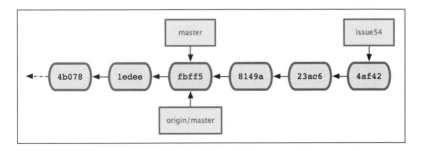

Figure 5-7. *Jessica's initial commit history*

Jessica wants to sync up with John, so she fetches:

```
# Jessica's Machine
$ git fetch origin
...
From jessica@githost:simplegit
   fbff5bc..72bbc59  master       -> origin/master
```

That pulls down the work John has pushed up in the meantime. Jessica's history now looks like Figure 5-8.

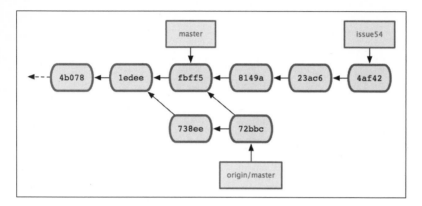

Figure 5-8. *Jessica's history after fetching John's changes*

Jessica thinks her topic branch is ready, but she wants to know what she has to merge her work into so that she can push. She runs git log to find out:

```
$ git log --no-merges origin/master ^issue54
commit 738ee872852dfaa9d6634e0dea7a324040193016
Author: John Smith <jsmith@example.com>
Date:   Fri May 29 16:01:27 2009 -0700

    removed invalid default value
```

Now, Jessica can merge her topic work into her master branch, merge John's work (origin/master) into her master branch, and then push back to the server again. First, she switches back to her master branch to integrate all this work:

```
$ git checkout master
Switched to branch "master"
Your branch is behind 'origin/master' by 2 commits, and can be fast-forwarded.
```

She can merge either origin/master or issue54 first—they're both upstream, so the order doesn't matter. The end snapshot should be identical no matter which order she chooses; only the history will be slightly different. She chooses to merge in issue54 first:

```
$ git merge issue54
Updating fbff5bc..4af4298
Fast forward
 README          |    1 +
 lib/simplegit.rb |    6 +++++-
 2 files changed, 6 insertions(+), 1 deletions(-)
```

No problems occur; as you can see, it was a simple fast-forward. Now Jessica merges in John's work (origin/master):

```
$ git merge origin/master
Auto-merging lib/simplegit.rb
Merge made by recursive.
 lib/simplegit.rb |    2 +-
 1 files changed, 1 insertions(+), 1 deletions(-)
```

Everything merges cleanly, and Jessica's history looks like Figure 5-9.

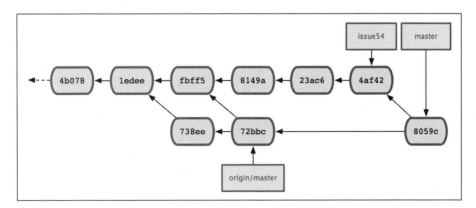

Figure 5-9. *Jessica's history after merging John's changes*

Now origin/master is reachable from Jessica's master branch, so she should be able to successfully push (assuming John hasn't pushed again in the meantime):

```
$ git push origin master
...
To jessica@githost:simplegit.git
   72bbc59..8059c15  master -> master
```

Each developer has committed a few times and merged each other's work successfully; see Figure 5-10.

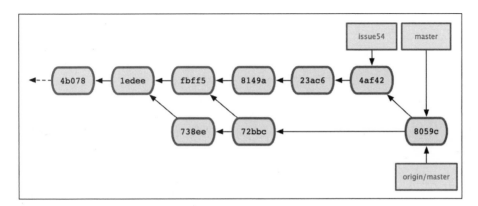

Figure 5-10. *Jessica's history after pushing all changes back to the server*

That is one of the simplest workflows. You work for a while, generally in a topic branch, and merge into your `master` branch when it's ready to be integrated. When you want to share that work, you merge it into your own `master` branch, then fetch and merge `origin/master` if it has changed, and finally push to the `master` branch on the server. The general sequence is something like that shown in Figure 5-11.

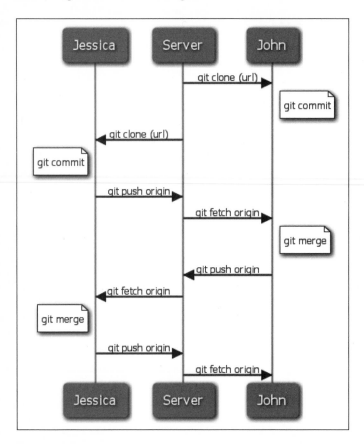

Figure 5-11. *General sequence of events for a simple multiple-developer Git workflow*

Private Managed Team

In this next scenario, you'll look at contributor roles in a larger private group. You'll learn how to work in an environment where small groups collaborate on features and then those team-based contributions are integrated by another party.

Let's say that John and Jessica are working together on one feature, while Jessica and Josie are working on a second. In this case, the company is using a type of integration-manager workflow where the work of the individual groups is integrated only by certain engineers, and the `master` branch of the main repository can be updated only by those engineers. In this scenario, all work is done in team-based branches and pulled together by the integrators later.

Let's follow Jessica's workflow as she works on her two features, collaborating in parallel with two different developers in this environment. Assuming she already has her repository cloned, she decides to work on featureA first. She creates a new branch for the feature and does some work on it there:

```
# Jessica's Machine
$ git checkout -b featureA
Switched to a new branch "featureA"
$ vim lib/simplegit.rb
$ git commit -am 'add limit to log function'
[featureA 3300904] add limit to log function
 1 files changed, 1 insertions(+), 1 deletions(-)
```

At this point, she needs to share her work with John, so she pushes her featureA branch commits up to the server. Jessica doesn't have push access to the master branch—only the integrators do—so she has to push to another branch in order to collaborate with John:

```
$ git push origin featureA
...
To jessica@githost:simplegit.git
 * [new branch]      featureA -> featureA
```

Jessica e-mails John to tell him that she's pushed some work into a branch named featureA and he can look at it now. While she waits for feedback from John, Jessica decides to start working on featureB with Josie. To begin, she starts a new feature branch, basing it off the server's master branch:

```
# Jessica's Machine
$ git fetch origin
$ git checkout -b featureB origin/master
Switched to a new branch "featureB"
```

Now, Jessica makes a couple of commits on the featureB branch:

```
$ vim lib/simplegit.rb
$ git commit -am 'made the ls-tree function recursive'
[featureB e5b0fdc] made the ls-tree function recursive
 1 files changed, 1 insertions(+), 1 deletions(-)
$ vim lib/simplegit.rb
$ git commit -am 'add ls-files'
[featureB 8512791] add ls-files
 1 files changed, 5 insertions(+), 0 deletions(-)
```

Jessica's repository looks like Figure 5-12.

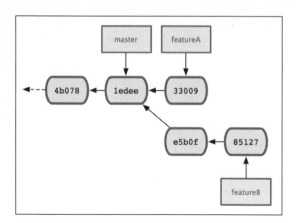

Figure 5-12. *Jessica's initial commit history*

She's ready to push up her work, but she gets an e-mail from Josie that a branch with some initial work on it was already pushed to the server as featureBee. Jessica first needs to merge those changes in with her own before she can push to the server. She can then fetch Josie's changes down with git fetch:

```
$ git fetch origin
...
From jessica@githost:simplegit
 * [new branch]      featureBee -> origin/featureBee
```

Jessica can now merge this into the work she did with git merge:

```
$ git merge origin/featureBee
Auto-merging lib/simplegit.rb
Merge made by recursive.
 lib/simplegit.rb |    4 ++++
 1 files changed, 4 insertions(+), 0 deletions(-)
```

There is a bit of a problem—she needs to push the merged work in her featureB branch to the featureBee branch on the server. She can do so by specifying the local branch followed by a colon (:) followed by the remote branch to the git push command:

```
$ git push origin featureB:featureBee
...
To jessica@githost:simplegit.git
   fba9af8..cd685d1  featureB -> featureBee
```

This is called a *refspec*. See Chapter 9 for a more detailed discussion of Git refspecs and different things you can do with them.

Next, John e-mails Jessica to say he's pushed some changes to the featureA branch and ask her to verify them. She runs a git fetch to pull down those changes:

```
$ git fetch origin
...
From jessica@githost:simplegit
   3300904..aad881d  featureA   -> origin/featureA
```

Then, she can see what has been changed with git log:

```
$ git log origin/featureA ^featureA
commit aad881d154acdaeb2b6b18ea0e827ed8a6d671e6
Author: John Smith <jsmith@example.com>
Date:   Fri May 29 19:57:33 2009 -0700

    changed log output to 30 from 25
```

Finally, she merges John's work into her own featureA branch:

```
$ git checkout featureA
Switched to branch "featureA"
$ git merge origin/featureA
Updating 3300904..aad881d
Fast forward
 lib/simplegit.rb |   10 +++++++++-
1 files changed, 9 insertions(+), 1 deletions(-)
```

Jessica wants to tweak something, so she commits again and then pushes this back up to the server:

```
$ git commit -am 'small tweak'
[featureA ed774b3] small tweak
 1 files changed, 1 insertions(+), 1 deletions(-)
$ git push origin featureA
...
To jessica@githost:simplegit.git
   3300904..ed774b3  featureA -> featureA
```

Jessica's commit history now looks something like Figure 5-13.

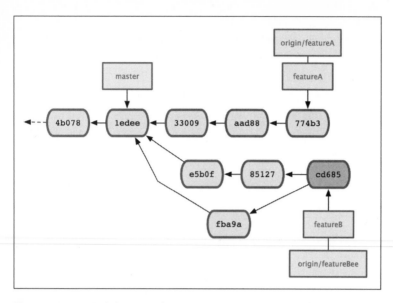

Figure 5-13. *Jessica's history after committing on a feature branch*

Jessica, Josie, and John inform the integrators that the featureA and featureBee branches on the server are ready for integration into the mainline. After they integrate these branches into the mainline, a fetch will bring down the new merge commits, making the commit history look like Figure 5-14.

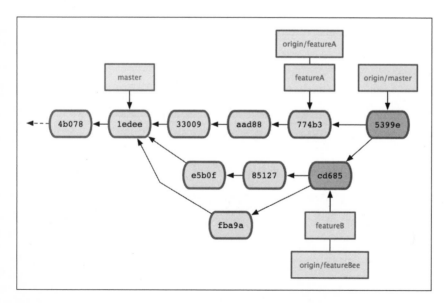

Figure 5-14. *Jessica's history after merging both her topic branches*

Many groups switch to Git because of this ability to have multiple teams working in parallel, merging the different lines of work late in the process. The ability of smaller subgroups of a team to collaborate via remote branches without necessarily having to involve or impede the entire team is a huge benefit of Git. The sequence for the workflow you saw here is something like Figure 5-15.

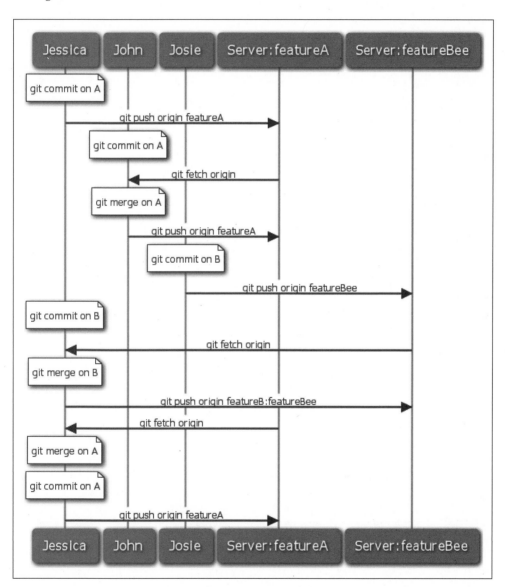

Figure 5-15. *Basic sequence of this managed-team workflow*

Public Small Project

Contributing to public projects is a bit different. Because you don't have the permissions to directly update branches on the project, you have to get the work to the maintainers some other way. This first example describes contributing via forking on Git hosts that support easy forking. The repo.or.cz and GitHub hosting sites both support this, and many project maintainers expect this style of contribution. The next section deals with projects that prefer to accept contributed patches via e-mail.

First, you'll probably want to clone the main repository, create a topic branch for the patch or patch series you're planning to contribute, and do your work there. The sequence looks basically like this:

```
$ git clone (url)
$ cd project
$ git checkout -b featureA
$ (work)
$ git commit
$ (work)
$ git commit
```

You may want to use `rebase -i` to squash your work down to a single commit, or rearrange the work in the commits to make the patch easier for the maintainer to review—see Chapter 6 for more information about interactive rebasing.

When your branch work is finished and you're ready to contribute it back to the maintainers, go to the original project page and click the Fork button, creating your own writable fork of the project. You then need to add in this new repository URL as a second remote, in this case named `myfork`:

```
$ git remote add myfork (url)
```

You need to push your work up to it. It's easiest to push the remote branch you're working on up to your repository, rather than merging into your `master` branch and pushing that up. The reason is that if the work isn't accepted or is cherry picked, you don't have to rewind your `master` branch. If the maintainers merge, rebase, or cherry-pick your work, you'll eventually get it back via pulling from their repository anyhow:

```
$ git push myfork featureA
```

When your work has been pushed up to your fork, you need to notify the maintainer. This is often called a *pull request,* and you can either generate it via the website—GitHub has a "pull request" button that automatically messages the maintainer—or run the `git request-pull` command and e-mail the output to the project maintainer manually.

The `request-pull` command takes the base branch into which you want your topic branch pulled and the Git repository URL you want them to pull from, and outputs a summary of all the changes you're asking to be pulled in. For instance, if Jessica wants to send John a pull request, and she's done two commits on the topic branch she just pushed up, she can run this:

```
$ git request-pull origin/master myfork
The following changes since commit 1edee6b1d61823a2de3b09c160d7080b8d1b3a40:
  John Smith (1):
        added a new function
```

```
are available in the git repository at:

  git://githost/simplegit.git featureA

Jessica Smith (2):
      add limit to log function
      change log output to 30 from 25

 lib/simplegit.rb |    10 +++++++++-
 1 files changed, 9 insertions(+), 1 deletions(-)
```

The output can be sent to the maintainer—it tells them where the work was branched from, summarizes the commits, and tells where to pull this work from.

On a project for which you're not the maintainer, it's generally easier to have a branch like master always track origin/master and to do your work in topic branches that you can easily discard if they're rejected. Having work themes isolated into topic branches also makes it easier for you to rebase your work if the tip of the main repository has moved in the meantime and your commits no longer apply cleanly. For example, if you want to submit a second topic of work to the project, don't continue working on the topic branch you just pushed up—start over from the main repository's master branch:

```
$ git checkout -b featureB origin/master
$ (work)
$ git commit
$ git push myfork featureB
$ (email maintainer)
$ git fetch origin
```

Now, each of your topics is contained within a silo—similar to a patch queue—that you can rewrite, rebase, and modify without the topics interfering or interdepending on each other, as in Figure 5-16.

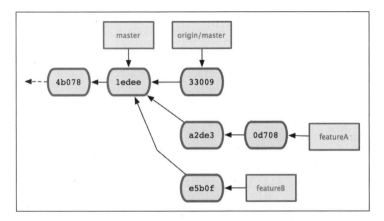

Figure 5-16. *Initial commit history with featureB work*

Let's say the project maintainer has pulled in a bunch of other patches and tried your first branch, but it no longer cleanly merges. In this case, you can try to rebase that branch on top of origin/master, resolve the conflicts for the maintainer, and then resubmit your changes:

```
$ git checkout featureA
$ git rebase origin/master
$ git push -f myfork featureA
```

This rewrites your history to now look like Figure 5-17.

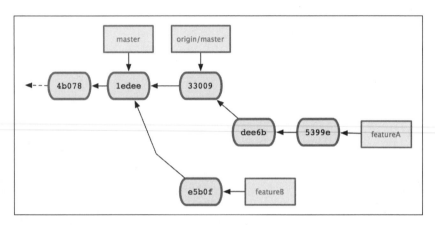

Figure 5-17. *Commit history after featureA work*

Because you rebased the branch, you have to specify the -f to your push command in order to be able to replace the featureA branch on the server with a commit that isn't a descendant of it. An alternative would be to push this new work to a different branch on the server (perhaps called featureAv2).

Let's look at one more possible scenario: the maintainer has looked at work in your second branch and likes the concept, but would like you to change an implementation detail. You'll also take this opportunity to move the work to be based off the project's current master branch. You start a new branch based off the current origin/master branch, squash the featureB changes there, resolve any conflicts, make the implementation change, and then push that up as a new branch:

```
$ git checkout -b featureBv2 origin/master
$ git merge --no-commit --squash featureB
$ (change implementation)
$ git commit
$ git push myfork featureBv2
```

The --squash option takes all the work on the merged branch and squashes it into one non-merge commit on top of the branch you're on. The --no-commit option tells Git not to automatically record a commit. This allows you to introduce all the changes from another branch and then make more changes before recording the new commit.

Now you can send the maintainer a message that you've made the requested changes and they can find those changes in your featureBv2 branch (see Figure 5-18).

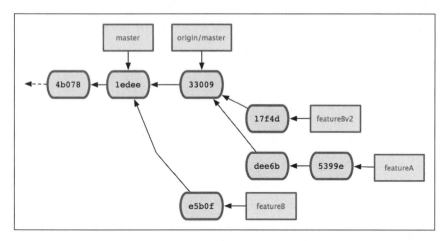

Figure 5-18. *Commit history after featureBv2 work*

Public Large Project

Many larger projects have established procedures for accepting patches—you'll need to check the specific rules for each project, because they will differ. However, many larger public projects accept patches via a developer mailing list, so I'll go over an example of that now.

The workflow is similar to the previous use case—you create topic branches for each patch series you work on. The difference is how you submit them to the project. Instead of forking the project and pushing to your own writable repository, you generate e-mail versions of each commit series and e-mail them to the developer mailing list:

```
$ git checkout -b topicA
$ (work)
$ git commit
$ (work)
$ git commit
```

Now you have two commits that you want to send to the mailing list. You use git format-patch to generate the mbox-formatted files that you can e-mail to the list—it turns each commit into an e-mail message with the first line of the commit message as the subject and the rest of the message plus the patch that the commit introduces as the body. The nice thing about this is that applying a patch from an e-mail generated with format-patch preserves all the commit information properly, as you'll see more of in the next section when you apply these commits:

```
$ git format-patch -M origin/master
0001-add-limit-to-log-function.patch
0002-changed-log-output-to-30-from-25.patch
```

The format-patch command prints out the names of the patch files it creates. The -M switch tells Git to look for renames. The files end up looking like this:

```
$ cat 0001-add-limit-to-log-function.patch
From 330090432754092d704da8e76ca5c05c198e71a8 Mon Sep 17 00:00:00 2001
From: Jessica Smith <jessica@example.com>
Date: Sun, 6 Apr 2008 10:17:23 -0700
Subject: [PATCH 1/2] add limit to log function

Limit log functionality to the first 20

---
 lib/simplegit.rb |    2 +-
 1 files changed, 1 insertions(+), 1 deletions(-)

diff --git a/lib/simplegit.rb b/lib/simplegit.rb
index 76f47bc..f9815f1 100644
--- a/lib/simplegit.rb
+++ b/lib/simplegit.rb
@@ -14,7 +14,7 @@ class SimpleGit
   end

   def log(treeish = 'master')
-    command("git log #{treeish}")
+    command("git log -n 20 #{treeish}")
   end

   def ls_tree(treeish = 'master')
--
1.6.2.rc1.20.g8c5b.dirty
```

You can also edit these patch files to add more information for the e-mail list that you don't want to show up in the commit message. If you add text between the --- line and the beginning of the patch (the lib/simplegit.rb line), then developers can read it; but applying the patch excludes it.

To e-mail this to a mailing list, you can either paste the file into your e-mail program or send it via a command-line program. Pasting the text often causes formatting issues, especially with "smarter" clients that don't preserve newlines and other whitespace appropriately. Luckily, Git provides a tool to help you send properly formatted patches via IMAP, which may be easier for you. I'll demonstrate how to send a patch via Gmail, which happens to be the e-mail agent I use; you can read detailed instructions for a number of mail programs at the end of the aforementioned Documentation/SubmittingPatches file in the Git source code.

First, you need to set up the imap section in your ~/.gitconfig file. You can set each value separately with a series of git config commands, or you can add them manually; but in the end, your config file should look something like this:

```
[imap]
  folder = "[Gmail]/Drafts"
  host = imaps://imap.gmail.com
```

```
user = user@gmail.com
pass = p4ssw0rd
port = 993
sslverify = false
```

If your IMAP server doesn't use SSL, the last two lines probably aren't necessary, and the host value will be `imap://` instead of `imaps://`.

When that is set up, you can use `git send-email` to place the patch series in the `Drafts` folder of the specified IMAP server:

```
$ git send-email *.patch
0001-added-limit-to-log-function.patch
0002-changed-log-output-to-30-from-25.patch
Who should the emails appear to be from? [Jessica Smith <jessica@example.com>]
Emails will be sent from: Jessica Smith <jessica@example.com>
Who should the emails be sent to? jessica@example.com
Message-ID to be used as In-Reply-To for the first email? y
```

Then, Git spits out a bunch of log information looking something like this for each patch you're sending:

```
(mbox) Adding cc: Jessica Smith <jessica@example.com> from
  \line 'From: Jessica Smith <jessica@example.com>'
OK. Log says:
Sendmail: /usr/sbin/sendmail -i jessica@example.com
From: Jessica Smith <jessica@example.com>
To: jessica@example.com
Subject: [PATCH 1/2] added limit to log function
Date: Sat, 30 May 2009 13:29:15 -0700
Message-Id: <1243715356-61726-1-git-send-email-jessica@example.com>
X-Mailer: git-send-email 1.6.2.rc1.20.g8c5b.dirty
In-Reply-To: <y>
References: <y>

Result: OK
```

At this point, you should be able to go to your `Drafts` folder, change the To field to the mailing list you're sending the patch to, possibly CC the maintainer or person responsible for that section, and send it off.

Summary

This section has covered a number of common workflows for dealing with several very different types of Git projects you're likely to encounter and introduced a couple of new tools to help you manage this process. Next, you'll see how to work the other side of the coin: maintaining a Git project. You'll learn how to *be* a benevolent dictator or integration manager.

Maintaining a Project

In addition to knowing how to effectively contribute to a project, you'll likely need to know how to maintain one. This can consist of accepting and applying patches generated via format-patch and e-mailed to you, or integrating changes in remote branches for repositories you've added as remotes to your project. Whether you maintain a canonical repository or want to help by verifying or approving patches, you need to know how to accept work in a way that is clearest for other contributors and sustainable by you over the long run.

Working in Topic Branches

When you're thinking of integrating new work, it's generally a good idea to try it out in a topic branch—a temporary branch specifically made to try out that new work. This way, it's easy to tweak a patch individually and leave it if it's not working until you have time to come back to it. If you create a simple branch name based on the theme of the work you're going to try, such as ruby_client or something similarly descriptive, you can easily remember it if you have to abandon it for a while and come back later. The maintainer of the Git project tends to namespace these branches as well—such as sc/ruby_client, where sc is short for the person who contributed the work.

As you'll remember, you can create the branch based off your master branch like this:

```
$ git branch sc/ruby_client master
```

Or, if you want to also switch to it immediately, you can use the checkout -b option:

```
$ git checkout -b sc/ruby_client master
```

Now you're ready to add your contributed work into this topic branch and determine if you want to merge it into your longer-term branches.

Applying Patches from E-mail

If you receive a patch over e-mail that you need to integrate into your project, you need to apply the patch in your topic branch to evaluate it. There are two ways to apply an e-mailed patch: with git apply or with git am.

Applying a Patch with apply

If you received the patch from someone who generated it with the git diff or a Unix diff command, you can apply it with the git apply command. Assuming you saved the patch at /tmp/patch-ruby-client.patch, you can apply the patch like this:

```
$ git apply /tmp/patch-ruby-client.patch
```

This modifies the files in your working directory. It's almost identical to running a patch -p1 command to apply the patch, although it's more paranoid and accepts fewer fuzzy matches then patch. It also handles file adds, deletes, and renames if they're described in the git diff format, which patch won't do. Finally, git apply is an "apply all or abort all" model where either everything is applied or nothing is, whereas patch can partially apply patchfiles, leaving your working directory in a weird state. git apply is over all much more paranoid than `patch`. It won't create a commit for you—after running it, you must stage and commit the changes introduced manually.

You can also use `git apply` to see if a patch applies cleanly before you try actually applying it—you can run `git apply --check` with the patch:

```
$ git apply --check 0001-seeing-if-this-helps-the-gem.patch
error: patch failed: ticgit.gemspec:1
error: ticgit.gemspec: patch does not apply
```

If there is no output, then the patch should apply cleanly. This command also exits with a non-zero status if the check fails, so you can use it in scripts if you want.

Applying a Patch with am

If the contributor is a Git user and was good enough to use the `format-patch` command to generate their patch, then your job is easier because the patch contains author information and a commit message for you. If you can, encourage your contributors to use `format-patch` instead of `diff` to generate patches for you. You should only have to use `git apply` for legacy patches and things like that.

To apply a patch generated by `format-patch`, you use `git am`. Technically, `git am` is built to read an mbox file, which is a simple, plain-text format for storing one or more e-mail messages in one text file. It looks something like this:

```
From 330090432754092d704da8e76ca5c05c198e71a8 Mon Sep 17 00:00:00 2001
From: Jessica Smith <jessica@example.com>
Date: Sun, 6 Apr 2008 10:17:23 -0700
Subject: [PATCH 1/2] add limit to log function

Limit log functionality to the first 20
```

This is the beginning of the output of the `format-patch` command that you saw in the previous section. This is also a valid mbox e-mail format. If someone has e-mailed you the patch properly using `git send-email`, and you download that into an mbox format, then you can point `git am` to that mbox file, and it will start applying all the patches it sees. If you run a mail client that can save several e-mails out in mbox format, you can save entire patch series into a file and then use `git am` to apply them one at a time.

However, if someone uploaded a patch file generated via `format-patch` to a ticketing system or something similar, you can save the file locally and then pass that file saved on your disk to `git am` to apply it:

```
$ git am 0001-limit-log-function.patch
Applying: add limit to log function
```

You can see that it applied cleanly and automatically created the new commit for you. The author information is taken from the e-mail's From and Date headers, and the message of the commit is taken from the Subject and body (before the patch) of the e-mail. For example, if this patch was applied from the mbox example I just showed, the commit generated would look something like this:

```
$ git log --pretty=fuller -1
commit 6c5e70b984a60b3cecd395edd5b48a7575bf58e0
```

```
Author:     Jessica Smith <jessica@example.com>
AuthorDate: Sun Apr 6 10:17:23 2008 -0700
Commit:     Scott Chacon <schacon@gmail.com>
CommitDate: Thu Apr 9 09:19:06 2009 -0700

    add limit to log function

    Limit log functionality to the first 20
```

The Commit information indicates the person who applied the patch and the time it was applied. The Author information is the individual who originally created the patch and when it was originally created.

But it's possible that the patch won't apply cleanly. Perhaps your main branch has diverged too far from the branch the patch was built from, or the patch depends on another patch you haven't applied yet. In that case, the git am process will fail and ask you what you want to do:

```
$ git am 0001-seeing-if-this-helps-the-gem.patch
Applying: seeing if this helps the gem
error: patch failed: ticgit.gemspec:1
error: ticgit.gemspec: patch does not apply
Patch failed at 0001.
When you have resolved this problem run "git am --resolved".
If you would prefer to skip this patch, instead run "git am --skip".
To restore the original branch and stop patching run "git am --abort".
```

This command puts conflict markers in any files it has issues with, much like a conflicted merge or rebase operation. You solve this issue much the same way—edit the file to resolve the conflict, stage the new file, and then run git am --resolved to continue to the next patch:

```
$ (fix the file)
$ git add ticgit.gemspec
$ git am --resolved
Applying: seeing if this helps the gem
```

If you want Git to try a bit more intelligently to resolve the conflict, you can pass a -3 option to it, which makes Git attempt a three-way merge. This option isn't on by default because it doesn't work if the commit the patch says it was based on isn't in your repository. If you do have that commit—if the patch was based on a public commit—then the -3 option is generally much smarter about applying a conflicting patch:

```
$ git am -3 0001-seeing-if-this-helps-the-gem.patch
Applying: seeing if this helps the gem
error: patch failed: ticgit.gemspec:1
error: ticgit.gemspec: patch does not apply
Using index info to reconstruct a base tree...
Falling back to patching base and 3-way merge...
No changes -- Patch already applied.
```

In this case, I was trying to apply a patch I had already applied. Without the -3 option, it looks like a conflict.

If you're applying a number of patches from an mbox, you can also run the am command in interactive mode, which stops at each patch it finds and asks if you want to apply it:

```
$ git am -3 -i mbox
Commit Body is:
--------------------------
seeing if this helps the gem
--------------------------
Apply? [y]es/[n]o/[e]dit/[v]iew patch/[a]ccept all
```

This is nice if you have a number of patches saved, because you can view the patch first if you don't remember what it is, or not apply the patch if you've already done so.

When all the patches for your topic are applied and committed into your branch, you can choose whether and how to integrate them into a longer-running branch.

Checking Out Remote Branches

If your contribution came from a Git user who set up their own repository, pushed a number of changes into it, and then sent you the URL to the repository and the name of the remote branch the changes are in, you can add them as a remote and do merges locally.

For instance, if Jessica sends you an e-mail saying that she has a great new feature in the ruby-client branch of her repository, you can test it by adding the remote and checking out that branch locally:

```
$ git remote add jessica git://github.com/jessica/myproject.git
$ git fetch jessica
$ git checkout -b rubyclient jessica/ruby-client
```

If she e-mails you again later with another branch containing another great feature, you can fetch and check out because you already have the remote setup.

This is most useful if you're working with a person consistently. If someone only has a single patch to contribute once in a while, then accepting it over e-mail may be less time consuming than requiring everyone to run their own server and having to continually add and remove remotes to get a few patches. You're also unlikely to want to have hundreds of remotes, each for someone who contributes only a patch or two. However, scripts and hosted services may make this easier—it depends largely on how you develop and how your contributors develop.

The other advantage of this approach is that you get the history of the commits as well. Although you may have legitimate merge issues, you know where in your history their work is based; a proper three-way merge is the default rather than having to supply a -3 and hope the patch was generated off a public commit to which you have access.

If you aren't working with a person consistently but still want to pull from them in this way, you can provide the URL of the remote repository to the git pull command. This does a one-time pull and doesn't save the URL as a remote reference:

```
$ git pull git://github.com/onetimeguy/project.git
From git://github.com/onetimeguy/project
 * branch            HEAD       -> FETCH_HEAD
Merge made by recursive.
```

Determining What Is Introduced

Now you have a topic branch that contains contributed work. At this point, you can determine what you'd like to do with it. This section revisits a couple of commands so you can see how you can use them to review exactly what you'll be introducing if you merge this into your main branch.

It's often helpful to get a review of all the commits that are in this branch but that aren't in your master branch. You can exclude commits in the master branch by adding the --not option before the branch name. For example, if your contributor sends you two patches and you create a branch called contrib and applied those patches there, you can run this:

```
$ git log contrib --not master
commit 5b6235bd297351589efc4d73316f0a68d484f118
Author: Scott Chacon <schacon@gmail.com>
Date:   Fri Oct 24 09:53:59 2008 -0700

    seeing if this helps the gem

commit 7482e0d16d04bea79d0dba8988cc78df655f16a0
Author: Scott Chacon <schacon@gmail.com>
Date:   Mon Oct 22 19:38:36 2008 -0700

    updated the gemspec to hopefully work better
```

To see what changes each commit introduces, remember that you can pass the -p option to git log and it will append the diff introduced to each commit.

To see a full diff of what would happen if you were to merge this topic branch with another branch, you may have to use a weird trick to get the correct results. You may think to run this:

```
$ git diff master
```

This command gives you a diff, but it may be misleading. If your master branch has moved forward since you created the topic branch from it, then you'll get seemingly strange results. This happens because Git directly compares the snapshots of the last commit of the topic branch you're on and the snapshot of the last commit on the master branch. For example, if you've added a line in a file on the master branch, a direct comparison of the snapshots will look like the topic branch is going to remove that line.

If master is a direct ancestor of your topic branch, this isn't a problem; but if the two histories have diverged, the diff will look like you're adding all the new stuff in your topic branch and removing everything new to the master branch.

What you really want to see are the changes added to the topic branch—the work you'll introduce if you merge this branch with master. You do that by having Git compare the last commit on your topic branch with the first common ancestor it has with the master branch.

Technically, you can do that by explicitly figuring out the common ancestor and then running your diff on it:

```
$ git merge-base contrib master
36c7dba2c95e6bbb78dfa822519ecfec6e1ca649
$ git diff 36c7db
```

However, that isn't convenient, so Git provides another shorthand for doing the same thing: the *triple-dot syntax*. In the context of the `diff` command, you can put three periods after another branch to do a diff between the last commit of the branch you're on and its common ancestor with another branch:

```
$ git diff master...topic
```

This command shows you only the work your topic branch has introduced since its common ancestor with `master`. That is a very useful syntax to remember.

Integrating Contributed Work

When all the work in your topic branch is ready to be integrated into a more mainline branch, the question is how to do it. Furthermore, what overall workflow do you want to use to maintain your project? You have a number of choices, so I'll cover a few of them.

Merging Workflows

One simple workflow merges your work into your `master` branch. In this scenario, you have a `master` branch that contains basically stable code. When you have work in a topic branch that you've done or that someone has contributed and you've verified, you merge it into your `master` branch, delete the topic branch, and then continue the process. If you have a repository that looks like Figure 5-19, with work in two branches named `ruby_client` and `php_client`, and you merge `ruby_client` first and then `php_client` next, your history will end up looking like Figure 5-20.

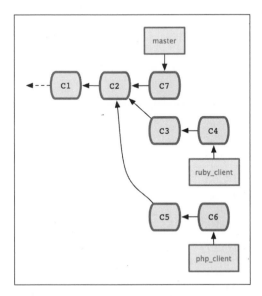

Figure 5-19. *History with several topic branches*

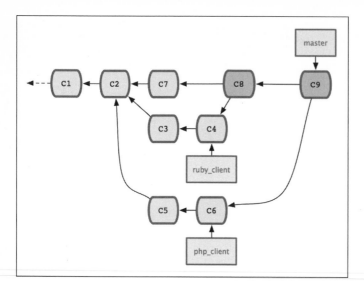

Figure 5-20. *After a topic branch merge*

That is probably the simplest workflow, but it's problematic if you're dealing with larger repositories or projects.

If you have more developers or a larger project, you'll probably want to use at least a two-phase merge cycle. In this scenario, you have two long-running branches, master and develop, in which you determine that master is updated only when a very stable release is cut and all new code is integrated into the develop branch. You regularly push both of these branches to the public repository. Each time you have a new topic branch to merge in (Figure 5-21), you merge it into develop (Figure 5-22); then, when you tag a release, you fast-forward master to wherever the now-stable develop branch is (Figure 5-23).

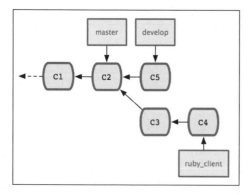

Figure 5-21. *Before a topic branch merge*

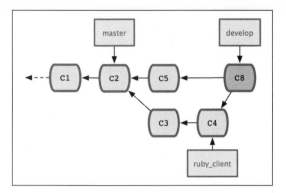

Figure 5-22. *After a topic branch merge*

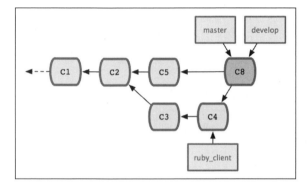

Figure 5-23. *After a topic branch release*

This way, when people clone your project's repository, they can either check out master to build the latest stable version and keep up to date on that easily, or they can check out develop, which is the more cutting-edge stuff.

You can also continue this concept, having an integrate branch where all the work is merged together. Then, when the codebase on that branch is stable and passes tests, you merge it into a develop branch; and when that has proven itself stable for a while, you fast-forward your master branch.

Large-Merging Workflows

The Git project has four long-running branches: master, next, and pu (proposed updates) for new work, and maint for maintenance backports. When new work is introduced by contributors, it's collected into topic branches in the maintainer's repository in a manner similar to what I've described (see Figure 5-24). At this point, the topics are evaluated to determine whether they're safe and ready for consumption or whether they need more work. If they're safe, they're merged into next, and that branch is pushed up so everyone can try the topics integrated together.

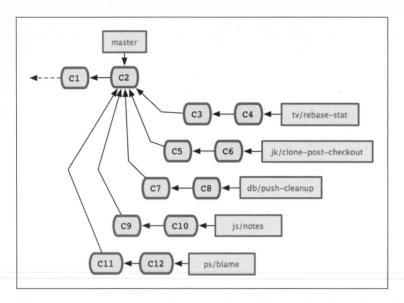

Figure 5-24. *Managing a complex series of parallel contributed topic branches*

If the topics still need work, they're merged into pu instead. When it's determined that they're totally stable, the topics are re-merged into master and are then rebuilt from the topics that were in next but didn't yet graduate to master. This means master almost always moves forward, next is rebased occasionally, and pu is rebased even more often (see Figure 5-25).

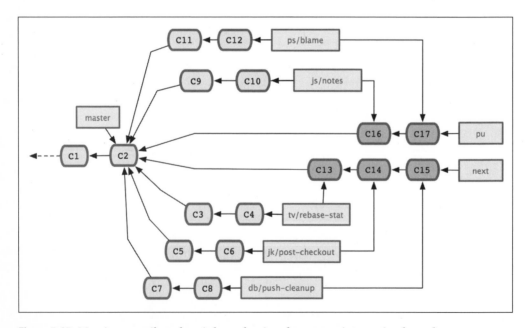

Figure 5-25. *Merging contributed topic branches into long-term integration branches*

When a topic branch has finally been merged into master, it's removed from the repository. The Git project also has a maint branch that is forked off from the last release to provide backported patches in case a maintenance release is required. Thus, when you clone the Git repository, you have four branches that you can check out to evaluate the project in different stages of development, depending on how cutting edge you want to be or how you want to contribute; and the maintainer has a structured workflow to help them vet new contributions.

Rebasing and Cherry-Picking Workflows

Other maintainers prefer to rebase or cherry-pick contributed work on top of their master branch, rather than merging it in, to keep a mostly linear history. When you have work in a topic branch and have determined that you want to integrate it, you move to that branch and run the rebase command to rebuild the changes on top of your current master (or develop, and so on) branch. If that works well, you can fast-forward your master branch, and you'll end up with a linear project history.

The other way to move introduced work from one branch to another is to cherry-pick it. A cherry-pick in Git is like a rebase for a single commit. It takes the patch that was introduced in a commit and tries to reapply it on the branch you're currently on. This is useful if you have a number of commits on a topic branch and you want to integrate only one of them, or if you only have one commit on a topic branch and you'd prefer to cherry-pick it rather than run rebase. For example, suppose you have a project that looks like Figure 5-26.

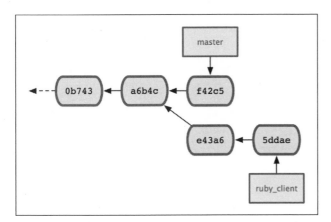

Figure 5-26. *Example history before a cherry-pick*

If you want to pull commit e43a6 into your master branch, you can run

```
$ git cherry-pick e43a6fd3e94888d76779ad79fb568ed180e5fcdf
Finished one cherry-pick.
[master]: created a0a41a9: "More friendly message when locking the index fails."
 3 files changed, 17 insertions(+), 3 deletions(-)
```

This pulls the same change introduced in e43a6, but you get a new commit SHA-1 value, because the date applied is different. Your history looks like Figure 5-27.

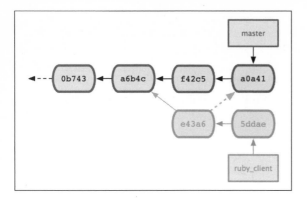

Figure 5-27. *History after cherry-picking a commit on a topic branch*

Now you can remove your topic branch and drop the commits you didn't want to pull in.

Tagging Your Releases

When you've decided to cut a release, you'll probably want to drop a tag so you can re-create that release at any point going forward. You can create a new tag as I discussed in Chapter 2. If you decide to sign the tag as the maintainer, the tagging may look something like this:

```
$ git tag -s v1.5 -m 'my signed 1.5 tag'
You need a passphrase to unlock the secret key for
user: "Scott Chacon <schacon@gmail.com>"
1024-bit DSA key, ID F721C45A, created 2009-02-09
```

If you do sign your tags, you may have the problem of distributing the public PGP key used to sign your tags. The maintainer of the Git project has solved this issue by including their public key as a blob in the repository and then adding a tag that points directly to that content. To do this, you can figure out which key you want by running gpg --list-keys:

```
$ gpg --list-keys
/Users/schacon/.gnupg/pubring.gpg
---------------------------------
pub   1024D/F721C45A 2009-02-09 [expires: 2010-02-09]
uid                  Scott Chacon <schacon@gmail.com>
sub   2048g/45D02282 2009-02-09 [expires: 2010-02-09]
```

Then, you can directly import the key into the Git database by exporting it and piping that through git hash-object, which writes a new blob with those contents into Git and gives you back the SHA-1 of the blob:

```
$ gpg -a --export F721C45A | git hash-object -w --stdin
659ef797d181633c87ec71ac3f9ba29fe5775b92
```

Now that you have the contents of your key in Git, you can create a tag that points directly to it by specifying the new SHA-1 value that the hash-object command gave you:

```
$ git tag -a maintainer-pgp-pub 659ef797d181633c87ec71ac3f9ba29fe5775b92
```

If you run git push --tags, the maintainer-pgp-pub tag will be shared with everyone. If anyone wants to verify a tag, they can directly import your PGP key by pulling the blob directly out of the database and importing it into GPG:

```
$ git show maintainer-pgp-pub | gpg --import
```

They can use that key to verify all your signed tags. Also, if you include instructions in the tag message, running git show <tag> will let you give the end user more specific instructions about tag verification.

Generating a Build Number

Because Git doesn't have monotonically increasing numbers like 'v123' or the equivalent to go with each commit, if you want to have a human-readable name to go with a commit, you can run git describe on that commit. Git gives you the name of the nearest tag with the number of commits on top of that tag and a partial SHA-1 value of the commit you're describing:

```
$ git describe master
v1.6.2-rc1-20-g8c5b85c
```

This way, you can export a snapshot or build and name it something understandable to people. In fact, if you build Git from source code cloned from the Git repository, git --version gives you something that looks like this. If you're describing a commit that you have directly tagged, it gives you the tag name.

The git describe command favors annotated tags (tags created with the -a or -s flag), so release tags should be created this way if you're using git describe, to ensure the commit is named properly when described. You can also use this string as the target of a checkout or show command, although it relies on the abbreviated SHA-1 value at the end, so it may not be valid forever. For instance, the Linux kernel recently jumped from 8 to 10 characters to ensure SHA-1 object uniqueness, so older git describe output names were invalidated.

Preparing a Release

Now you want to release a build. One of the things you'll want to do is create an archive of the latest snapshot of your code for those poor souls who don't use Git. The command to do this is git archive:

```
$ git archive master --prefix='project/' | gzip > `git describe master`.tar.gz
$ ls *.tar.gz
v1.6.2-rc1-20-g8c5b85c.tar.gz
```

If someone opens that tarball, they get the latest snapshot of your project under a project directory. You can also create a zip archive in much the same way, but by passing the --format=zip option to git archive:

```
$ git archive master --prefix='project/' --format=zip > `git describe master`.zip
```

You now have a nice tarball and a zip archive of your project release that you can upload to your website or e-mail to people.

The Shortlog

It's time to e-mail your mailing list of people who want to know what's happening in your project. A nice way of quickly getting a sort of changelog of what has been added to your project since your last release or e-mail is to use the `git shortlog` command. It summarizes all the commits in the range you give it; for example, the following gives you a summary of all the commits since your last release, if your last release was named v1.0.1:

```
$ git shortlog --no-merges master --not v1.0.1
Chris Wanstrath (8):
      Add support for annotated tags to Grit::Tag
      Add packed-refs annotated tag support.
      Add Grit::Commit#to_patch
      Update version and History.txt
      Remove stray 'puts'
      Make ls_tree ignore nils

Tom Preston-Werner (4):
      fix dates in history
      dynamic version method
      Version bump to 1.0.2
      Regenerated gemspec for version 1.0.2
```

You get a clean summary of all the commits since v1.0.1, grouped by author, that you can e-mail to your list.

Summary

You should feel fairly comfortable contributing to a project in Git as well as maintaining your own project or integrating other users' contributions. Congratulations on being an effective Git developer! In the next chapter, you'll learn more powerful tools and tips for dealing with complex situations, which will truly make you a Git master.

■ ■ ■

## CHAPTER 6

Git Tools

By now, you've learned most of the day-to-day commands and workflows that you need to manage or maintain a Git repository for your source-code control. You've accomplished the basic tasks of tracking and committing files, and you've harnessed the power of the staging area and lightweight topic branching and merging.

Now you'll explore a number of very powerful things that Git can do that you may not necessarily use on a day-to-day basis but that you may need at some point.

Revision Selection

Git allows you to specify specific commits or a range of commits in several ways. They aren't necessarily obvious but are helpful to know.

Single Revisions

You can obviously refer to a commit by the SHA-1 hash that it's given, but there are more human-friendly ways to refer to commits as well. This section outlines the various ways you can refer to a single commit.

Short SHA

Git is smart enough to figure out what commit you meant to type if you provide the first few characters, as long as your partial SHA-1 is at least four characters long and unambiguous—that is, only one object in the current repository begins with that partial SHA-1.

For example, to see a specific commit, suppose you run a `git log` command and identify the commit where you added certain functionality:

```
$ git log
commit 734713bc047d87bf7eac9674765ae793478c50d3
Author: Scott Chacon <schacon@gmail.com>
Date:   Fri Jan 2 18:32:33 2009 -0800

    fixed refs handling, added gc auto, updated tests

commit d921970aadf03b3cf0e71becdaab3147ba71cdef
Merge: 1c002dd... 35cfb2b...
Author: Scott Chacon <schacon@gmail.com>
Date:   Thu Dec 11 15:08:43 2008 -0800
```

```
    Merge commit 'phedders/rdocs'
```

```
commit 1c002dd4b536e7479fe34593e72e6c6c1819e53b
Author: Scott Chacon <schacon@gmail.com>
Date:   Thu Dec 11 14:58:32 2008 -0800
```

```
    added some blame and merge stuff
```

In this case, choose 1c002dd.... If you git show that commit, the following commands are equivalent (assuming the shorter versions are unambiguous):

```
$ git show 1c002dd4b536e7479fe34593e72e6c6c1819e53b
$ git show 1c002dd4b536e7479f
$ git show 1c002d
```

Git can figure out a short, unique abbreviation for your SHA-1 values. If you pass --abbrev-commit to the git log command, the output will use shorter values but keep them unique; it defaults to using seven characters but makes them longer if necessary to keep the SHA-1 unambiguous:

```
$ git log --abbrev-commit --pretty=oneline
ca82a6d changed the version number
085bb3b removed unnecessary test code
a11bef0 first commit
```

Generally, eight to ten characters are more than enough to be unique within a project. One of the largest Git projects, the Linux kernel, is beginning to need 12 characters out of the possible 40 to stay unique.

A SHORT NOTE ABOUT SHA-1

A lot of people become concerned at some point that they will, by random happenstance, have two objects in their repository that hash to the same SHA-1 value. What then?

If you do happen to commit an object that hashes to the same SHA-1 value as a previous object in your repository, Git will see the previous object in your Git database and assume it was already written. If you try to check out that object again at some point, you'll always get the data of the first object.

However, you should be aware of how ridiculously unlikely this scenario is. The SHA-1 digest is 20 bytes or 160 bits. The number of randomly hashed objects needed to ensure a 50% probability of a single collision is about 2^{80} (the formula for determining collision probability is $p = (n(n-1)/2) * (1/2^{160})$). 2^{80} is 1.2×10^{24} or 1 million billion billion. That's 1,200 times the number of grains of sand on Earth.

Here's an example to give you an idea of what it would take to get a SHA-1 collision. If all 6.5 billion humans on Earth were programming, and every *second*, each one was producing code that was the equivalent of the entire Linux kernel history (1 million Git objects) and pushing it into one enormous Git repository, it would take 5 years until that repository contained enough objects to have a 50% probability of a single SHA-1 object collision. A higher probability exists that every member of your programming team will be attacked and killed by wolves in unrelated incidents on the same night.

Branch References

The most straightforward way to specify a commit requires that it have a branch reference pointed at it. Then, you can use a branch name in any Git command that expects a commit object or SHA-1 value. For instance, if you want to show the last commit object on a branch, the following commands are equivalent, assuming that the topic1 branch points to ca82a6d:

```
$ git show ca82a6dff817ec66f44342007202690a93763949
$ git show topic1
```

If you want to see which specific SHA a branch points to, or if you want to see what any of these examples boils down to in terms of SHAs, you can use a Git plumbing tool called rev-parse. You can see Chapter 9 for more information about plumbing tools; basically, rev-parse exists for lower-level operations and isn't designed to be used in day-to-day operations. However, it can be helpful sometimes when you need to see what's really going on. Here you can run rev-parse on your branch.

```
$ git rev-parse topic1
ca82a6dff817ec66f44342007202690a93763949
```

RefLog Shortnames

One of the things Git does in the background while you're working away is keep a *reflog*—a log of where your HEAD and branch references have been for the last few months.

You can see your reflog by using git reflog:

```
$ git reflog
734713b... HEAD@{0}: commit: fixed refs handling, added gc auto, updated
d921970... HEAD@{1}: merge phedders/rdocs: Merge made by recursive.
1c002dd... HEAD@{2}: commit: added some blame and merge stuff
1c36188... HEAD@{3}: rebase -i (squash): updating HEAD
95df984... HEAD@{4}: commit: # This is a combination of two commits.
1c36188... HEAD@{5}: rebase -i (squash): updating HEAD
7e05da5... HEAD@{6}: rebase -i (pick): updating HEAD
```

Every time your branch tip is updated for any reason, Git stores that information for you in this temporary history. And you can specify older commits with this data, as well. If you want to see the fifth prior value of the HEAD of your repository, you can use the @{n} reference that you see in the reflog output:

```
$ git show HEAD@{5}
```

You can also use this syntax to see where a branch was some specific amount of time ago. For instance, to see where your master branch was yesterday, you can type

```
$ git show master@{yesterday}
```

That shows you where the branch tip was yesterday. This technique only works for data that's still in your reflog, so you can't use it to look for commits older than a few months.

To see reflog information inline with your normal log information, you can run git log -g:

```
$ git log -g master
commit 734713bc047d87bf7eac9674765ae793478c50d3
Reflog: master@{0} (Scott Chacon <schacon@gmail.com>)
Reflog message: commit: fixed refs handling, added gc auto, updated
Author: Scott Chacon <schacon@gmail.com>
Date:   Fri Jan 2 18:32:33 2009 -0800

    fixed refs handling, added gc auto, updated tests

commit d921970aadf03b3cf0e71becdaab3147ba71cdef
Reflog: master@{1} (Scott Chacon <schacon@gmail.com>)
Reflog message: merge phedders/rdocs: Merge made by recursive.
Author: Scott Chacon <schacon@gmail.com>
Date:   Thu Dec 11 15:08:43 2008 -0800

    Merge commit 'phedders/rdocs'
```

It's important to note that the reflog information is strictly local—it's a log of what you've done in your repository. The references won't be the same on someone else's copy of the repository; and right after you initially clone a repository, you'll have an empty reflog, because no activity has occurred yet in your repository. Running git show HEAD@{2.months.ago} will work only if you cloned the project at least two months ago—if you cloned it five minutes ago, you'll get no results.

Ancestry References

The other main way to specify a commit is via its ancestry. If you place a ^ at the end of a reference, Git resolves it to mean the parent of that commit.

Suppose you look at the history of your project:

```
$ git log --pretty=format:'%h %s' --graph
* 734713b fixed refs handling, added gc auto, updated tests
*   d921970 Merge commit 'phedders/rdocs'
|\
| * 35cfb2b Some rdoc changes
* | 1c002dd added some blame and merge stuff
|/
* 1c36188 ignore *.gem
* 9b29157 add open3_detach to gemspec file list
```

Then, you can see the previous commit by specifying HEAD^, which means "the parent of HEAD":

```
$ git show HEAD^
commit d921970aadf03b3cf0e71becdaab3147ba71cdef
Merge: 1c002dd... 35cfb2b...
Author: Scott Chacon <schacon@gmail.com>
Date:   Thu Dec 11 15:08:43 2008 -0800

    Merge commit 'phedders/rdocs'
```

You can also specify a number after the ^—for example, d921970^2 means "the second parent of d921970." This syntax is only useful for merge commits, which have more than one parent. The first parent is the branch you were on when you merged, and the second is the commit on the branch that you merged in:

```
$ git show d921970^
commit 1c002dd4b536e7479fe34593e72e6c6c1819e53b
Author: Scott Chacon <schacon@gmail.com>
Date:   Thu Dec 11 14:58:32 2008 -0800

    added some blame and merge stuff

$ git show d921970^2
commit 35cfb2b795a55793d7cc56a6cc2060b4bb732548
Author: Paul Hedderly <paul+git@mjr.org>
Date:   Wed Dec 10 22:22:03 2008 +0000

    Some rdoc changes
```

The other main ancestry specification is the ~. This also refers to the first parent, so HEAD~ and HEAD^ are equivalent. The difference becomes apparent when you specify a number. HEAD~2 means "the first parent of the first parent," or "the grandparent"—it traverses the first parents the number of times you specify. For example, in the history listed earlier, HEAD~3 would be

```
$ git show HEAD~3
commit 1c3618887afb5fbcbea25b7c013f4e2114448b8d
Author: Tom Preston-Werner <tom@mojombo.com>
Date:   Fri Nov 7 13:47:59 2008 -0500

    ignore *.gem
```

This can also be written HEAD^^^, which again is the first parent of the first parent of the first parent:

```
$ git show HEAD^^^
commit 1c3618887afb5fbcbea25b7c013f4e2114448b8d
Author: Tom Preston-Werner <tom@mojombo.com>
Date:   Fri Nov 7 13:47:59 2008 -0500

    ignore *.gem
```

You can also combine these syntaxes—you can get the second parent of the previous reference (assuming it was a merge commit) by using HEAD~3^2, and so on.

Commit Ranges

Now that you can specify individual commits, let's see how to specify ranges of commits. This is particularly useful for managing your branches—if you have a lot of branches, you can use range specifications to answer questions such as, "What work is on this branch that I haven't yet merged into my main branch?"

Double Dot

The most common range specification is the double-dot syntax. This basically asks Git to resolve a range of commits that are reachable from one commit but aren't reachable from another. For example, say you have a commit history that looks like Figure 6-1.

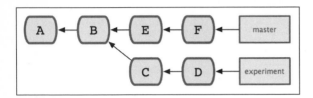

Figure 6-1. *Example history for range selection*

You want to see what is in your `experiment` branch that hasn't yet been merged into your `master` branch. You can ask Git to show you a log of just those commits with `master..experiment`—that means "all commits reachable by `experiment` that aren't reachable by `master`." For the sake of brevity and clarity in these examples, I'll use the letters of the commit objects from the diagram in place of the actual log output in the order that they would display:

```
$ git log master..experiemnt
D
C
```

If, on the other hand, you want to see the opposite—all commits in `master` that aren't in `experiment`—you can reverse the branch names. `experiment..master` shows you everything in `master` not reachable from `experiment`:

```
$ git log experiment..master
F
E
```

This is useful if you want to keep the `experiment` branch up to date and preview what you're about to merge in. Another very frequent use of this syntax is to see what you're about to push to a remote:

```
$ git log origin/master..HEAD
```

This command shows you any commits in your current branch that aren't in the `master` branch on your `origin` remote. If you run a `git push` and your current branch is tracking `origin/master`, the commits listed by `git log origin/master..HEAD` are the commits that will be transferred to the server.

You can also leave off one side of the syntax to have Git assume `HEAD`. For example, by typing `git log origin/master..` you can get the same results as in the previous example; Git substitutes `HEAD` if one side is missing.

Multiple Points

The double-dot syntax is useful as shorthand; but perhaps you want to specify more than two branches to indicate your revision, such as seeing what commits are in any of several branches that aren't in the branch you're currently on. Git allows you to do this by using either the ^ character or `--not` before any reference from which you don't want to see reachable commits. Thus these three commands are equivalent:

```
$ git log refA..refB
$ git log ^refA refB
$ git log refB --not refA
```

This is nice because with this syntax, you can specify more than two references in your query, which you can't do with the double-dot syntax. For instance, if you want to see all commits that are reachable from refA or refB but not from refC, you can type one of these:

```
$ git log refA refB ^refC
$ git log refA refB --not refC
```

This makes for a very powerful revision query system that should help you figure out what is in your branches.

Triple Dot

The last major range-selection syntax is the triple-dot syntax, which specifies all the commits that are reachable by either of two references but not by both of them. Look back at the example commit history in Figure 6-1.

If you want to see what is in master or experiment but not any common references, you can run

```
$ git log master...experiment
F
E
D
C
```

Again, this gives you normal log output but shows you only the commit information for those four commits, appearing in the traditional commit date ordering.

A common switch to use with the log command in this case is `--left-right`, which shows you which side of the range each commit is in. This helps make the data more useful:

```
$ git log --left-right master...experiment
< F
< E
> D
> C
```

With these tools, you can much more easily let Git know what commit or commits you want to inspect.

Interactive Staging

Git comes with a couple of scripts that make some command-line tasks easier. Here, you'll look at a few interactive commands that can help you easily craft your commits to include only certain combinations and parts of files. These tools are very helpful if you modify a bunch of files and then decide that you want those changes to be in several focused commits rather than one big messy commit. This way, you can make sure your commits are logically separate changesets and can be easily reviewed by the developers working with you.

If you run git add with the -i or --interactive option, Git goes into an interactive shell mode, displaying something like this:

```
$ git add -i
           staged      unstaged path
  1:     unchanged        +0/-1 TODO
  2:     unchanged        +1/-1 index.html
  3:     unchanged        +5/-1 lib/simplegit.rb

*** Commands ***
  1: status      2: update      3: revert      4: add untracked
  5: patch       6: diff        7: quit        8: help
What now>
```

You can see that this command shows you a much different view of your staging area—basically the same information you get with git status but a bit more succinct and informative. It lists the changes you've staged on the left and unstaged changes on the right.

After this comes a Commands section. Here you can do a number of things, including staging files, unstaging files, staging parts of files, adding untracked files, and seeing diffs of what has been staged.

Staging and Unstaging Files

If you type 2 or **u** at the What now> prompt, the script prompts you for which files you want to stage:

```
What now> 2
           staged      unstaged path
  1:     unchanged        +0/-1 TODO
  2:     unchanged        +1/-1 index.html
  3:     unchanged        +5/-1 lib/simplegit.rb
Update>>
```

To stage the TODO and index.html files, you can type the numbers:

```
Update>> 1,2
           staged      unstaged path
* 1:     unchanged        +0/-1 TODO
* 2:     unchanged        +1/-1 index.html
  3:     unchanged        +5/-1 lib/simplegit.rb
Update>>
```

The * next to each file means the file is selected to be staged. If you press Enter after typing nothing at the Update>> prompt, Git takes anything selected and stages it for you:

```
Update>>
updated 2 paths

*** Commands ***
  1: status     2: update     3: revert     4: add untracked
  5: patch      6: diff       7: quit       8: help
What now> 1
          staged      unstaged path
  1:        +0/-1       nothing TODO
  2:        +1/-1       nothing index.html
  3:     unchanged       +5/-1 lib/simplegit.rb
```

Now you can see that the TODO and index.html files are staged and the simplegit.rb file is still unstaged. If you want to unstage the TODO file at this point, you use the 3 or r (for *revert*) option:

```
*** Commands ***
  1: status     2: update     3: revert     4: add untracked
  5: patch      6: diff       7: quit       8: help
What now> 3
          staged      unstaged path
  1:        +0/-1       nothing TODO
  2:        +1/-1       nothing index.html
  3:     unchanged       +5/-1 lib/simplegit.rb
Revert>> 1
          staged      unstaged path
* 1:        +0/-1       nothing TODO
  2:        +1/-1       nothing index.html
  3:     unchanged       +5/-1 lib/simplegit.rb
Revert>> [enter]
reverted one path
```

Looking at your Git status again, you can see that you've unstaged the TODO file:

```
*** Commands ***
  1: status     2: update     3: revert     4: add untracked
  5: patch      6: diff       7: quit       8: help
What now> 1
          staged      unstaged path
  1:     unchanged       +0/-1 TODO
  2:        +1/-1       nothing index.html
  3:     unchanged       +5/-1 lib/simplegit.rb
```

To see the diff of what you've staged, you can use the 6 or d (for *diff*) command. It shows you a list of your staged files, and you can select the ones for which you would like to see the staged diff. This is much like specifying git diff --cached on the command line:

```
*** Commands ***
  1: status      2: update     3: revert     4: add untracked
  5: patch       6: diff       7: quit       8: help
What now> 6
           staged      unstaged path
  1:          +1/-1      nothing index.html
Review diff>> 1
diff --git a/index.html b/index.html
index 4d07108..4335f49 100644
--- a/index.html
+++ b/index.html
@@ -16,7 +16,7 @@ Date Finder

 <p id="out">...</p>

-<div id="footer">contact : support@github.com</div>
+<div id="footer">contact : email.support@github.com</div>

 <script type="text/javascript">
```

With these basic commands, you can use the interactive add mode to deal with your staging area a little more easily.

Staging Patches

It's also possible for Git to stage certain parts of files and not the rest. For example, if you make two changes to your simplegit.rb file and want to stage one of them and not the other, doing so is very easy in Git. From the interactive prompt, type **5** or **p** (for *patch*). Git will ask you which files you would like to partially stage; then, for each section of the selected files, it will display hunks of the file diff and ask if you would like to stage them, one by one:

```
diff --git a/lib/simplegit.rb b/lib/simplegit.rb
index dd5ecc4..57399e0 100644
--- a/lib/simplegit.rb
+++ b/lib/simplegit.rb
@@ -22,7 +22,7 @@ class SimpleGit
   end

   def log(treeish = 'master')
-    command("git log -n 25 #{treeish}")
+    command("git log -n 30 #{treeish}")
   end
```

```
      def blame(path)
Stage this hunk [y,n,a,d,/,j,J,g,e,?]?
```

You have a lot of options at this point. Typing **?** shows a list of what you can do:

```
Stage this hunk [y,n,a,d,/,j,J,g,e,?]? ?
y - stage this hunk
n - do not stage this hunk
a - stage this and all the remaining hunks in the file
d - do not stage this hunk nor any of the remaining hunks in the file
g - select a hunk to go to
/ - search for a hunk matching the given regex
j - leave this hunk undecided, see next undecided hunk
J - leave this hunk undecided, see next hunk
k - leave this hunk undecided, see previous undecided hunk
K - leave this hunk undecided, see previous hunk
s - split the current hunk into smaller hunks
e - manually edit the current hunk
? - print help
```

Generally, you'll type **y** or **n** if you want to stage each hunk, but staging all of them in certain files or skipping a hunk decision until later can be helpful too. If you stage one part of the file and leave another part unstaged, your status output will look like this:

```
What now> 1
           staged     unstaged path
  1:    unchanged        +0/-1 TODO
  2:        +1/-1      nothing index.html
  3:        +1/-1        +4/-0 lib/simplegit.rb
```

The status of the `simplegit.rb` file is interesting. It shows you that a couple of lines are staged and a couple are unstaged. You've partially staged this file. At this point, you can exit the interactive adding script and run `git commit` to commit the partially staged files.

Finally, you don't need to be in interactive add mode to do the partial-file staging—you can start the same script by using `git add -p` or `git add --patch` on the command line.

Stashing

Often, when you've been working on part of your project, things are in a messy state and you want to switch branches for a bit to work on something else. The problem is, you don't want to do a commit of half-done work just so you can get back to this point later. The answer to this issue is the `git stash` command.

Stashing takes the dirty state of your working directory—that is, your modified tracked files and staged changes—and saves it on a stack of unfinished changes that you can reapply at any time.

Stashing Your Work

To demonstrate, you'll go into your project and start working on a couple of files and possibly stage one of the changes. If you run git status, you can see your dirty state:

```
$ git status
# On branch master
# Changes to be committed:
#   (use "git reset HEAD <file>..." to unstage)
#
#       modified:   index.html
#
# Changed but not updated:
#   (use "git add <file>..." to update what will be committed)
#
#       modified:   lib/simplegit.rb
#
```

Now you want to switch branches, but you don't want to commit what you've been working on yet; so you'll stash the changes. To push a new stash onto your stack, run git stash:

```
$ git stash
Saved working directory and index state \
  "WIP on master: 049d078 added the index file"
HEAD is now at 049d078 added the index file
(To restore them type "git stash apply")
```

Your working directory is clean:

```
$ git status
# On branch master
nothing to commit (working directory clean)
```

At this point, you can easily switch branches and do work elsewhere; your changes are stored on your stack. To see which stashes you've stored, you can use git stash list:

```
$ git stash list
stash@{0}: WIP on master: 049d078 added the index file
stash@{1}: WIP on master: c264051... Revert "added file_size"
stash@{2}: WIP on master: 21d80a5... added number to log
```

In this case, two stashes were done previously, so you have access to three different stashed works. You can reapply the one you just stashed by using the command shown in the help output of the original stash command: git stash apply. If you want to apply one of the older stashes, you can specify it by naming it, like this: git stash apply stash@{2}. If you don't specify a stash, Git assumes the most recent stash and tries to apply it:

```
$ git stash apply
# On branch master
# Changed but not updated:
#   (use "git add <file>..." to update what will be committed)
#
#       modified:   index.html
#       modified:   lib/simplegit.rb
#
```

You can see that Git re-modifies the files you uncommitted when you saved the stash. In this case, you had a clean working directory when you tried to apply the stash, and you tried to apply it on the same branch you saved it from; but having a clean working directory and applying it on the same branch aren't necessary to successfully apply a stash. You can save a stash on one branch, switch to another branch later, and try to reapply the changes. You can also have modified and uncommitted files in your working directory when you apply a stash—Git gives you merge conflicts if anything no longer applies cleanly.

The changes to your files were reapplied, but the file you staged before wasn't restaged. To do that, you must run the git stash apply command with a --index option to tell the command to try to reapply the staged changes. If you had run that instead, you'd have gotten back to your original position:

```
$ git stash apply --index
# On branch master
# Changes to be committed:
#   (use "git reset HEAD <file>..." to unstage)
#
#       modified:   index.html
#
# Changed but not updated:
#   (use "git add <file>..." to update what will be committed)
#
#       modified:   lib/simplegit.rb
#
```

The apply option only tries to apply the stashed work—you continue to have it on your stack. To remove it, you can run git stash drop with the name of the stash to remove:

```
$ git stash list
stash@{0}: WIP on master: 049d078 added the index file
stash@{1}: WIP on master: c264051... Revert "added file_size"
stash@{2}: WIP on master: 21d80a5... added number to log
$ git stash drop stash@{0}
Dropped stash@{0} (364e91f3f268f0900bc3ee613f9f733e82aaed43)
```

You can also run git stash pop to apply the stash and then immediately drop it from your stack.

Creating a Branch from a Stash

If you stash some work, leave it there for a while, and continue on the branch from which you stashed the work, you may have a problem reapplying the work. If the apply tries to modify a file that you've since modified, you'll get a merge conflict and will have to try to resolve it. If you want an easier way to test the stashed changes again, you can run `git stash branch`, which creates a new branch for you, checks out the commit you were on when you stashed your work, reapplies your work there, and then drops the stash if it applies successfully:

```
$ git stash branch testchanges
Switched to a new branch "testchanges"
# On branch testchanges
# Changes to be committed:
#   (use "git reset HEAD <file>..." to unstage)
#
#       modified:   index.html
#
# Changed but not updated:
#   (use "git add <file>..." to update what will be committed)
#
#       modified:   lib/simplegit.rb
#
Dropped refs/stash@{0} (f0dfc4d5dc332d1cee34a634182e168c4efc3359)
```

This is a nice shortcut to recover stashed work easily and work on it in a new branch.

Rewriting History

Many times, when working with Git, you may want to revise your commit history for some reason. One of the great things about Git is that it allows you to make decisions at the last possible moment. You can decide what files go into which commits right before you commit with the staging area, you can decide that you didn't mean to be working on something yet with the `stash` command, and you can rewrite commits that already happened so they look like they happened in a different way. This can involve changing the order of the commits, changing messages or modifying files in a commit, squashing together or splitting apart commits, or removing commits entirely—all before you share your work with others.

In this section, you'll cover how to accomplish these very useful tasks so that you can make your commit history look the way you want before you share it with others.

Changing the Last Commit

Changing your last commit is probably the most common rewriting of history that you'll do. You'll often want to do two basic things to your last commit: change the commit message, or change the snapshot you just recorded by adding, changing. and removing files.

If you only want to modify your last commit message, it's very simple:

```
$ git commit --amend
```

That drops you into your text editor, which has your last commit message in it, ready for you to modify the message. When you save and close the editor, the editor writes a new commit containing that message and makes it your new last commit.

If you've committed and then you want to change the snapshot you committed by adding or changing files, possibly because you forgot to add a newly created file when you originally committed, the process works basically the same way. You stage the changes you want by editing a file and running `git add` on it or `git rm` to a tracked file, and the subsequent `git commit --amend` takes your current staging area and makes it the snapshot for the new commit.

You need to be careful with this technique because amending changes the SHA-1 of the commit. It's like a very small rebase—don't amend your last commit if you've already pushed it.

Changing Multiple Commit Messages

To modify a commit that is farther back in your history, you must move to more complex tools. Git doesn't have a modify-history tool, but you can use the `rebase` tool to rebase a series of commits onto the HEAD they were originally based on instead of moving them to another one. With the interactive `rebase` tool, you can then stop after each commit you want to modify and change the message, add files, or do whatever you wish. You can run `rebase` interactively by adding the `-i` option to `git rebase`. You must indicate how far back you want to rewrite commits by telling the command which commit to rebase onto.

For example, if you want to change the last three commit messages, or any of the commit messages in that group, you supply as an argument to `git rebase -i` the parent of the last commit you want to edit, which is HEAD~2^ or HEAD~3. It may be easier to remember the ~3 because you're trying to edit the last three commits; but keep in mind that you're actually designating four commits ago, the *parent* of the last commit you want to edit:

```
$ git rebase -i HEAD~3
```

Remember again that this is a rebasing command—every commit included in the range HEAD~3..HEAD will be rewritten, whether you change the message or not. Don't include any commit you've already pushed to a central server—doing so will confuse other developers by providing an alternate version of the same change.

Running this command gives you a list of commits in your text editor that looks something like this:

```
pick f7f3f6d changed my name a bit
pick 310154e updated README formatting and added blame
pick a5f4a0d added cat-file

# Rebase 710f0f8..a5f4a0d onto 710f0f8
#
# Commands:
#  p, pick = use commit
#  e, edit = use commit, but stop for amending
#  s, squash = use commit, but meld into previous commit
#
# If you remove a line here THAT COMMIT WILL BE LOST.
# However, if you remove everything, the rebase will be aborted.
#
```

It's important to note that these commits are listed in the opposite order than you normally see them using the log command. If you run a log, you see something like this:

```
$ git log --pretty=format:"%h %s HEAD~3..HEAD"
a5f4a0d added cat-file
310154e updated README formatting and added blame
f7f3f6d changed my name a bit
```

Notice the reverse order. The interactive rebase gives you a script that it's going to run. It will start at the commit you specify on the command line (HEAD~3) and replay the changes introduced in each of these commits from top to bottom. It lists the oldest at the top, rather than the newest, because that's the first one it will replay.

You need to edit the script so that it stops at the commit you want to edit. To do so, change the word pick to the word edit for each of the commits you want the script to stop after. For example, to modify only the third commit message, you change the file to look like this:

```
edit f7f3f6d changed my name a bit
pick 310154e updated README formatting and added blame
pick a5f4a0d added cat-file
```

When you save and exit the editor, Git rewinds you back to the last commit in that list and drops you on the command line with the following message:

```
$ git rebase -i HEAD~3
Stopped at 7482e0d... updated the gemspec to hopefully work better
You can amend the commit now, with

      git commit --amend

Once you're satisfied with your changes, run

      git rebase --continue
```

These instructions tell you exactly what to do. Type the following:

```
$ git commit --amend
```

Change the commit message, and exit the editor. Then, run this:

```
$ git rebase --continue
```

This command will apply the other two commits automatically, and then you're done. If you change pick to edit on more lines, you can repeat these steps for each commit you change to edit. Each time, Git will stop, let you amend the commit, and continue when you're finished.

Reordering Commits

You can also use interactive rebases to reorder or remove commits entirely. If you want to remove the added cat-file commit and change the order in which the other two commits are introduced, you can change the rebase script from this:

```
pick f7f3f6d changed my name a bit
pick 310154e updated README formatting and added blame
pick a5f4a0d added cat-file
```

to this:

```
pick 310154e updated README formatting and added blame
pick f7f3f6d changed my name a bit
```

When you save and exit the editor, Git rewinds your branch to the parent of these commits, applies 310154e and then f7f3f6d, and then stops. You effectively change the order of those commits and remove the cat-file commit completely.

Squashing a Commit

It's also possible to take a series of commits and squash them down into a single commit with the interactive rebasing tool. The script puts helpful instructions in the rebase message:

```
#
# Commands:
#  p, pick = use commit
#  e, edit = use commit, but stop for amending
#  s, squash = use commit, but meld into previous commit
#
# If you remove a line here THAT COMMIT WILL BE LOST.
# However, if you remove everything, the rebase will be aborted.
#
```

If, instead of pick or edit, you specify squash, Git applies both that change and the change directly before it and makes you merge the commit messages together. So, if you want to make a single commit from these three commits, you make the script look like this:

```
pick f7f3f6d changed my name a bit
squash 310154e updated README formatting and added blame
squash a5f4a0d added cat-file
```

When you save and exit the editor, Git applies all three changes and then puts you back into the editor to merge the three commit messages:

```
# This is a combination of 3 commits.
# The first commit's message is:
changed my name a bit

# This is the 2nd commit message:

updated README formatting and added blame

# This is the 3rd commit message:

added cat-file
```

When you save that, you have a single commit that introduces the changes of all three previous commits.

Splitting a Commit

Splitting a commit undoes a commit and then partially stages and commits as many times as commits you want to end up with. For example, suppose you want to split the middle commit of your three commits. Instead of updated README formatting and added blame, you want to split it into two commits: updated README formatting for the first, and added blame for the second. You can do that in the rebase -i script by changing the instruction on the commit you want to split to edit:

```
pick f7f3f6d changed my name a bit
edit 310154e updated README formatting and added blame
pick a5f4a0d added cat-file
```

Then, when the script drops you to the command line, you reset that commit, take the changes that have been reset, and create multiple commits out of them. When you save and exit the editor, Git rewinds to the parent of the first commit in your list, applies the first commit (f7f3f6d), applies the second (310154e), and drops you to the console. There, you can do a mixed reset of that commit with git reset HEAD^, which effectively undoes that commit and leaves the modified files unstaged. Now you can stage and commit files until you have several commits, and run git rebase --continue when you're done:

```
$ git reset HEAD^
$ git add README
$ git commit -m 'updated README formatting'
$ git add lib/simplegit.rb
$ git commit -m 'added blame'
$ git rebase --continue
```

Git applies the last commit (a5f4a0d) in the script, and your history looks like this:

```
$ git log -4 --pretty=format:"%h %s"
1c002dd added cat-file
9b29157 added blame
35cfb2b updated README formatting
f3cc40e changed my name a bit
```

Once again, this changes the SHAs of all the commits in your list, so make sure no commit shows up in that list that you've already pushed to a shared repository.

The Nuclear Option: filter-branch

There is another history-rewriting option that you can use if you need to rewrite a larger number of commits in some scriptable way—for instance, changing your e-mail address globally or removing a file from every commit. The command is filter-branch, and it can rewrite huge swaths of your history, so you probably shouldn't use it unless your project isn't yet public and other people haven't based work off the commits you're about to rewrite. However, it can be very useful. You'll learn a few of the common uses so you can get an idea of some of the things it's capable of.

Removing a File from Every Commit

This occurs fairly commonly. Someone accidentally commits a huge binary file with a thought-less `git add .`, and you want to remove it everywhere. Perhaps you accidentally committed a file that contained a password, and you want to make your project open source. `filter-branch` is the tool you probably want to use to scrub your entire history. To remove a file named `passwords.txt` from your entire history, you can use the `--tree-filter` option to `filter-branch`:

```
$ git filter-branch --tree-filter 'rm -f passwords.txt' HEAD
Rewrite 6b9b3cf04e7c5686a9cb838c3f36a8cb6a0fc2bd (21/21)
Ref 'refs/heads/master' was rewritten
```

The `--tree-filter` option runs the specified command after each checkout of the project and then recommits the results. In this case, you remove a file called `passwords.txt` from every snapshot, whether it exists or not. If you want to remove all accidentally committed editor backup files, you can run something like `git filter-branch --tree-filter 'rm -f *~' HEAD`.

You'll be able to watch Git rewriting trees and commits and then move the branch pointer at the end. It's generally a good idea to do this in a testing branch and then hard-reset your `master` branch after you've determined the outcome is what you really want. To run `filter-branch` on all your branches, you can pass `--all` to the command.

Making a Subdirectory the New Root

Suppose you've done an import from another source control system and have subdirectories that make no sense (trunk, tags, and so on). If you want to make the `trunk` subdirectory be the new project root for every commit, `filter-branch` can help you do that, too:

```
$ git filter-branch --subdirectory-filter trunk HEAD
Rewrite 856f0bf61e41a27326cdae8f09fe708d679f596f (12/12)
Ref 'refs/heads/master' was rewritten
```

Now your new project root is what was in the `trunk` subdirectory each time. Git will also automatically remove commits that didn't affect the subdirectory.

Changing E-mail Addresses Globally

Another common case is that you forgot to run `git config` to set your name and e-mail address before you started working, or perhaps you want to open-source a project at work and change all your work e-mail addresses to your personal address. In any case, you can change e-mail addresses in multiple commits in a batch with `filter-branch` as well. You need to be careful to change only the e-mail addresses that are yours, so you use `--commit-filter`:

```
$ git filter-branch --commit-filter '
        if [ "$GIT_AUTHOR_EMAIL" = "schacon@localhost" ];
        then
                GIT_AUTHOR_NAME="Scott Chacon";
                GIT_AUTHOR_EMAIL="schacon@example.com";
```

```
        git commit-tree "$@";
    else
        git commit-tree "$@";
    fi' HEAD
```

This goes through and rewrites every commit to have your new address. Because commits contain the SHA-1 values of their parents, this command changes every commit SHA in your history, not just those that have the matching e-mail address.

Debugging with Git

Git also provides a couple of tools to help you debug issues in your projects. Because Git is designed to work with nearly any type of project, these tools are pretty generic, but they can often help you hunt for a bug or culprit when things go wrong.

File Annotation

If you track down a bug in your code and want to know when it was introduced and why, file annotation is often your best tool. It shows you what commit was the last to modify each line of any file. So, if you see that a method in your code is buggy, you can annotate the file with git blame to see when each line of the method was last edited and by whom. This example uses the -L option to limit the output to lines 12 through 22:

```
$ git blame -L 12,22 simplegit.rb
^4832fe2 (Scott Chacon  2008-03-15 10:31:28 -0700 12)  def show(tree = 'master')
^4832fe2 (Scott Chacon  2008-03-15 10:31:28 -0700 13)   command("git show #{tree}")
^4832fe2 (Scott Chacon  2008-03-15 10:31:28 -0700 14)  end
^4832fe2 (Scott Chacon  2008-03-15 10:31:28 -0700 15)
9f6560e4 (Scott Chacon  2008-03-17 21:52:20 -0700 16)  def log(tree = 'master')
79eaf55d (Scott Chacon  2008-04-06 10:15:08 -0700 17)   command("git log #{tree}")
9f6560e4 (Scott Chacon  2008-03-17 21:52:20 -0700 18)  end
9f6560e4 (Scott Chacon  2008-03-17 21:52:20 -0700 19)
42cf2861 (Magnus Chacon 2008-04-13 10:45:01 -0700 20)  def blame(path)
42cf2861 (Magnus Chacon 2008-04-13 10:45:01 -0700 21)   command("git blame #{path}")
42cf2861 (Magnus Chacon 2008-04-13 10:45:01 -0700 22)  end
```

Notice that the first field is the partial SHA-1 of the commit that last modified that line. The next two fields are values extracted from that commit—the author name and the authored date of that commit—so you can easily see who modified that line and when. After that come the line number and the content of the file. Also note the ^4832fe2 commit lines, which designate that those lines were in this file's original commit. That commit is when this file was first added to this project, and those lines have been unchanged since. This is a tad confusing, because now you've seen at least three different ways that Git uses the ^ to modify a commit SHA, but that is what it means here.

Another cool thing about Git is that it doesn't track file renames explicitly. It records the snapshots and then tries to figure out what was renamed implicitly, after the fact. One of the interesting features of this is that you can ask it to figure out all sorts of code movement as well. If you pass -C to git blame, Git analyzes the file you're annotating and tries to figure out where snippets of code within it originally came from if they were copied from elsewhere. Recently, I was refactoring a file named `GITServerHandler.m` into multiple files, one of which was `GITPackUpload.m`. By blaming `GITPackUpload.m` with the `-C` option, I could see where sections of the code originally came from:

```
$ git blame -C -L 141,153 GITPackUpload.m
f344f58d GITServerHandler.m (Scott 2009-01-04 141)
f344f58d GITServerHandler.m (Scott 2009-01-04 142) - (void) gatherObjectShasFromC
f344f58d GITServerHandler.m (Scott 2009-01-04 143) {
70befddd GITServerHandler.m (Scott 2009-03-22 144)          //NSLog(@"GATHER COMMI
ad11ac80 GITPackUpload.m    (Scott 2009-03-24 145)
ad11ac80 GITPackUpload.m    (Scott 2009-03-24 146)          NSString *parentSha;
ad11ac80 GITPackUpload.m    (Scott 2009-03-24 147)          GITCommit *commit = [g
ad11ac80 GITPackUpload.m    (Scott 2009-03-24 148)
ad11ac80 GITPackUpload.m    (Scott 2009-03-24 149)          //NSLog(@"GATHER COMMI
ad11ac80 GITPackUpload.m    (Scott 2009-03-24 150)
56ef2caf GITServerHandler.m (Scott 2009-01-05 151)          if(commit) {
56ef2caf GITServerHandler.m (Scott 2009-01-05 152)                  [refDict setOb
56ef2caf GITServerHandler.m (Scott 2009-01-05 153)
```

This is really useful. Normally, you get as the original commit the commit where you copied the code over, because that is the first time you touched those lines in this file. Git tells you the original commit where you wrote those lines, even if it was in another file.

Binary Search

Annotating a file helps if you know where the issue is to begin with. If you don't know what is breaking, and there have been dozens or hundreds of commits since the last state where you know the code worked, you'll likely turn to `git bisect` for help. The `bisect` command does a binary search through your commit history to help you identify as quickly as possible which commit introduced an issue.

Let's say you just pushed out a release of your code to a production environment, you're getting bug reports about something that wasn't happening in your development environment, and you can't imagine why the code is doing that. You go back to your code, and it turns out you can reproduce the issue, but you can't figure out what is going wrong. You can bisect the code to find out. First you run `git bisect start` to get things going, and then you use `git bisect bad` to tell the system that the current commit you're on is broken. Then, you must tell `bisect` when the last known good state was, using `git bisect good [good_commit]`:

```
$ git bisect start
$ git bisect bad
$ git bisect good v1.0
Bisecting: 6 revisions left to test after this
[ecb6e1bc347ccecc5f9350d878ce677feb13d3b2] error handling on repo
```

Git figured out that about 12 commits came between the commit you marked as the last good commit (v1.0) and the current bad version, and it checked out the middle one for you. At this point, you can run your test to see if the issue exists as of this commit. If it does, then it was introduced sometime before this middle commit; if it doesn't, then the problem was introduced sometime after the middle commit. It turns out there is no issue here, and you tell Git that by typing git bisect good and continue your journey:

```
$ git bisect good
Bisecting: 3 revisions left to test after this
[b047b02ea83310a70fd603dc8cd7a6cd13d15c04] secure this thing
```

Now you're on another commit, halfway between the one you just tested and your bad commit. You run your test again and find that this commit is broken, so you tell Git that with git bisect bad:

```
$ git bisect bad
Bisecting: 1 revisions left to test after this
[f71ce38690acf49c1f3c9bea38e09d82a5ce6014] drop exceptions table
```

This commit is fine, and now Git has all the information it needs to determine where the issue was introduced. It tells you the SHA-1 of the first bad commit and shows some of the commit information and which files were modified in that commit so you can figure out what happened that may have introduced this bug:

```
$ git bisect good
b047b02ea83310a70fd603dc8cd7a6cd13d15c04 is first bad commit
commit b047b02ea83310a70fd603dc8cd7a6cd13d15c04
Author: PJ Hyett <pjhyett@example.com>
Date:   Tue Jan 27 14:48:32 2009 -0800

    secure this thing

:040000 040000 40ee3e7821b895e52c1695092db9bdc4c61d1730
f24d3c6ebcfc639b1a3814550e62d60b8e68a8e4 M  config
```

When you're finished, you should run git bisect reset to reset your HEAD to where you were before you started, or you'll end up in a weird state:

```
$ git bisect reset
```

This is a powerful tool that can help you check hundreds of commits for an introduced bug in minutes. In fact, if you have a script that will exit 0 if the project is good or non-0 if the project is bad, you can fully automate git bisect. First, you again tell it the scope of the bisect by providing the known bad and good commits. You can do this by listing them with the bisect start command if you want, listing the known bad commit first and the known good commit second:

```
$ git bisect start HEAD v1.0
$ git bisect run test-error.sh
```

Doing so automatically runs test-error.sh on each checked-out commit until Git finds the first broken commit. You can also run something like make or make tests or whatever you have that runs automated tests for you.

Submodules

It often happens that while working on one project, you need to use another project from within it. Perhaps it's a library that a third party developed or that you're developing separately and using in multiple parent projects. A common issue arises in these scenarios: you want to be able to treat the two projects as separate yet still be able to use one from within the other.

Here's an example. Suppose you're developing a web site and creating Atom feeds. Instead of writing your own Atom-generating code, you decide to use a library. You're likely to have to either include this code from a shared library like a CPAN install or Ruby gem, or copy the source code into your own project tree. The issue with including the library is that it's difficult to customize the library in any way and often more difficult to deploy it, because you need to make sure every client has that library available. The issue with vendoring the code into your own project is that any custom changes you make are difficult to merge when upstream changes become available.

Git addresses this issue using *submodules*. Submodules allow you to keep a Git repository as a subdirectory of another Git repository. This lets you clone another repository into your project and keep your commits separate.

Starting with Submodules

Suppose you want to add the Rack library (a Ruby web server gateway interface) to your project, possibly maintain your own changes to it, but continue to merge in upstream changes. The first thing you should do is clone the external repository into your subdirectory. You add external projects as submodules with the git submodule add command:

```
$ git submodule add git://github.com/chneukirchen/rack.git rack
Initialized empty Git repository in /opt/subtest/rack/.git/
remote: Counting objects: 3181, done.
remote: Compressing objects: 100% (1534/1534), done.
remote: Total 3181 (delta 1951), reused 2623 (delta 1603)
Receiving objects: 100% (3181/3181), 675.42 KiB | 422 KiB/s, done.
Resolving deltas: 100% (1951/1951), done.
```

Now you have the Rack project under a subdirectory named rack within your project. You can go into that subdirectory, make changes, add your own writable remote repository to push your changes into, fetch and merge from the original repository, and more. If you run git status right after you add the submodule, you see two things:

```
$ git status
# On branch master
# Changes to be committed:
#   (use "git reset HEAD <file>..." to unstage)
#
#       new file:   .gitmodules
#       new file:   rack
#
```

First you notice the `.gitmodules` file. This is a configuration file that stores the mapping between the project's URL and the local subdirectory you've pulled it into:

```
$ cat .gitmodules
[submodule "rack"]
      path = rack
      url = git://github.com/chneukirchen/rack.git
```

If you have multiple submodules, you'll have multiple entries in this file. It's important to note that this file is version-controlled with your other files, like your `.gitignore` file. It's pushed and pulled with the rest of your project. This is how other people who clone this project know where to get the submodule projects from.

The other listing in the `git status` output is the `rack` entry. If you run `git diff` on that, you see something interesting:

```
$ git diff --cached rack
diff --git a/rack b/rack
new file mode 160000
index 0000000..08d709f
--- /dev/null
+++ b/rack
@@ -0,0 +1 @@
+Subproject commit 08d709f78b8c5b0fbeb7821e37fa53e69afcf433
```

Although `rack` is a subdirectory in your working directory, Git sees it as a submodule and doesn't track its contents when you're not in that directory. Instead, Git records it as a particular commit from that repository. When you make changes and commit in that subdirectory, the superproject notices that the `HEAD` there has changed and records the exact commit you're currently working off of; that way, when others clone this project, they can re-create the environment exactly.

This is an important point with submodules: you record them as the exact commit they're at. You can't record a submodule at `master` or some other symbolic reference.

When you commit, you see something like this:

```
$ git commit -m 'first commit with submodule rack'
[master 0550271] first commit with submodule rack
 2 files changed, 4 insertions(+), 0 deletions(-)
 create mode 100644 .gitmodules
 create mode 160000 rack
```

Notice the 160000 mode for the `rack` entry. That is a special mode in Git that basically means you're recording a commit as a directory entry rather than a subdirectory or a file.

You can treat the `rack` directory as a separate project and then update your superproject from time to time with a pointer to the latest commit in that subproject. All the Git commands work independently in the two directories:

```
$ git log -1
commit 0550271328a0038865aad6331e620cd7238601bb
Author: Scott Chacon <schacon@gmail.com>
Date:   Thu Apr 9 09:03:56 2009 -0700
```

```
    first commit with submodule rack
$ cd rack/
$ git log -1
commit 08d709f78b8c5b0fbeb7821e37fa53e69afcf433
Author: Christian Neukirchen <chneukirchen@gmail.com>
Date:   Wed Mar 25 14:49:04 2009 +0100

    Document version change
```

Cloning a Project with Submodules

Here you'll clone a project with a submodule in it. When you receive such a project, you get the directories that contain submodules, but none of the files yet:

```
$ git clone git://github.com/schacon/myproject.git
Initialized empty Git repository in /opt/myproject/.git/
remote: Counting objects: 6, done.
remote: Compressing objects: 100% (4/4), done.
remote: Total 6 (delta 0), reused 0 (delta 0)
Receiving objects: 100% (6/6), done.
$ cd myproject
$ ls -l
total 8
-rw-r--r--  1 schacon  admin   3 Apr  9 09:11 README
drwxr-xr-x  2 schacon  admin  68 Apr  9 09:11 rack
$ ls rack/
$
```

The rack directory is there, but empty. You must run two commands: git submodule init to initialize your local configuration file, and git submodule update to fetch all the data from that project and check out the appropriate commit listed in your superproject:

```
$ git submodule init
Submodule 'rack' (git://github.com/chneukirchen/rack.git) registered for path 'rack'
$ git submodule update
Initialized empty Git repository in /opt/myproject/rack/.git/
remote: Counting objects: 3181, done.
remote: Compressing objects: 100% (1534/1534), done.
remote: Total 3181 (delta 1951), reused 2623 (delta 1603)
Receiving objects: 100% (3181/3181), 675.42 KiB | 173 KiB/s, done.
Resolving deltas: 100% (1951/1951), done.
Submodule path 'rack': checked out '08d709f78b8c5b0fbeb7821e37fa53e69afcf433'
```

Now your rack subdirectory is at the exact state it was in when you committed earlier. If another developer makes changes to the rack code and commits, and you pull that reference down and merge it in, you get something a bit odd:

```
$ git merge origin/master
Updating 0550271..85a3eee
```

```
Fast forward
 rack |     2 +-
 1 files changed, 1 insertions(+), 1 deletions(-)
[master*]$ git status
# On branch master
# Changed but not updated:
#   (use "git add <file>..." to update what will be committed)
#   (use "git checkout -- <file>..." to discard changes in working directory)
#
#       modified:  rack
#
```

You merged in what is basically a change to the pointer for your submodule; but it doesn't update the code in the submodule directory, so it looks like you have a dirty state in your working directory:

```
$ git diff
diff --git a/rack b/rack
index 6c5e70b..08d709f 160000
--- a/rack
+++ b/rack
@@ -1 +1 @@
-Subproject commit 6c5e70b984a60b3cecd395edd5b48a7575bf58e0
+Subproject commit 08d709f78b8c5b0fbeb7821e37fa53e69afcf433
```

This is the case because the pointer you have for the submodule isn't what is actually in the submodule directory. To fix this, you must run `git submodule update` again:

```
$ git submodule update
remote: Counting objects: 5, done.
remote: Compressing objects: 100% (3/3), done.
remote: Total 3 (delta 1), reused 2 (delta 0)
Unpacking objects: 100% (3/3), done.
From git@github.com:schacon/rack
   08d709f..6c5e70b  master     -> origin/master
Submodule path 'rack': checked out '6c5e70b984a60b3cecd395edd5b48a7575bf58e0'
```

You have to do this every time you pull down a submodule change in the main project. It's strange, but it works.

One common problem happens when a developer makes a change locally in a submodule but doesn't push it to a public server. Then, they commit a pointer to that non-public state and push up the superproject. When other developers try to run `git submodule update`, the submodule system can't find the commit that is referenced, because it exists only on the first developer's system. If that happens, you see an error like this:

```
$ git submodule update
fatal: reference isn't a tree: 6c5e70b984a60b3cecd395edd5b48a7575bf58e0
Unable to checkout '6c5e70b984a60b3cecd395edd5ba7575bf58e0' in submodule path 'rack'
```

You have to see who last changed the submodule:

```
$ git log -1 rack
commit 85a3eee996800fcfa91e2119372dd4172bf76678
Author: Scott Chacon <schacon@gmail.com>
Date:   Thu Apr 9 09:19:14 2009 -0700

    added a submodule reference I will never make public. hahahahaha!
```

Then, you e-mail that guy and yell at him.

Superprojects

Sometimes, developers want to get a combination of a large project's subdirectories, depending on what team they're on. This is common if you're coming from CVS or Subversion, where you've defined a module or collection of subdirectories, and you want to keep this type of workflow.

A good way to do this in Git is to make each of the subfolders a separate Git repository and then create superproject Git repositories that contain multiple submodules. A benefit of this approach is that you can more specifically define the relationships between the projects with tags and branches in the superprojects.

Issues with Submodules

Using submodules isn't without hiccups, however. First, you must be relatively careful when working in the submodule directory. When you run `git submodule update`, it checks out the specific version of the project, but not within a branch. This is called having a *detached head*—it means the HEAD file points directly to a commit, not to a symbolic reference. The issue is that you generally don't want to work in a detached head environment, because it's easy to lose changes. If you do an initial submodule update, commit in that submodule directory without creating a branch to work in, and then run `git submodule update` again from the superproject without committing in the meantime, Git will overwrite your changes without telling you. Technically, you won't lose the work; but you won't have a branch pointing to it, so it will be difficult to retrieve.

To avoid this issue, create a branch when you work in a submodule directory with `git checkout -b work` or something equivalent. When you do the submodule update a second time, it will still revert your work, but at least you have a pointer to get back to.

Switching branches with submodules in them can also be tricky. If you create a new branch, add a submodule there, and then switch back to a branch without that submodule, you still have the submodule directory as an untracked directory:

```
$ git checkout -b rack
Switched to a new branch "rack"
$ git submodule add git@github.com:schacon/rack.git rack
Initialized empty Git repository in /opt/myproj/rack/.git/
...
Receiving objects: 100% (3184/3184), 677.42 KiB | 34 KiB/s, done.
Resolving deltas: 100% (1952/1952), done.
$ git commit -am 'added rack submodule'
```

```
[rack cc49a69] added rack submodule
 2 files changed, 4 insertions(+), 0 deletions(-)
 create mode 100644 .gitmodules
 create mode 160000 rack
$ git checkout master
Switched to branch "master"
$ git status
# On branch master
# Untracked files:
#   (use "git add <file>..." to include in what will be committed)
#
#       rack/
```

You have to either move it out of the way or remove it, in which case you have to clone it again when you switch back—and you may lose local changes or branches that you didn't push up.

The last main caveat that many people run into involves switching from subdirectories to submodules. If you've been tracking files in your project and you want to move them out into a submodule, you must be careful or Git will get angry at you. Assume that you have the rack files in a subdirectory of your project, and you want to switch it to a submodule. If you delete the subdirectory and then run submodule add, Git yells at you:

```
$ rm -Rf rack/
$ git submodule add git@github.com:schacon/rack.git rack
'rack' already exists in the index
```

You have to unstage the rack directory first. Then you can add the submodule:

```
$ git rm -r rack
$ git submodule add git@github.com:schacon/rack.git rack
Initialized empty Git repository in /opt/testsub/rack/.git/
remote: Counting objects: 3184, done.
remote: Compressing objects: 100% (1465/1465), done.
remote: Total 3184 (delta 1952), reused 2770 (delta 1675)
Receiving objects: 100% (3184/3184), 677.42 KiB | 88 KiB/s, done.
Resolving deltas: 100% (1952/1952), done.
```

Now suppose you did that in a branch. If you try to switch back to a branch where those files are still in the actual tree rather than a submodule—you get this error:

```
$ git checkout master
error: Untracked working tree file 'rack/AUTHORS' would be overwritten by merge.
```

You have to move the rack submodule directory out of the way before you can switch to a branch that doesn't have it:

```
$ mv rack /tmp/
$ git checkout master
Switched to branch "master"
$ ls
README    rack
```

Then, when you switch back, you get an empty rack directory. You can either run git submodule update to reclone, or you can move your /tmp/rack directory back into the empty directory.

Subtree Merging

Now that you've seen the difficulties of the submodule system, let's look at an alternate way to solve the same problem. When Git merges, it looks at what it has to merge together and then chooses an appropriate merging strategy to use. If you're merging two branches, Git uses a recursive strategy. If you're merging more than two branches, Git picks the octopus strategy. These strategies are automatically chosen for you because the recursive strategy can handle complex three-way merge situations—for example, more than one common ancestor—but it can only handle merging two branches. The octopus merge can handle multiple branches but is more cautious to avoid difficult conflicts, so it's chosen as the default strategy if you're trying to merge more than two branches.

However, there are other strategies you can choose as well. One of them is the *subtree merge*, and you can use it to deal with the subproject issue. Here you'll see how to do the same rack embedding as in the last section, but using subtree merges instead.

The idea of the subtree merge is that you have two projects, and one of the projects maps to a subdirectory of the other one and vice versa. When you specify a subtree merge, Git is smart enough to figure out that one is a subtree of the other and merge appropriately—it's pretty amazing.

You first add the Rack application to your project. You add the Rack project as a remote reference in your own project and then check it out into its own branch:

```
$ git remote add rack_remote git@github.com:schacon/rack.git
$ git fetch rack_remote
warning: no common commits
remote: Counting objects: 3184, done.
remote: Compressing objects: 100% (1465/1465), done.
remote: Total 3184 (delta 1952), reused 2770 (delta 1675)
Receiving objects: 100% (3184/3184), 677.42 KiB | 4 KiB/s, done.
Resolving deltas: 100% (1952/1952), done.
From git@github.com:schacon/rack
 * [new branch]      build        -> rack_remote/build
 * [new branch]      master       -> rack_remote/master
 * [new branch]      rack-0.4     -> rack_remote/rack-0.4
 * [new branch]      rack-0.9     -> rack_remote/rack-0.9
$ git checkout -b rack_branch rack_remote/master
Branch rack_branch set up to track remote branch refs/remotes/rack_remote/master.
Switched to a new branch "rack_branch"
```

Now you have the root of the Rack project in your rack_branch branch and your own project in the master branch. If you check out one and then the other, you can see that they have different project roots:

```
$ ls
AUTHORS        KNOWN-ISSUES   Rakefile     contrib      lib
```

```
COPYING        README       bin        example     test
$ git checkout master
Switched to branch "master"
$ ls
README
```

You want to pull the Rack project into your master project as a subdirectory. You can do that in Git with git read-tree. You'll learn more about read-tree and its friends in Chapter 9, but for now know that it reads the root tree of one branch into your current index and working directory. You just switched back to your master branch, and you pull the rack branch into the rack subdirectory of your master branch main project:

```
$ git read-tree --prefix=rack/ -u rack_branch
```

When you commit, it looks like you have all the Rack files under that subdirectory—as though you copied them in from a tarball. What gets interesting is that you can fairly easily merge changes from one of the branches to the other. So, if the Rack project updates, you can pull in upstream changes by switching to that branch and pulling:

```
$ git checkout rack_branch
$ git pull
```

Then, you can merge those changes back into your master branch. You can use git merge -s subtree and it will work fine; but Git will also merge the histories together, which you probably don't want. To pull in the changes and prepopulate the commit message, use the --squash and --no-commit options as well as the -s subtree strategy option:

```
$ git checkout master
$ git merge --squash -s subtree --no-commit rack_branch
Squash commit -- not updating HEAD
Automatic merge went well; stopped before committing as requested
```

All the changes from your Rack project are merged in and ready to be committed locally. You can also do the opposite—make changes in the rack subdirectory of your master branch and then merge them into your rack_branch branch later to submit them to the maintainers or push them upstream.

To get a diff between what you have in your rack subdirectory and the code in your rack_branch branch—to see if you need to merge them—you can't use the normal diff command. Instead, you must run git diff-tree with the branch you want to compare to:

```
$ git diff-tree -p rack_branch
```

Or, to compare what is in your rack subdirectory with what the master branch on the server was the last time you fetched, you can run the following:

```
$ git diff-tree -p rack_remote/master
```

Summary

You've seen a number of advanced tools that allow you to manipulate your commits and staging area more precisely. When you notice issues, you should be able to easily figure out what commit introduced them, when, and by whom. If you want to use subprojects in your project, you've learned a few ways to accommodate those needs. At this point, you should be able to do most of the things in Git that you'll need on the command line day to day and feel comfortable doing so.

CHAPTER 7

■■■

Customizing Git

So far, I've covered the basics of how Git works and how to use it, and I've introduced a number of tools that Git provides to help you use it easily and efficiently. In this chapter, I'll go through some operations that you can use to make Git operate in a more customized fashion by introducing several important configuration settings and the hooks system. With these tools, it's easy to get Git to work exactly the way you, your company, or your group needs it to.

Git Configuration

As you briefly saw in Chapter 1, you can specify Git configuration settings with the `git config` command. One of the first things you did was set up your name and e-mail address:

```
$ git config --global user.name "John Doe"
$ git config --global user.email johndoe@example.com
```

Now you'll learn a few of the more interesting options that you can set in this manner to customize your Git usage.

You saw some simple Git configuration details in the first chapter, but I'll go over them again quickly here. Git uses a series of configuration files to determine non-default behavior that you may want. The first place Git looks for these values is in an `/etc/gitconfig` file, which contains values for every user on the system and all of their repositories. If you pass the option `--system` to `git config`, it reads and writes from this file specifically.

The next place Git looks is the `~/.gitconfig` file, which is specific to each user. You can make Git read and write to this file by passing the `--global` option.

Finally, Git looks for configuration values in the `config` file in the Git directory (`.git/config`) of whatever repository you're currently using. These values are specific to that single repository. Each level overwrites values in the previous level, so values in `.git/config` trump those in `/etc/sysconfig`, for instance. You can also set these values by manually editing the file and inserting the correct syntax, but it's generally easier to run the `git config` command.

Basic Client Configuration

The configuration options recognized by Git fall into two categories: client side and server side. The majority of the options are client side—configuring your personal working preferences. Although tons of options are available, I'll only cover the few that either are commonly used or can significantly affect your workflow. Many options are useful only in edge cases that I won't go over here. If you want to see a list of all the options your version of Git recognizes, you can run

```
$ git config --help
```

The manual page for git config lists all the available options in quite a bit of detail.

core.editor

By default, Git uses whatever you've set as your default text editor or else falls back to the Vi editor to create and edit your commit and tag messages. To change that default to something else, you can use the core.editor setting:

```
$ git config --global core.editor emacs
```

Now, no matter what is set as your default shell editor variable, Git will fire up Emacs to edit messages.

commit.template

If you set this to the path of a file on your system, Git will use that file as the default message when you commit. For instance, suppose you create a template file at $HOME/.gitmessage.txt that looks like this:

```
subject line

what happened

[ticket: X]
```

To tell Git to use it as the default message that appears in your editor when you run git commit, set the commit.template configuration value:

```
$ git config --global commit.template $HOME/.gitmessage.txt
$ git commit
```

Then, your editor will open to something like this for your placeholder commit message when you commit:

```
subject line

what happened

[ticket: X]
# Please enter the commit message for your changes. Lines starting
# with '#' will be ignored, and an empty message aborts the commit.
# On branch master
# Changes to be committed:
#   (use "git reset HEAD <file>..." to unstage)
#
# modified:   lib/test.rb
#
~
~
".git/COMMIT_EDITMSG" 14L, 297C
```

If you have a commit-message policy in place, then putting a template for that policy on your system and configuring Git to use it by default can help increase the chance of that policy being followed regularly.

core.pager

The core.pager setting determines what pager is used when Git pages output such as log and diff. You can set it to more or to your favorite pager (by default, it's less), or you can turn it off by setting it to a blank string:

```
$ git config --global core.pager ''
```

If you run that, Git will show the entire output of all commands without paging, no matter how long they are.

user.signingkey

If you're making signed annotated tags (as discussed in Chapter 2), setting your GPG signing key as a configuration setting makes things easier. Set your key ID like so:

```
$ git config --global user.signingkey <gpg-key-id>
```

Now, you can sign tags without having to specify your key every time with the git tag command:

```
$ git tag -s <tag-name>
```

core.excludesfile

You can put patterns in your project's `.gitignore` file to have Git not see them as untracked files or try to stage them when you run `git add` on them, as discussed in Chapter 2. However, if you want another file outside of your project to hold those values or have extra values, you can tell Git where that file is with the `core.excludesfile` setting. Simply set it to the path of a file that has content similar to what a `.gitignore` file would have.

help.autocorrect

This option is available only in Git 1.6.1 and later. If you mistype a command in Git 1.6, it shows you something like this:

```
$ git com
git: 'com' is not a git-command. See 'git --help'.

Did you mean this?
    commit
```

If you set `help.autocorrect` to 1, Git will automatically run the command if it has only one match under this scenario.

Colors in Git

Git can color its output to your terminal, which can help you visually parse the output quickly and easily. A number of options can help you set the coloring to your preference.

color.ui

Git automatically colors most of its output if you ask it to. You can get very specific about what you want colored and how; but to turn on all the default terminal coloring, set `color.ui` to true:

```
$ git config --global color.ui true
```

When that value is set, Git colors its output if the output goes to a terminal. Other possible settings are `false`, which never colors the output, and `always`, which sets colors all the time, even if you're redirecting Git commands to a file or piping them to another command. This setting was added in Git version 1.5.5; if you have an older version, you'll have to specify all the color settings individually.

You'll rarely want `color.ui = always`. In most scenarios, if you want color codes in your redirected output, you can instead pass a `--color` flag to the Git command to force it to use color codes. The `color.ui = true` setting is almost always what you'll want to use.

color.*

If you want to be more specific about which commands are colored and how, or you have an older version, Git provides verb-specific coloring settings. Each of these can be set to `true`, `false`, or `always`:

```
color.branch
color.diff
color.interactive
color.status
```

In addition, each of these has subsettings you can use to set specific colors for parts of the output, if you want to override each color. For example, to set the meta information in your diff output to blue foreground, black background, and bold text, you can run

```
$ git config --global color.diff.meta "blue black bold"
```

You can set the color to any of the following values: normal, black, red, green, yellow, blue, magenta, cyan, or white. If you want an attribute like bold in the previous example, you can choose from bold, dim, ul, blink, and reverse.

See the git config manpage for all the subsettings you can configure, if you want to do that.

External Merge and Diff Tools

Although Git has an internal implementation of diff, which is what you've been using, you can set up an external tool instead. You can also set up a graphical merge conflict–resolution tool instead of having to resolve conflicts manually. I'll demonstrate setting up the Perforce Visual Merge Tool (P4Merge) to do your diffs and merge resolutions, because it's a nice graphical tool and it's free.

If you want to try this, P4Merge works on all major platforms, so you should be able to do so. I'll use path names in the examples that work on Mac and Linux systems; for Windows, you'll have to change /usr/local/bin to an executable path in your environment.

You can download P4Merge here:

```
http://www.perforce.com/perforce/downloads/component.html
```

To begin, you'll set up external wrapper scripts to run your commands. I'll use the Mac path for the executable; in other systems, it will be where your p4merge binary is installed. Set up a merge wrapper script named extMerge that calls your binary with all the arguments provided:

```
$ cat /usr/local/bin/extMerge
#!/bin/sh
/Applications/p4merge.app/Contents/MacOS/p4merge $*
```

The diff wrapper checks to make sure seven arguments are provided and passes two of them to your merge script. By default, Git passes the following arguments to the diff program:

```
path old-file old-hex old-mode new-file new-hex new-mode
```

Because you only want the old-file and new-file arguments, you use the wrapper script to pass the ones you need.

```
$ cat /usr/local/bin/extDiff
#!/bin/sh
[ $# -eq 7 ] && /usr/local/bin/extMerge "$2" "$5"
```

You also need to make sure these tools are executable:

```
$ sudo chmod +x /usr/local/bin/extMerge
$ sudo chmod +x /usr/local/bin/extDiff
```

Now you can set up your config file to use your custom merge resolution and diff tools. This takes a number of custom settings: merge.tool to tell Git what strategy to use, mergetool.*.cmd to specify how to run the command, mergetool.trustExitCode to tell Git if the exit code of that program indicates a successful merge resolution or not, and diff.external to tell Git what command to run for diffs. So, either you can run four config commands

```
$ git config --global merge.tool extMerge
$ git config --global mergetool.extMerge.cmd \
    'extMerge "$BASE" "$LOCAL" "$REMOTE" "$MERGED"'
$ git config --global mergetool.trustExitCode false
$ git config --global diff.external extDiff
```

or you can edit your ~/.gitconfig file to add these lines:

```
[merge]
  tool = extMerge
[mergetool "extMerge"]
  cmd = extMerge "$BASE" "$LOCAL" "$REMOTE" "$MERGED"
  trustExitCode = false
[diff]
  external = extDiff
```

After all this is set, if you run diff commands such as this:

```
$ git diff 32d1776b1^ 32d1776b1
```

Instead of getting the diff output on the command line, Git fires up P4Merge, which looks something like Figure 7-1.

If you try to merge two branches and subsequently have merge conflicts, you can run the command git mergetool; it starts P4Merge to let you resolve the conflicts through that GUI tool.

The nice thing about this wrapper setup is that you can change your diff and merge tools easily. For example, to change your extDiff and extMerge tools to run the KDiff3 tool instead, all you have to do is edit your extMerge file:

```
$ cat /usr/local/bin/extMerge
#!/bin/sh
/Applications/kdiff3.app/Contents/MacOS/kdiff3 $*
```

Now, Git will use the KDiff3 tool for diff viewing and merge conflict resolution.

Git comes preset to use a number of other merge-resolution tools without your having to set up the cmd configuration. You can set your merge tool to kdiff3, opendiff, tkdiff, meld, xxdiff, emerge, vimdiff, or gvimdiff. If you're not interested in using KDiff3 for diff but rather want to use it just for merge resolution, and the kdiff3 command is in your path, then you can run

```
$ git config --global merge.tool kdiff3
```

If you run this instead of setting up the `extMerge` and `extDiff` files, Git will use KDiff3 for merge resolution and the normal Git `diff` tool for diffs.

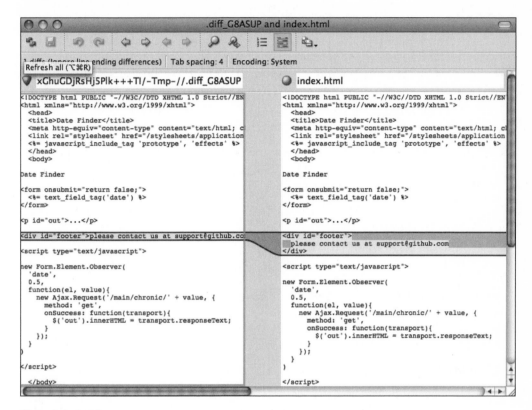

Figure 7-1. *P4Merge*

Formatting and Whitespace

Formatting and whitespace issues are some of the more frustrating and subtle problems that many developers encounter when collaborating, especially cross-platform. It's very easy for patches or other collaborated work to introduce subtle whitespace changes because editors silently introduce them or Windows programmers add carriage returns at the end of lines they touch in cross-platform projects. Git has a few configuration options to help with these issues.

core.autocrlf

If you're programming on Windows or using another system but working with people who are programming on Windows, you'll probably run into line-ending issues at some point. This is because Windows uses both a carriage-return character and a linefeed character for newlines in its files, whereas Mac and Linux systems use only the linefeed character. This is a subtle but incredibly annoying fact of cross-platform work.

Git can handle this by auto-converting CRLF line endings into LF when you commit, and vice versa when it checks out code onto your filesystem. You can turn on this functionality with the `core.autocrlf` setting. If you're on a Windows machine, set it to `true`—this converts LF endings into CRLF when you check out code:

```
$ git config --global core.autocrlf true
```

If you're on a Linux or Mac system that uses LF line endings, then you don't want Git to automatically convert them when you check out files; however, if a file with CRLF endings accidentally gets introduced, then you may want Git to fix it. You can tell Git to convert CRLF to LF on commit but not the other way around by setting `core.autocrlf` to `input`:

```
$ git config --global core.autocrlf input
```

This setup should leave you with CRLF endings in Windows checkouts but LF endings on Mac and Linux systems and in the repository.

If you're a Windows programmer doing a Windows-only project, then you can turn off this functionality, recording the carriage returns in the repository by setting the `config` value to `false`:

```
$ git config --global core.autocrlf false
```

core.whitespace

Git comes preset to detect and fix some whitespace issues. It can look for four primary whitespace issues—two are enabled by default and can be turned off, and two aren't enabled by default but can be activated.

The two that are turned on by default are `trailing-space`, which looks for spaces at the end of a line, and `space-before-tab`, which looks for spaces before tabs at the beginning of a line.

The two that are disabled by default but can be turned on are `indent-with-non-tab`, which looks for lines that begin with eight or more spaces instead of tabs, and `cr-at-eol`, which tells Git that carriage returns at the end of lines are OK.

You can tell Git which of these you want enabled by setting `core.whitespace` to the values you want on or off, separated by commas. You can disable settings by either leaving them out of the setting string or prepending a - in front of the value. For example, if you want all but `cr-at-eol` to be set, you can do this:

```
$ git config --global core.whitespace \
    trailing-space,space-before-tab,indent-with-non-tab
```

Git will detect these issues when you run a `git diff` command and try to color them so you can possibly fix them before you commit. It will also use these values to help you when you apply patches with `git apply`. When you're applying patches, you can ask Git to warn you if it's applying patches with the specified whitespace issues:

```
$ git apply --whitespace=warn <patch>
```

Or you can have Git try to automatically fix the issue before applying the patch:

```
$ git apply --whitespace=fix <patch>
```

Server Configuration

Not nearly as many configuration options are available for the server side of Git, but there are a few interesting ones you may want to take note of.

receive.fsckObjects

By default, Git doesn't check for consistency all the objects it receives during a push. Although Git can check to make sure each object still matches its SHA-1 checksum and points to valid objects, it doesn't do that by default on every push. This is a relatively expensive operation and may add a lot of time to each push, depending on the size of the repo or the push. If you want Git to check object consistency on every push, you can force it to do so by setting `receive.fsckObjects` to `true`:

```
$ git config --system receive.fsckObjects true
```

Now, Git will check the integrity of your repository before each push is accepted to make sure faulty clients aren't introducing corrupt data.

receive.denyNonFastForwards

If you rebase commits that you've already pushed and then try to push again, or otherwise try to push a commit to a remote branch that doesn't contain the commit that the remote branch currently points to, you'll be denied. This is generally good policy; but in the case of the rebase, you may determine that you know what you're doing and can force-update the remote branch with a `-f` flag to your `push` command.

To disable the ability to force-update remote branches to non-fast-forward references, set `receive.denyNonFastForwards`:

```
$ git config --system receive.denyNonFastForwards true
```

The other way you can do this is via server-side receive hooks, which I'll cover in a bit. That approach lets you do more complex things like deny non-fast-forwards to a certain subset of users.

receive.denyDeletes

One of the workarounds to the `denyNonFastForwards` policy is for the user to delete the branch and then push it back up with the new reference. In newer versions of Git (beginning with version 1.6.1), you can set `receive.denyDeletes` to `true`:

```
$ git config --system receive.denyDeletes true
```

This denies branch and tag deletion over a push across the board—no user can do it. To remove remote branches, you must remove the ref files from the server manually. There are also more interesting ways to do this on a per-user basis via ACLs, as you'll learn at the end of this chapter.

Git Attributes

Some of these settings can also be specified for a path, so that Git applies those settings only for a subdirectory or subset of files. These path-specific settings are called Git *attributes* and are set either in a `.gitattribute` file in one of your directories (normally the root of your project) or in the `.git/info/attributes` file if you don't want the attributes file committed with your project.

Using attributes, you can do things like specify separate merge strategies for individual files or directories in your project, tell Git how to diff non-text files, or have Git filter content before you check it into or out of Git. In this section, you'll learn about some of the attributes you can set on your paths in your Git project and see a few examples of using this feature in practice.

Binary Files

One cool trick for which you can use Git attributes is telling Git which files are binary (in cases it otherwise may not be able to figure out) and giving Git special instructions about how to handle those files. For instance, some text files may be machine generated and not diffable, whereas some binary files can be diffed—you'll see how to tell Git which is which.

Identifying Binary Files

Some files look like text files but for all intents and purposes are to be treated as binary data. For instance, Xcode projects on the Mac contain a file that ends in `.pbxproj`, which is basically a JSON (plain-text JavaScript data format) dataset written out to disk by the IDE that records your build settings and so on. Although it's technically a text file, because it's all ASCII, you don't want to treat it as such because it's really a lightweight database—you can't merge the contents if two people changed it, and diffs generally aren't helpful. The file is meant to be consumed by a machine. In essence, you want to treat it like a binary file.

To tell Git to treat all `pbxproj` files as binary data, add the following line to your `.gitattributes` file:

```
*.pbxproj -crlf -diff
```

Now, Git won't try to convert or fix CRLF issues; nor will it try to compute or print a diff for changes in this file when you run `git show` or `git diff` on your project. In the 1.6 series of Git, you can also use a macro that is provided that means `-crlf -diff`:

```
*.pbxproj binary
```

Diffing Binary Files

In the 1.6 series of Git, you can use the Git attributes functionality to effectively diff binary files. You do this by telling Git how to convert your binary data to a text format that can be compared via the normal `diff`.

Because this is a pretty cool and not widely known feature, I'll go over a few examples. First, you'll use this technique to solve one of the most annoying problems known to humanity: version-controlling Word documents. Everyone knows that Word is the most horrific editor around; but, oddly, everyone uses it. If you want to version-control Word documents, you can stick them in a Git repository and commit every once in a while; but what good does that do? If you run git diff normally, you only see something like this:

```
$ git diff
diff --git a/chapter1.doc b/chapter1.doc
index 88839c4..4afcb7c 100644
Binary files a/chapter1.doc and b/chapter1.doc differ
```

You can't directly compare two versions unless you check them out and scan them manually, right? It turns out you can do this fairly well using Git attributes. Put the following line in your .gitattributes file:

```
*.doc diff=word
```

This tells Git that any file that matches this pattern (.doc) should use the "word" filter when you try to view a diff that contains changes. What is the "word" filter? You have to set it up. Here you'll configure Git to use the strings program to convert Word documents into readable text files, which it will then diff properly:

```
$ git config diff.word.textconv strings
```

Now Git knows that if it tries to do a diff between two snapshots, and any of the files end in .doc, it should run those files through the "word" filter, which is defined as the strings program. This effectively makes nice text-based versions of your Word files before attempting to diff them.

Here's an example. I put Chapter 1 of this book into Git, added some text to a paragraph, and saved the document. Then, I ran git diff to see what changed:

```
$ git diff
diff --git a/chapter1.doc b/chapter1.doc
index c1c8a0a..b93c9e4 100644
--- a/chapter1.doc
+++ b/chapter1.doc
@@ -8,7 +8,8 @@ re going to cover Version Control Systems (VCS) and Git basics
 re going to cover how to get it and set it up for the first time if you don
 t already have it on your system.
 In Chapter Two we will go over basic Git usage - how to use Git for the 80%
-s going on, modify stuff and contribute changes. If the book spontaneously
+s going on, modify stuff and contribute changes. If the book spontaneously
+Let's see if this works.
 Chapter Three is about the branching model in Git, often described as Git
```

Git successfully and succinctly tells me that I added the string "Let's see if this works", which is correct. It's not perfect—it adds a bunch of random stuff at the end—but it certainly works. If you can find or write a Word-to-plain-text converter that works well enough, that solution will likely be incredibly effective. However, `strings` is available on most Mac and Linux systems, so it may be a good first try to do this with many binary formats.

Another interesting problem you can solve this way involves diffing image files. One way to do this is to run JPEG files through a filter that extracts their EXIF information—metadata that is recorded with most image formats. If you download and install the `exiftool` program, you can use it to convert your images into text about the metadata, so at least the diff will show you a textual representation of any changes that happened:

```
$ echo '*.png diff=exif' >> .gitattributes
$ git config diff.exif.textconv exiftool
```

If you replace an image in your project and run `diff`, you see something like this:

```
diff --git a/image.png b/image.png
index 88839c4..4afcb7c 100644
--- a/image.png
+++ b/image.png
@@ -1,12 +1,12 @@
 ExifTool Version Number       : 7.74
-File Size                     : 70 kB
-File Modification Date/Time    : 2009:04:21 07:02:45-07:00
+File Size                     : 94 kB
+File Modification Date/Time    : 2009:04:21 07:02:43-07:00
 File Type                     : PNG
 MIME Type                     : image/png
-Image Width                   : 1058
-Image Height                  : 889
+Image Width                   : 1056
+Image Height                  : 827
 Bit Depth                     : 8
 Color Type                    : RGB with Alpha
```

You can easily see that the file size and image dimensions have both changed.

Keyword Expansion

SVN- or CVS-style keyword expansion is often requested by developers used to those systems. The main problem with this in Git is that you can't modify a file with information about the commit after you've committed, because Git checksums the file first. However, you can inject text into a file when it's checked out and remove it again before it's added to a commit. Git attributes offers you two ways to do this.

First, you can inject the SHA-1 checksum of a blob into an Id field in the file automatically. If you set this attribute on a file or set of files, then the next time you check out that branch, Git will replace that field with the SHA-1 of the blob. It's important to notice that it isn't the SHA of the commit, but of the blob itself:

```
$ echo '*.txt ident' >> .gitattributes
$ echo '$Id$' > test.txt
```

The next time you check out this file, Git injects the SHA of the blob:

```
$ rm text.txt
$ git checkout -- text.txt
$ cat test.txt
$Id: 42812b7653c7b88933f8a9d6cad0ca16714b9bb3 $
```

However, that result is of limited use. If you've used keyword substitution in CVS or Subversion, you can include a datestamp—the SHA isn't all that helpful, because it's fairly random and you can't tell if one SHA is older or newer than another.

It turns out that you can write your own filters for doing substitutions in files on commit/checkout. These are the "clean" and "smudge" filters. In the .gitattributes file, you can set a filter for particular paths and then set up scripts that will process files just before they're committed ("clean"; see Figure 7-2) and just before they're checked out ("smudge"; see Figure 7-3). These filters can be set to do all sorts of fun things.

The original commit message for this functionality gives a simple example of running all your C source code through the indent program before committing. You can set it up by setting the filter attribute in your .gitattributes file to filter *.c files with the "indent" filter:

```
*.c     filter=indent
```

Then, tell Git what the "indent" filter does on smudge and clean:

```
$ git config --global filter.indent.clean indent
$ git config --global filter.indent.smudge cat
```

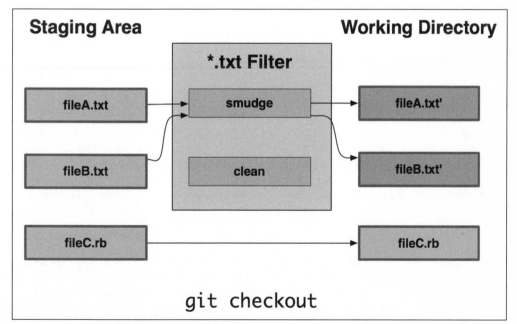

Figure 7-2. *The "smudge" filter is run on checkout.*

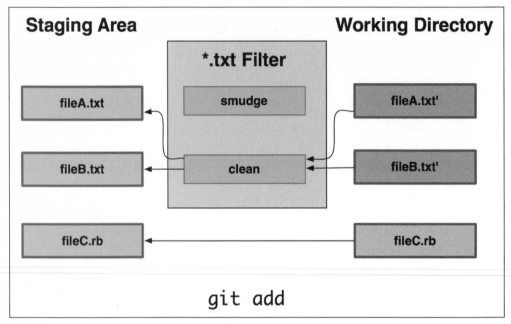

Figure 7-3. *The "clean" filter is run when files are staged.*

In this case, when you commit files that match *.c, Git will run them through the indent program before it commits them and then run them through the cat program before it checks them back out onto disk. The cat program is basically a no-op: it spits out the same data that it gets in. This combination effectively filters all C source code files through indent before committing.

Another interesting example gets $Date$ keyword expansion, RCS style. To do this properly, you need a small script that takes a file through stdin, figures out the last commit date for this project, and inserts the date into the file. Here is a small Ruby script that does that:

```
#! /usr/bin/env ruby
data = STDIN.read
last_date = 'git log --pretty=format:"%ad" -1'
puts data.gsub('$Date$', '$Date: ' + last_date.to_s + '$')
```

All the script does is get the latest commit date from the git log command, stick that into any $Date$ strings it sees in stdin, and print the results—it should be simple to do in whatever language you're most comfortable in. You can name this script expand_date and put it in your path. Now, you need to set up a filter in Git (call it dater) and tell it to use your "expand_date" filter to smudge the files on checkout. You'll use a Perl expression to clean that up on commit:

```
$ git config filter.dater.smudge expand_date
$ git config filter.dater.clean 'perl -pe "s/\\\$Date[^\\\$]*\\\$/\\\$Date\\\$/"'
```

This Perl snippet strips out anything it sees in a $Date$ string, to get back to where you started. Now that your filter is ready, you can test it by setting up a file with your $Date$ keyword and then setting up a Git attribute for that file that engages the new filter:

```
$ echo '# $Date$' > date_test.txt
$ echo 'date*.txt filter=dater' >> .gitattributes
```

If you commit those changes and check out the file again, you see the keyword properly substituted:

```
$ git add date_test.txt .gitattributes
$ git commit -m "Testing date expansion in Git"
$ rm date_test.txt
$ git checkout date_test.txt
$ cat date_test.txt
# $Date: Tue Apr 21 07:26:52 2009 -0700$
```

You can see how powerful this technique can be for customized applications. You have to be careful, though, because the .gitattributes file is committed and passed around with the project but the driver (in this case, dater) isn't; so, it won't automatically work everywhere. When you design these filters, they should be able to fail gracefully and have the project still work properly.

Exporting Your Repository

Git attribute data also allows you to do some interesting things when exporting an archive of your project.

export-ignore

You can tell Git not to export certain files or directories when generating an archive. If there is a subdirectory or file that you don't want to include in your archive file but that you do want checked into your project, you can determine that file via the export-ignore attribute.

For example, say you have some test files in a test/ subdirectory, and it doesn't make sense to include them in the tarball export of your project. You can add the following line to your Git attributes file:

```
test/ export-ignore
```

Now, when you run git archive to create a tarball of your project, that directory won't be included in the archive.

export-subst

Another thing you can do for your archives is some simple keyword substitution. Git lets you put the string $Format:$ in any file with any of the --pretty=format formatting shortcodes, many of which you saw in Chapter 2. For instance, if you want to include a file named LAST_COMMIT in your project, and the last commit date was automatically injected into it when git archive ran, you can set up the file like this:

```
$ echo 'Last commit date: $Format:%cd$' > LAST_COMMIT
$ echo "LAST_COMMIT export-subst" >> .gitattributes
$ git add LAST_COMMIT .gitattributes
$ git commit -am 'adding LAST_COMMIT file for archives'
```

When you run git archive, the contents of that file when people open the archive file will look like this:

```
$ cat LAST_COMMIT
Last commit date: $Format:Tue Apr 21 08:38:48 2009 -0700$
```

Merge Strategies

You can also use Git attributes to tell Git to use different merge strategies for specific files in your project. One very useful option is to tell Git to not try to merge specific files when they have conflicts, but rather to use your side of the merge over someone else's.

This is helpful if a branch in your project has diverged or is specialized, but you want to be able to merge changes back in from it, and you want to ignore certain files. Say you have a database settings file called database.xml that is different in two branches, and you want to merge in your other branch without messing up the database file. You can set up an attribute like this:

```
database.xml merge=ours
```

If you merge in the other branch, instead of having merge conflicts with the database.xml file, you see something like this:

```
$ git merge topic
Auto-merging database.xml
Merge made by recursive.
```

In this case, database.xml stays at whatever version you originally had.

Git Hooks

Like many other Version Control Systems, Git has a way to fire off custom scripts when certain important actions occur. There are two groups of these hooks: client side and server side. The *client-side hooks* are for client operations such as committing and merging. The *server-side hooks* are for Git server operations such as receiving pushed commits. You can use these hooks for all sorts of reasons, and you'll learn about a few of them here.

Installing a Hook

The hooks are all stored in the hooks subdirectory of the Git directory. In most projects, that's .git/hooks. By default, Git populates this directory with a bunch of example scripts, many of which are useful by themselves; but they also document the input values of each script. All the examples are written as shell scripts, with some Perl thrown in, but any properly named executable scripts will work fine—you can write them in Ruby or Python or what have you. For post-1.6 versions of Git, these example hook files end with .sample; you'll need to rename them. For pre-1.6 versions of Git, the example files are named properly but are not executable.

To enable a hook script, put a file in the hooks subdirectory of your Git directory that is named appropriately and is executable. From that point forward, it should be called. I'll cover most of the major hook filenames here.

Client-Side Hooks

There are a lot of client-side hooks. This section splits them into committing-workflow hooks, e-mail workflow scripts, and the rest of the client-side scripts.

Committing-Workflow Hooks

The first four hooks have to do with the committing process. The `pre-commit` hook is run first, before you even type in a commit message. It's used to inspect the snapshot that's about to be committed, to see if you've forgotten something, to make sure tests run, or to examine whatever you need to inspect in the code. Exiting non-zero from this hook aborts the commit, although you can bypass it with `git commit --no-verify`. You can do things like check for code style (run `lint` or something equivalent), check for trailing whitespace (the default hook does exactly that), or check for appropriate documentation on new methods.

The `prepare-commit-msg` hook is run before the commit message editor is fired up but after the default message is created. It lets you edit the default message before the commit author sees it. This hook takes a few options: the path to the file that holds the commit message so far, the type of commit, and the commit SHA-1 if this is an amended commit. This hook generally isn't useful for normal commits; rather, it's good for commits where the default message is auto-generated, such as templated commit messages, merge commits, squashed commits, and amended commits. You may use it in conjunction with a commit template to programmatically insert information.

The `commit-msg` hook takes one parameter, which again is the path to a temporary file that contains the current commit message. If this script exits non-zero, Git aborts the commit process, so you can use it to validate your project state or commit message before allowing a commit to go through. In the last section of this chapter, I'll demonstrate using this hook to check that your commit message is conformant to a required pattern.

After the entire commit process is completed, the `post-commit` hook runs. It doesn't take any parameters, but you can easily get the last commit by running `git log -1 HEAD`. Generally, this script is used for notification or something similar.

The committing-workflow client-side scripts can be used in just about any workflow. They're often used to enforce certain policies, although it's important to note that these scripts aren't transferred during a clone. You can enforce policy on the server side to reject pushes of commits that don't conform to some policy, but it's entirely up to the developer to use these scripts on the client side. So, these are scripts to help developers, and they must be set up and maintained by them, although they can be overridden or modified by them at any time.

E-mail Workflow Hooks

You can set up three client-side hooks for an e-mail-based workflow. They're all invoked by the `git am` command, so if you aren't using that command in your workflow, you can safely skip to the next section. If you're taking patches over e-mail prepared by `git format-patch`, then some of these may be helpful to you.

The first hook that is run is `applypatch-msg`. It takes a single argument: the name of the temporary file that contains the proposed commit message. Git aborts the patch if this script exits non-zero. You can use this to make sure a commit message is properly formatted or to normalize the message by having the script edit it in place.

The next hook to run when applying patches via `git am` is `pre-applypatch`. It takes no arguments and is run after the patch is applied, so you can use it to inspect the snapshot before making the commit. You can run tests or otherwise inspect the working tree with this script. If something is missing or the tests don't pass, exiting non-zero also aborts the `git am` script without committing the patch.

The last hook to run during a `git am` operation is `post-applypatch`. You can use it to notify a group or the author of the patch you pulled in that you've done so. You can't stop the patching process with this script.

Other Client Hooks

The `pre-rebase` hook runs before you rebase anything and can halt the process by exiting non-zero. You can use this hook to disallow rebasing any commits that have already been pushed. The example `pre-rebase` hook that Git installs does this, although it assumes that next is the name of the branch you publish. You'll likely need to change that to whatever your stable, published branch is.

After you run a successful `git checkout`, the `post-checkout` hook runs; you can use it to set up your working directory properly for your project environment. This may mean moving in large binary files that you don't want source controlled, auto-generating documentation, or something along those lines.

Finally, the `post-merge` hook runs after a successful `merge` command. You can use it to restore data in the working tree that Git can't track, such as permissions data. This hook can likewise validate the presence of files external to Git control that you may want copied in when the working tree changes.

Server-Side Hooks

In addition to the client-side hooks, you can use a couple of important server-side hooks as a system administrator to enforce nearly any kind of policy for your project. These scripts run before and after pushes to the server. The pre hooks can exit non-zero at any time to reject the push as well as print an error message back to the client; you can set up a push policy that's as complex as you wish.

pre-receive and post-receive

The first script to run when handling a push from a client is `pre-receive`. It takes a list of references that are being pushed from stdin; if it exits non-zero, none of them are accepted. You can use this hook to do things like make sure none of the updated references are non-fast-forwards; or to check that the user doing the pushing has create, delete, or push access or access to push updates to all the files they're modifying with the push.

The `post-receive` hook runs after the entire process is completed and can be used to update other services or notify users. It takes the same stdin data as the `pre-receive` hook. Examples include e-mailing a list, notifying a continuous integration server, or updating a ticket-tracking system—you can even parse the commit messages to see if any tickets need to be opened, modified, or closed. This script can't stop the push process, but the client doesn't disconnect until it has completed; so, be careful when you try to do anything that may take a long time.

update

The `update` script is very similar to the `pre-receive` script, except that it's run once for each branch the pusher is trying to update. If the pusher is trying to push to multiple branches, `pre-receive` runs only once, whereas `update` runs once per branch they're pushing to. Instead of reading from stdin, this script takes three arguments: the name of the reference (branch), the SHA-1 that reference pointed to before the push, and the SHA-1 the user is trying to push. If the update script exits non-zero, only that reference is rejected; other references can still be updated.

An Example Git-Enforced Policy

In this section, you'll use what you've learned to establish a Git workflow that checks for a custom commit message format, enforces fast-forward-only pushes, and allows only certain users to modify certain subdirectories in a project. You'll build client scripts that help the developer know if their push will be rejected and server scripts that actually enforce the policies.

I used Ruby to write these, both because it's my preferred scripting language and because I feel it's the most pseudocode-looking of the scripting languages; thus you should be able to roughly follow the code even if you don't use Ruby. However, any language will work fine. All the sample hook scripts distributed with Git are in either Perl or Bash scripting, so you can also see plenty of examples of hooks in those languages by looking at the samples.

Server-Side Hook

All the server-side work will go into the `update` file in your `hooks` directory. The `update` file runs once per branch being pushed and takes the reference being pushed to, the old revision where that branch was, and the new revision being pushed. You also have access to the user doing the pushing if the push is being run over SSH. If you've allowed everyone to connect with a single user (like "git") via public-key authentication, you may have to give that user a shell wrapper that determines which user is connecting based on the public key, and set an environment variable specifying that user. Here I assume the connecting user is in the $USER environment variable, so your `update` script begins by gathering all the information you need:

```ruby
#!/usr/bin/env ruby

$refname = ARGV[0]
$oldrev  = ARGV[1]
$newrev  = ARGV[2]
$user    = ENV['USER']

puts "Enforcing Policies... \n(#{$refname}) (#{$oldrev[0,6]}) (#{$newrev[0,6]})"
```

Yes, I'm using global variables. Don't judge me—it's easier to demonstrate in this manner.

Enforcing a Specific Commit-Message Format

Your first challenge is to enforce that each commit message must adhere to a particular format. Just to have a target, assume that each message has to include a string that looks like "ref: 1234" because you want each commit to link to a work item in your ticketing system. You must look at each commit being pushed up, see if that string is in the commit message, and, if the string is absent from any of the commits, exit non-zero so the push is rejected.

You can get a list of the SHA-1 values of all the commits that are being pushed by taking the $newrev and $oldrev values and passing them to a Git plumbing command that is called git rev-list. This is basically the git log command, but by default it prints out only the SHA-1 values and no other information. So, to get a list of all the commit SHAs introduced between one commit SHA and another, you can run something like this:

```
$ git rev-list 538c33..d14fc7
d14fc7c847ab946ec39590d87783c69b031bdfb7
9f585da4401b0a3999e84113824d15245c13f0be
234071a1be950e2a8d078e6141f5cd20c1e61ad3
dfa04c9ef3d5197182f13fb5b9b1fb7717d2222a
17716ec0f1ff5c77eff40b7fe912f9f6cfd0e475
```

You can take that output, loop through each of those commit SHAs, grab the message for it, and test that message against a regular expression that looks for a pattern.

You have to figure out how to get the commit message from each of these commits to test. To get the raw commit data, you can use another plumbing command called git cat-file. I'll go over all these plumbing commands in detail in Chapter 9; but for now, here's what that command gives you:

```
$ git cat-file commit ca82a6
tree cfda3bf379e4f8dba8717dee55aab78aef7f4daf
parent 085bb3bcb608e1e8451d4b2432f8ecbe6306e7e7
author Scott Chacon <schacon@gmail.com> 1205815931 -0700
committer Scott Chacon <schacon@gmail.com> 1240030591 -0700

changed the version number
```

A simple way to get the commit message from a commit when you have the SHA-1 value is to go to the first blank line and take everything after that. You can do so with the sed command on Unix systems:

```
$ git cat-file commit ca82a6 | sed '1,/^$/d'
changed the version number
```

You can use that incantation to grab the commit message from each commit that is trying to be pushed and exit if you see anything that doesn't match. To exit the script and reject the push, exit non-zero. The whole method looks like this:

```
$regex = /\[ref: (\d+)\]/

# enforced custom commit message format
def check_message_format
  missed_revs = 'git rev-list #{$oldrev}..#{$newrev}'.split("\n")
```

```
  missed_revs.each do |rev|
    message = 'git cat-file commit #{rev} | sed '1,/^$/d''
    if !$regex.match(message)
      puts "[POLICY] Your message is not formatted correctly"
      exit 1
    end
  end
end
check_message_format
```

Putting that in your update script will reject updates that contain commits that have messages that don't adhere to your rule.

Enforcing a User-Based ACL System

Suppose you want to add a mechanism that uses an access control list (ACL) that specifies which users are allowed to push changes to which parts of your projects. Some people have full access, and others only have access to push changes to certain subdirectories or specific files. To enforce this, you'll write those rules to a file named acl that lives in your bare Git repository on the server. You'll have the update hook look at those rules, see what files are being introduced for all the commits being pushed, and determine whether the user doing the push has access to update all those files.

The first thing you'll do is write your ACL. Here you'll use a format very much like the CVS ACL mechanism: it uses a series of lines, where the first field is avail or unavail, the next field is a comma-delimited list of the users to which the rule applies, and the last field is the path to which the rule applies (blank meaning open access). All of these fields are delimited by a pipe (|) character.

In this case, you have a couple of administrators, some documentation writers with access to the doc directory, and one developer who only has access to the lib and tests directories, and your ACL file looks like this:

```
avail|nickh,pjhyett,defunkt,tpw
avail|usinclair,cdickens,ebronte|doc
avail|schacon|lib
avail|schacon|tests
```

You begin by reading this data into a structure that you can use. In this case, to keep the example simple, you'll only enforce the avail directives. Here is a method that gives you an associative array where the key is the user name and the value is an array of paths to which the user has write access:

```
def get_acl_access_data(acl_file)
  # read in ACL data
  acl_file = File.read(acl_file).split("\n").reject { |line| line == '' }
  access = {}
  acl_file.each do |line|
    avail, users, path = line.split('|')
    next unless avail == 'avail'
    users.split(',').each do |user|
```

```
      access[user] ||= []
      access[user] << path
    end
  end
  access
end
```

On the ACL file you looked at earlier, this get_acl_access_data method returns a data structure that looks like this:

```
{"defunkt"=>[nil],
 "tpw"=>[nil],
 "nickh"=>[nil],
 "pjhyett"=>[nil],
 "schacon"=>["lib", "tests"],
 "cdickens"=>["doc"],
 "usinclair"=>["doc"],
 "ebronte"=>["doc"]}
```

Now that you have the permissions sorted out, you need to determine what paths the commits being pushed have modified, so you can make sure the user who's pushing has access to all of them.

You can pretty easily see what files have been modified in a single commit with the --name-only option to the git log command (mentioned briefly in Chapter 2):

```
$ git log -1 --name-only --pretty=format:'' 9f585d

README
lib/test.rb
```

If you use the ACL structure returned from the get_acl_access_data method and check it against the listed files in each of the commits, you can determine whether the user has access to push all of their commits:

```
# only allows certain users to modify certain subdirectories in a project
def check_directory_perms
  access = get_acl_access_data('acl')

  # see if anyone is trying to push something they can't
  new_commits = 'git rev-list #{$oldrev}..#{$newrev}'.split("\n")
  new_commits.each do |rev|
    files_modified = 'git log -1 --name-only --pretty=format:'' #{rev}'.split("\n")
    files_modified.each do |path|
      next if path.size == 0
      has_file_access = false
      access[$user].each do |access_path|
        if !access_path # user has access to everything
          || (path.index(access_path) == 0) # access to this path
          has_file_access = true
        end
```

```
      end
      if !has_file_access
        puts "[POLICY] You do not have access to push to #{path}"
        exit 1
      end
    end
  end
end

check_directory_perms
```

Most of that should be easy to follow. You get a list of new commits being pushed to your server with `git rev-list`. Then, for each of those, you find which files are modified and make sure the user who's pushing has access to all the paths being modified. One Rubyism that may not be clear is `path.index(access_path) == 0`, which is true if `path` begins with `access_path`— this ensures that `access_path` is not just in one of the allowed paths, but each accessed path begins with an allowed path..

Now your users can't push any commits with badly formed messages or with modified files outside of their designated paths.

Enforcing Fast-Forward-Only Pushes

The only thing left is to enforce fast-forward-only pushes. In Git versions 1.6 or newer, you can set the `receive.denyDeletes` and `receive.denyNonFastForwards` settings. But enforcing this with a hook will work in older versions of Git, and you can modify it to do so only for certain users or whatever else you come up with later.

The logic for checking this is to see if any commits are reachable from the older revision that aren't reachable from the newer one. If there are none, then it was a fast-forward push; otherwise, you deny it:

```
# enforces fast-forward only pushes
def check_fast_forward
  missed_refs = 'git rev-list #{$newrev}..#{$oldrev}'
  missed_ref_count = missed_refs.split("\n").size
  if missed_ref_count > 0
    puts "[POLICY] Cannot push a non fast-forward reference"
    exit 1
  end
end

check_fast_forward
```

Everything is set up. If you run `chmod u+x .git/hooks/update`, which is the file into which you should have put all this code, and then try to push a non-fast-forwarded reference, you get something like this:

```
$ git push -f origin master
Counting objects: 5, done.
```

```
Compressing objects: 100% (3/3), done.
Writing objects: 100% (3/3), 323 bytes, done.
Total 3 (delta 1), reused 0 (delta 0)
Unpacking objects: 100% (3/3), done.
Enforcing Policies...
(refs/heads/master) (8338c5) (c5b616)
[POLICY] Cannot push a non-fast-forward reference
error: hooks/update exited with error code 1
error: hook declined to update refs/heads/master
To git@gitserver:project.git
 ! [remote rejected] master -> master (hook declined)
error: failed to push some refs to 'git@gitserver:project.git'
```

There are a couple of interesting things here. First, you see this where the hook starts running.

```
Enforcing Policies...
(refs/heads/master) (fb8c72) (c56860)
```

Notice that you printed that out to stdout at the very beginning of your update script. It's important to note that anything your script prints to stdout will be transferred to the client.

The next thing you'll notice is the error message.

```
[POLICY] Cannot push a non fast-forward reference
error: hooks/update exited with error code 1
error: hook declined to update refs/heads/master
```

The first line was printed out by you, the other two were Git telling you that the update script exited non-zero and that is what is declining your push. Lastly, you have this:

```
To git@gitserver:project.git
 ! [remote rejected] master -> master (hook declined)
error: failed to push some refs to 'git@gitserver:project.git'
```

You'll see a remote rejected message for each reference that your hook declined, and it tells you that it was declined specifically because of a hook failure.

Furthermore, if the ref marker isn't there in any of your commits, you'll see the error message you're printing out for that.

```
[POLICY] Your message is not formatted correctly
```

Or if someone tries to edit a file they don't have access to and push a commit containing it, they will see something similar. For instance, if a documentation author tries to push a commit modifying something in the lib directory, they see

```
[POLICY] You do not have access to push to lib/test.rb
```

That's all. From now on, as long as that update script is there and executable, your repository will never be rewound and will never have a commit message without your pattern in it, and your users will be sandboxed.

Client-Side Hooks

The downside to this approach is the whining that will inevitably result when your users' commit pushes are rejected. Having their carefully crafted work rejected at the last minute can be extremely frustrating and confusing; and furthermore, they will have to edit their history to correct it, which isn't always for the faint of heart.

The answer to this dilemma is to provide some client-side hooks that users can use to notify them when they're doing something that the server is likely to reject. That way, they can correct any problems before committing and before those issues become more difficult to fix. Because hooks aren't transferred with a clone of a project, you must distribute these scripts some other way and then have your users copy them to their .git/hooks directory and make them executable. You can distribute these hooks within the project or in a separate project, but there is no way to set them up automatically.

To begin, you should check your commit message just before each commit is recorded, so you know the server won't reject your changes due to badly formatted commit messages. To do this, you can add the commit-msg hook. If you have it read the message from the file passed as the first argument and compare that to the pattern, you can force Git to abort the commit if there is no match:

```ruby
#!/usr/bin/env ruby
message_file = ARGV[0]
message = File.read(message_file)

$regex = /\[ref: (\d+)\]/

if !$regex.match(message)
  puts "[POLICY] Your message is not formatted correctly"
  exit 1
end
```

If that script is in place (in .git/hooks/commit-msg) and executable, and you commit with a message that isn't properly formatted, you see this:

```
$ git commit -am 'test'
[POLICY] Your message is not formatted correctly
```

No commit was completed in that instance. However, if your message contains the proper pattern, Git allows you to commit:

```
$ git commit -am 'test [ref: 132]'
[master e05c914] test [ref: 132]
 1 files changed, 1 insertions(+), 0 deletions(-)
```

Next, you want to make sure you aren't modifying files that are outside your ACL scope. If your project's .git directory contains a copy of the ACL file you used previously, then the following pre-commit script will enforce those constraints for you:

```ruby
#!/usr/bin/env ruby

$user      = ENV['USER']

# [ insert acl_access_data method from above ]

# only allows certain users to modify certain subdirectories in a project
def check_directory_perms
  access = get_acl_access_data('.git/acl')

  files_modified = 'git diff-index --cached --name-only HEAD'.split("\n")
  files_modified.each do |path|
    next if path.size == 0
    has_file_access = false
    access[$user].each do |access_path|
    if !access_path || (path.index(access_path) == 0)
      has_file_access = true
    end
    if !has_file_access
      puts "[POLICY] You do not have access to push to #{path}"
      exit 1
    end
  end
end
end

check_directory_perms
```

This is roughly the same script as the server-side part, but with two important differences. First, the ACL file is in a different place, because this script runs from your working directory, not from your Git directory. You have to change the path to the ACL file from this

```ruby
access = get_acl_access_data('acl')
```

to this:

```ruby
access = get_acl_access_data('.git/acl')
```

The other important difference is the way you get a listing of the files that have been changed. Because the server-side method looks at the log of commits, and, at this point, the commit hasn't been recorded yet, you must get your file listing from the staging area instead. Instead of

```ruby
files_modified = 'git log -1 --name-only --pretty=format:'' #{ref}'
```

you have to use

```ruby
files_modified = 'git diff-index --cached --name-only HEAD'
```

But those are the only two differences—otherwise, the script works the same way. One caveat is that it expects you to be running locally as the same user you push as to the remote machine. If that is different, you must set the $user variable manually.

The last thing you have to do is check that you're not trying to push non-fast-forwarded references, but that is a bit less common. To get a reference that isn't a fast-forward, you either have to rebase past a commit you've already pushed up or try pushing a different local branch up to the same remote branch.

Because the server will tell you that you can't push a non-fast-forward anyway, and the hook prevents forced pushes, the only accidental thing you can try to catch is rebasing commits that have already been pushed.

Here is an example pre-rebase script that checks for that. It gets a list of all the commits you're about to rewrite and checks whether they exist in any of your remote references. If it sees one that is reachable from one of your remote references, it aborts the rebase:

```ruby
#!/usr/bin/env ruby

base_branch = ARGV[0]
if ARGV[1]
  topic_branch = ARGV[1]
else
  topic_branch = "HEAD"
end

target_shas = 'git rev-list #{base_branch}..#{topic_branch}'.split("\n")
remote_refs = 'git branch -r'.split("\n").map { |r| r.strip }

target_shas.each do |sha|
  remote_refs.each do |remote_ref|
    shas_pushed = 'git rev-list ^#{sha}^@ refs/remotes/#{remote_ref}'
    if shas_pushed.split("\n").include?(sha)
      puts "[POLICY] Commit #{sha} has already been pushed to #{remote_ref}"
      exit 1
    end
  end
end
```

This script uses a syntax that wasn't covered in the "Revision Selection" section of Chapter 6. You get a list of commits that have already been pushed up by running this:

```
git rev-list ^#{sha}^@ refs/remotes/#{remote_ref}
```

The SHA^@ syntax resolves to all the parents of that commit. You're looking for any commit that is reachable from the last commit on the remote and that isn't reachable from any parent of any of the SHAs you're trying to push up—meaning it's a fast-forward.

The main drawback to this approach is that it can be very slow and is often unnecessary—if you don't try to force the push with -f, the server will warn you and not accept the push. However, it's an interesting exercise and can in theory help you avoid a rebase that you might later have to go back and fix.

Summary

You've covered most of the major ways that you can customize your Git client and server to best fit your workflow and projects. You've learned about all sorts of configuration settings, file-based attributes, and event hooks, and you've built an example policy-enforcing server. You should now be able to make Git fit nearly any workflow you can dream up.

■ ■ ■

## CHAPTER 8

Git and Other Systems

The world isn't perfect. Usually, you can't immediately switch every project you come in contact with to Git. Sometimes you're stuck on a project using another VCS, and many times that system is Subversion. You'll spend the first part of this chapter learning about `git svn`, the bidirectional Subversion gateway tool in Git.

At some point, you may want to convert your existing project to Git. The second part of this chapter covers how to migrate your project into Git: first from Subversion, then from Perforce, and finally via a custom import script for a nonstandard importing case.

Git and Subversion

Currently, the majority of open source development projects and a large number of corporate projects use Subversion to manage their source code. It's the most popular open source VCS and has been around for nearly a decade. It's also very similar in many ways to CVS, which was the big boy of the source-control world before that.

One of Git's great features is a bidirectional bridge to Subversion called `git svn`. This tool allows you to use Git as a valid client to a Subversion server, so you can use all the local features of Git and then push to a Subversion server as if you were using Subversion locally. This means you can do local branching and merging, use the staging area, use rebasing and cherry-picking, and so on, while your collaborators continue to work in their dark and ancient ways. It's a good way to sneak Git into the corporate environment and help your fellow developers become more efficient while you lobby to get the infrastructure changed to support Git fully. The Subversion bridge is the gateway drug to the DVCS world.

git svn

The base command in Git for all the Subversion bridging commands is `git svn`. You preface everything with that. It takes quite a few commands, so you'll learn about the common ones while going through a few small workflows.

It's important to note that when you're using `git svn`, you're interacting with Subversion, which is a system that is far less sophisticated than Git. Although you can easily do local branching and merging, it's generally best to keep your history as linear as possible by rebasing your work and avoiding doing things like simultaneously interacting with a Git remote repository.

Don't rewrite your history and try to push again, and don't push to a parallel Git repository to collaborate with fellow Git developers at the same time. Subversion can have only a single linear history, and confusing it is very easy. If you're working with a team, and some are using SVN and others are using Git, make sure everyone is using the SVN server to collaborate—doing so will make your life easier.

Setting Up

To demonstrate this functionality, you need a typical SVN repository that you have write access to. If you want to copy these examples, you'll have to make a writeable copy of my test repository. In order to do that easily, you can use a tool called svnsync that comes with more recent versions of Subversion—it should be distributed with at least 1.4. For these tests, I created a new Subversion repository on Google code that was a partial copy of the protobuf project, which is a tool that encodes structured data for network transmission.

To follow along, you first need to create a new local Subversion repository:

```
$ mkdir /tmp/test-svn
$ svnadmin create /tmp/test-svn
```

Then, enable all users to change revprops—the easy way is to add a pre-revprop-change script that always exits 0:

```
$ cat /tmp/test-svn/hooks/pre-revprop-change
#!/bin/sh
exit 0;
$ chmod +x /tmp/test-svn/hooks/pre-revprop-change
```

You can now sync this project to your local machine by calling svnsync init with the to and from repositories.

```
$ svnsync init file:///tmp/test-svn http://progit-example.googlecode.com/svn/
```

This sets up the properties to run the sync. You can then clone the code by running

```
$ svnsync sync file:///tmp/test-svn
Committed revision 1.
Copied properties for revision 1.
Committed revision 2.
Copied properties for revision 2.
Committed revision 3.
...
```

Although this operation may take only a few minutes, if you try to copy the original repository to another remote repository instead of a local one, the process will take nearly an hour, even though there are fewer than 100 commits. Subversion has to clone one revision at a time and then push it back into another repository—it's ridiculously inefficient, but it's the only easy way to do this.

Getting Started

Now that you have a Subversion repository to which you have write access, you can go through a typical workflow. You'll start with the git svn clone command, which imports an entire Subversion repository into a local Git repository. Remember that if you're importing from a real hosted Subversion repository, you should replace the `file:///tmp/test-svn` here with the URL of your Subversion repository:

```
$ git svn clone file:///tmp/test-svn -T trunk -b branches -t tags
Initialized empty Git repository in /Users/schacon/projects/testsvnsync/svn/.git/
r1 = b4e387bc68740b5af56c2a5faf4003ae42bd135c (trunk)
        A    m4/acx_pthread.m4
        A    m4/stl_hash.m4
...
r75 = d1957f3b307922124eec6314e15bcda59e3d9610 (trunk)
Found possible branch point: file:///tmp/test-svn/trunk => \
    file:///tmp/test-svn /branches/my-calc-branch, 75
Found branch parent: (my-calc-branch) d1957f3b307922124eec6314e15bcda59e3d9610
Following parent with do_switch
Successfully followed parent
r76 = 8624824ecc0badd73f40ea2f01fce51894189b01 (my-calc-branch)
Checked out HEAD:
 file:///tmp/test-svn/branches/my-calc-branch r76
```

This runs the equivalent of two commands—git svn init followed by git svn fetch—on the URL you provide. This can take a while. The test project has only about 75 commits and the codebase isn't that big, so it takes just a few minutes. However, Git has to check out each version, one at a time, and commit it individually. For a project with hundreds or thousands of commits, this can literally take hours or even days to finish.

The -T trunk -b branches -t tags part tells Git that this Subversion repository follows the basic branching and tagging conventions. If you name your trunk, branches, or tags differently, you can change these options. Because this is so common, you can replace this entire part with -s, which means *standard layout* and implies all those options. The following command is equivalent:

```
$ git svn clone file:///tmp/test-svn -s
```

At this point, you should have a valid Git repository that has imported your branches and tags:

```
$ git branch -a
* master
  my-calc-branch
  tags/2.0.2
  tags/release-2.0.1
  tags/release-2.0.2
  tags/release-2.0.2rc1
  trunk
```

It's important to note how this tool namespaces your remote references differently. When you're cloning a normal Git repository, you get all the branches on that remote server available locally as something like origin/[*branch*], namespaced by the name of the remote. However, git svn assumes that you won't have multiple remotes and saves all its references to points on the remote server with no namespacing. You can use the Git plumbing command show-ref to look at all your full reference names:

```
$ git show-ref
1cbd4904d9982f386d87f88fce1c24ad7c0f0471 refs/heads/master
aee1ecc26318164f355a883f5d99cff0c852d3c4 refs/remotes/my-calc-branch
03d09b0e2aad427e34a6d50ff147128e76c0e0f5 refs/remotes/tags/2.0.2
50d02cc0adc9da4319eeba0900430ba219b9c376 refs/remotes/tags/release-2.0.1
4caaa711a50c77879a91b8b90380060f672745cb refs/remotes/tags/release-2.0.2
1c4cb508144c513ff1214c3488abe66dcb92916f refs/remotes/tags/release-2.0.2rc1
1cbd4904d9982f386d87f88fce1c24ad7c0f0471 refs/remotes/trunk
```

A normal Git repository looks more like this:

```
$ git show-ref
83e38c7a0af325a9722f2fdc56b10188806d83a1 refs/heads/master
3e15e38c198baac84223acfc6224bb8b99ff2281 refs/remotes/gitserver/master
0a30dd3b0c795b80212ae723640d4e5d48cabdff refs/remotes/origin/master
25812380387fdd55f916652be4881c6f11600d6f refs/remotes/origin/testing
```

You have two remote servers: one named `gitserver` with a `master` branch; and another named `origin` with two branches, `master` and `testing`.

Notice how in the example of remote references imported from `git svn`, tags are added as remote branches, not as real Git tags. Your Subversion import looks like it has a remote named `tags` with branches under it.

Committing Back to Subversion

Now that you have a working repository, you can do some work on the project and push your commits back upstream, using Git effectively as a SVN client. If you edit one of the files and commit it, you have a commit that exists in Git locally that doesn't exist on the Subversion server:

```
$ git commit -am 'Adding git-svn instructions to the README'
[master 97031e5] Adding git-svn instructions to the README
 1 files changed, 1 insertions(+), 1 deletions(-)
```

Next, you need to push your change upstream. Notice how this changes the way you work with Subversion—you can do several commits offline and then push them all at once to the Subversion server. To push to a Subversion server, you run the `git svn dcommit` command:

```
$ git svn dcommit
Committing to file:///tmp/test-svn/trunk ...
        M        README.txt
Committed r79
        M        README.txt
r79 = 938b1a547c2cc92033b74d32030e86468294a5c8 (trunk)
No changes between current HEAD and refs/remotes/trunk
Resetting to the latest refs/remotes/trunk
```

This takes all the commits you've made on top of the Subversion server code, does a Subversion commit for each, and then rewrites your local Git commit to include a unique identifier. This is important because it means that all the SHA-1 checksums for your commits change. Partly for this reason, working with Git-based remote versions of your projects concurrently with a Subversion server isn't a good idea. If you look at the last commit, you can see the new `git-svn-id` that was added:

```
$ git log -1
commit 938b1a547c2cc92033b74d32030e86468294a5c8
Author: schacon <schacon@4c93b258-373f-11de-be05-5f7a86268029>
Date:    Sat May 2 22:06:44 2009 +0000

    Adding git-svn instructions to the README

    git-svn-id: file:///tmp/test-svn/trunk@79 4c93b258-373f-11de-be05-5f7a86268029
```

Notice that the SHA checksum that originally started with 97031e5 when you committed now begins with 938b1a5. If you want to push to both a Git server and a Subversion server, you have to push (dcommit) to the Subversion server first, because that action changes your commit data.

Pulling in New Changes

If you're working with other developers, then at some point one of you will push, and then the other one will try to push a change that conflicts. That change will be rejected until you merge in their work. In git svn, it looks like this:

```
$ git svn dcommit
Committing to file:///tmp/test-svn/trunk ...
Merge conflict during commit: Your file or directory 'README.txt' is probably \
out-of-date: resource out of date; try updating at /Users/schacon/libexec/git-\
core/git-svn line 482
```

To resolve this situation, you can run git svn rebase, which pulls down any changes on the server that you don't have yet and rebases any work you have on top of what is on the server:

```
$ git svn rebase
        M        README.txt
r80 = ff829ab914e8775c7c025d741beb3d523ee30bc4 (trunk)
First, rewinding head to replay your work on top of it...
Applying: first user change
```

Now, all your work is on top of what is on the Subversion server, so you can successfully dcommit:

```
$ git svn dcommit
Committing to file:///tmp/test-svn/trunk ...
        M        README.txt
Committed r81
        M        README.txt
r81 = 456cbe6337abe49154db70106d1836bc1332deed (trunk)
No changes between current HEAD and refs/remotes/trunk
Resetting to the latest refs/remotes/trunk
```

It's important to remember that unlike Git, which requires you to merge upstream work you don't yet have locally before you can push, `git svn` makes you do that only if the changes conflict. If someone else pushes a change to one file and then you push a change to another file, your dcommit will work fine:

```
$ git svn dcommit
Committing to file:///tmp/test-svn/trunk ...
        M       configure.ac
Committed r84
        M       autogen.sh
r83 = 8aa54a74d452f82eee10076ab2584c1fc424853b (trunk)
        M       configure.ac
r84 = cdbac939211ccb18aa744e581e46563af5d962d0 (trunk)
W: d2f23b80f67aaaa1f6f5aaef48fce3263ac71a92 and refs/remotes/trunk differ, \
  using rebase:
:100755 100755 efa5a59965fbbb5b2b0a12890f1b351bb5493c18 \
  015e4c98c482f0fa71e4d5434338014530b37fa6 M     autogen.sh
First, rewinding head to replay your work on top of it...
Nothing to do.
```

This is important to remember, because the outcome is a project state that didn't exist on either of your computers when you pushed. If the changes are incompatible but don't conflict, you may get issues that are difficult to diagnose. This is different than using a Git server—in Git, you can fully test the state on your client system before publishing it, whereas in SVN, you can't ever be certain that the states immediately before commit and after commit are identical.

You should also run this command to pull in changes from the Subversion server, even if you're not ready to commit yourself. You can run `git svn fetch` to grab the new data, but `git svn rebase` does the fetch and then updates your local commits:

```
$ git svn rebase
        M       generate_descriptor_proto.sh
r82 = bd16df9173e424c6f52c337ab6efa7f7643282f1 (trunk)
First, rewinding head to replay your work on top of it...
Fast-forwarded master to refs/remotes/trunk.
```

Running `git svn rebase` every once in a while makes sure your code is always up to date. You need to be sure your working directory is clean when you run this, though. If you have local changes, you must either stash your work or temporarily commit it before running `git svn rebase`—otherwise, the command will stop if it sees that the rebase will result in a merge conflict.

Git Branching Issues

When you've become comfortable with a Git workflow, you'll likely create topic branches, do work on them, and then merge them in. If you're pushing to a Subversion server via `git svn`, you may want to rebase your work onto a single branch each time instead of merging branches together. The reason to prefer rebasing is that Subversion has a linear history and doesn't deal with merges like Git does, so `git svn` follows only the first parent when converting the snapshots into Subversion commits.

Suppose your history looks like the following: you created an `experiment` branch, did two commits, and then merged them back into `master`. When you dcommit, you see output like this:

```
$ git svn dcommit
Committing to file:///tmp/test-svn/trunk ...
        M       CHANGES.txt
Committed r85
        M       CHANGES.txt
r85 = 4bfebeec434d156c36f2bcd18f4e3d97dc3269a2 (trunk)
No changes between current HEAD and refs/remotes/trunk
Resetting to the latest refs/remotes/trunk
COPYING.txt: locally modified
INSTALL.txt: locally modified
        M       COPYING.txt
        M       INSTALL.txt
Committed r86
        M       INSTALL.txt
        M       COPYING.txt
r86 = 2647f6b86ccfcaad4ec58c520e369ec81f7c283c (trunk)
No changes between current HEAD and refs/remotes/trunk
Resetting to the latest refs/remotes/trunk
```

Running `dcommit` on a branch with merged history works fine, except that when you look at your Git project history, it hasn't rewritten either of the commits you made on the `experiment` branch—instead, all those changes appear in the SVN version of the single merge commit.

When someone else clones that work, all they see is the merge commit with all the work squashed into it; they don't see the commit data about where it came from or when it was committed.

Subversion Branching

Branching in Subversion isn't the same as branching in Git; if you can avoid using it much, that's probably best. However, you can create and commit to branches in Subversion using `git svn`.

Creating a New SVN Branch

To create a new branch in Subversion, you run `git svn branch [`*branchname*`]`:

```
$ git svn branch opera
Copying file:///tmp/test-svn/trunk at r87 to file:///tmp/test-svn/branches/opera...
Found possible branch point: file:///tmp/test-svn/trunk => \
  file:///tmp/test-svn/branches/opera, 87
Found branch parent: (opera) 1f6bfe471083cbca06ac8d4176f7ad4de0d62e5f
Following parent with do_switch
Successfully followed parent
r89 = 9b6fe0b90c5c9adf9165f700897518dbc54a7cbf (opera)
```

This does the equivalent of the `svn copy trunk branches/opera` command in Subversion and operates on the Subversion server. It's important to note that it doesn't check you out into that branch; if you commit at this point, that commit will go to `trunk` on the server, not `opera`.

Switching Active Branches

Git figures out what branch your dcommits go to by looking for the tip of any of your Subversion branches in your history—you should have only one, and it should be the last one with a `git-svn-id` in your current branch history.

If you want to work on more than one branch simultaneously, you can set up local branches to dcommit to specific Subversion branches by starting them at the imported Subversion commit for that branch. If you want an `opera` branch that you can work on separately, you can run

```
$ git branch opera remotes/opera
```

Now, if you want to merge your `opera` branch into `trunk` (your `master` branch), you can do so with a normal `git merge`. But you need to provide a descriptive commit message (via -m), or the merge will say `Merge branch opera` instead of something useful.

Remember that although you're using `git merge` to do this operation, and the merge likely will be much easier than it would be in Subversion (because Git will automatically detect the appropriate merge base for you), this isn't a normal Git merge commit. You have to push this data back to a Subversion server that can't handle a commit that tracks more than one parent; so, after you push it up, it will look like a single commit that squashed in all the work of another branch under a single commit. After you merge one branch into another, you can't easily go back and continue working on that branch, as you normally can in Git. The `dcommit` command that you run erases any information that says what branch was merged in, so subsequent merge-base calculations will be wrong—the `dcommit` makes your `git merge` result look like you ran `git merge --squash`. Unfortunately, there's no good way to avoid this situation—Subversion can't store this information, so you'll always be crippled by its limitations while you're using it as your server. To avoid issues, you should delete the local branch (in this case, `opera`) after you merge it into `trunk`.

Subversion Commands

The `git svn` toolset provides a number of commands to help ease the transition to Git by providing some functionality that's similar to what you had in Subversion. Here are a few commands that give you what Subversion used to.

SVN Style History

If you're used to Subversion and want to see your history in SVN output style, you can run `git svn log` to view your commit history in SVN formatting:

```
$ git svn log
------------------------------------------------------------------------
r87 | schacon | 2009-05-02 16:07:37 -0700 (Sat, 02 May 2009) | 2 lines

autogen change
```

```
------------------------------------------------------------------------
r86 | schacon | 2009-05-02 16:00:21 -0700 (Sat, 02 May 2009) | 2 lines

Merge branch 'experiment'

------------------------------------------------------------------------
r85 | schacon | 2009-05-02 16:00:09 -0700 (Sat, 02 May 2009) | 2 lines

updated the changelog
```

You should know two important things about git svn log. First, it works offline, unlike the real svn log command, which asks the Subversion server for the data. Second, it only shows you commits that have been committed up to the Subversion server. Local Git commits that you haven't dcommited don't show up; neither do commits that people have made to the Subversion server in the meantime. It's more like the last known state of the commits on the Subversion server.

SVN Annotation

Much as the git svn log command simulates the svn log command offline, you can get the equivalent of svn annotate by running git svn blame [FILE]. The output looks like this:

```
$ git svn blame README.txt
  2    temporal Protocol Buffers - Google's data interchange format
  2    temporal Copyright 2008 Google Inc.
  2    temporal http://code.google.com/apis/protocolbuffers/
  2    temporal
 22    temporal C++ Installation - Unix
 22    temporal =========================
  2    temporal
 79     schacon Committing in git-svn.
 78     schacon
  2    temporal To build and install the C++ Protocol Buffer runtime and the Protocol
  2    temporal Buffer compiler (protoc) execute the following:
  2    temporal
```

Again, it doesn't show commits that you did locally in Git or that have been pushed to Subversion in the meantime.

SVN Server Information

You can also get the same sort of information that svn info gives you by running git svn info:

```
$ git svn info
Path: .
URL: https://schacon-test.googlecode.com/svn/trunk
Repository Root: https://schacon-test.googlecode.com/svn
Repository UUID: 4c93b258-373f-11de-be05-5f7a86268029
Revision: 87
```

```
Node Kind: directory
Schedule: normal
Last Changed Author: schacon
Last Changed Rev: 87
Last Changed Date: 2009-05-02 16:07:37 -0700 (Sat, 02 May 2009)
```

This is like `blame` and `log` in that it runs offline and is up to date only as of the last time you communicated with the Subversion server.

Ignoring What Subversion Ignores

If you clone a Subversion repository that has `svn:ignore` properties set anywhere, you'll likely want to set corresponding `.gitignore` files so you don't accidentally commit files that you shouldn't. `git svn` has two commands to help with this issue. The first is `git svn create-ignore`, which automatically creates corresponding `.gitignore` files for you so your next commit can include them.

The second command is `git svn show-ignore`, which prints to stdout the lines you need to put in a `.gitignore` file so you can redirect the output into your project exclude file:

```
$ git svn show-ignore > .git/info/exclude
```

That way, you don't litter the project with `.gitignore` files. This is a good option if you're the only Git user on a Subversion team, and your teammates don't want `.gitignore` files in the project.

Git-Svn Summary

The `git svn` tools are useful if you're stuck with a Subversion server for now or are otherwise in a development environment that necessitates running a Subversion server. You should consider it crippled Git, however, or you'll hit issues in translation that may confuse you and your collaborators. To stay out of trouble, try to follow these guidelines:

- Keep a linear Git history that doesn't contain merge commits made by `git merge`. Rebase any work you do outside of your mainline branch back onto it; don't merge it in.

- Don't set up and collaborate on a separate Git server. Possibly have one to speed up clones for new developers, but don't push anything to it that doesn't have a `git-svn-id` entry. You may even want to add a pre-receive hook that checks each commit message for a `git-svn-id` and rejects pushes that contain commits without it.

If you follow those guidelines, working with a Subversion server can be more bearable. However, if it's possible to move to a real Git server, doing so can gain your team a lot more.

Migrating to Git

If you have an existing codebase in another VCS but you've decided to start using Git, you must migrate your project one way or another. This section goes over some importers that are included with Git for common systems and then demonstrates how to develop your own custom importer.

Importing

You'll learn how to import data from two of the bigger professionally used SCM systems—
Subversion and Perforce—both because they make up the majority of users I hear of who are
currently switching, and because high-quality tools for both systems are distributed with Git.

Subversion

If you read the previous section about using git svn, you can easily use those instructions to
git svn clone a repository; then, stop using the Subversion server, push to a new Git server,
and start using that. If you want the history, you can accomplish that as quickly as you can pull
the data out of the Subversion server (which may take a while).

However, the import isn't perfect; and because it will take so long, you may as well do it
right. The first problem is the author information. In Subversion, each person committing has
a user on the system who is recorded in the commit information. The examples in the previous
section show schacon in some places, such as the blame output and the git svn log. If you want
to map this to better Git author data, you need a mapping from the Subversion users to the Git
authors. Create a file called users.txt that has this mapping in a format like this:

```
schacon = Scott Chacon <schacon@geemail.com>
selse = Someo Nelse <selse@geemail.com>
```

To get a list of the author names that SVN uses, you can run this:

```
$ svn log --xml | grep author | sort -u | perl -pe 's/.>(.?)<./$1 = /'
```

That gives you the log output in XML format—then it looks for the authors, creates
a unique list, and then strips out the XML. (Obviously this only works on a machine with grep,
sort, and perl installed.) Then, redirect that output into your users.txt file so you can add the
equivalent Git user data next to each entry.

You can provide this file to git svn to help it map the author data more accurately. You
can also tell git svn not to include the metadata that Subversion normally imports, by passing
--no-metadata to the clone or init command. This makes your import command look like this:

```
$ git-svn clone http://my-project.googlecode.com/svn/ \
    --authors-file=users.txt --no-metadata -s my_project
```

Now you should have a nicer Subversion import in your my_project directory. Instead of
commits that look like this:

```
commit 37efa680e8473b615de980fa935944215428a35a
Author: schacon <schacon@4c93b258-373f-11de-be05-5f7a86268029>
Date:   Sun May 3 00:12:22 2009 +0000

    fixed install - go to trunk

    git-svn-id: https://my-project.googlecode.com/svn/trunk@94 4c93b258-373f-11de-
    be05-5f7a86268029
```

they look like this:

```
commit 03a8785f44c8ea5cdb0e8834b7c8e6c469be2ff2
Author: Scott Chacon <schacon@geemail.com>
Date:    Sun May 3 00:12:22 2009 +0000

    fixed install - go to trunk
```

Not only does the `Author` field look a lot better, but the `git-svn-id` is no longer there, either.

You then need to do a bit of post-import cleanup. For one thing, you should clean up the weird references that `git svn` set up. First you'll move the tags so they're actual tags rather than strange remote branches, and then you'll move the rest of the branches so they're local.

To move the tags to be proper Git tags, run

```
$ cp -Rf .git/refs/remotes/tags/* .git/refs/tags/
$ rm -Rf .git/refs/remotes/tags
```

This takes the references that were remote branches that started with `tag/` and makes them real (lightweight) tags.

Next, move the rest of the references under `refs/remotes` to be local branches:

```
$ cp -Rf .git/refs/remotes/* .git/refs/heads/
$ rm -Rf .git/refs/remotes
```

Now all the old branches are real Git branches and all the old tags are real Git tags. The last thing to do is add your new Git server as a remote and push to it. Because you want all your branches and tags to go up, you can run this:

```
$ git push origin --all
```

All your branches and tags should be on your new Git server in a nice, clean import.

Perforce

The next system you'll look at importing from is Perforce. A Perforce importer is also distributed with Git, but only in the `contrib` section of the source code—it isn't available by default like `git svn`. To run it, you must get the Git source code, which you can download from `git.kernel.org`:

```
$ git clone git://git.kernel.org/pub/scm/git/git.git
$ cd git/contrib/fast-import
```

In this `fast-import` directory, you should find an executable Python script named `git-p4`. You must have Python and the `p4` tool installed on your machine for this import to work. For example, you'll import the Jam project from the Perforce Public Depot. To set up your client, you must export the `P4PORT` environment variable to point to the Perforce depot:

```
$ export P4PORT=public.perforce.com:1666
```

Run the `git-p4 clone` command to import the Jam project from the Perforce server, supplying the depot and project path and the path into which you want to import the project:

```
$ git-p4 clone //public/jam/src@all /opt/p4import
Importing from //public/jam/src@all into /opt/p4import
Reinitialized existing Git repository in /opt/p4import/.git/
Import destination: refs/remotes/p4/master
Importing revision 4409 (100%)
```

If you go to the /opt/p4import directory and run git log, you can see your imported work:

```
$ git log -2
commit 1fd4ec126171790efd2db83548b85b1bbbc07dc2
Author: Perforce staff <support@perforce.com>
Date:   Thu Aug 19 10:18:45 2004 -0800

    Drop 'rc3' moniker of jam-2.5.  Folded rc2 and rc3 RELNOTES into
    the main part of the document.  Built new tar/zip balls.

    Only 16 months later.

    [git-p4: depot-paths = "//public/jam/src/": change = 4409]

commit ca8870db541a23ed867f38847eda65bf4363371d
Author: Richard Geiger <rmg@perforce.com>
Date:   Tue Apr 22 20:51:34 2003 -0800

    Update derived jamgram.c

    [git-p4: depot-paths = "//public/jam/src/": change = 3108]
```

You can see the git-p4 identifier in each commit. It's fine to keep that identifier there, in case you need to reference the Perforce change number later. However, if you'd like to remove the identifier, now is the time to do so—before you start doing work on the new repository. You can use git filter-branch to remove the identifier strings en masse:

```
$ git filter-branch --msg-filter '
        sed -e "/^\[git-p4:/d"
'
Rewrite 1fd4ec126171790efd2db83548b85b1bbbc07dc2 (123/123)
Ref 'refs/heads/master' was rewritten
```

If you run git log, you can see that all the SHA-1 checksums for the commits have changed, but the git-p4 strings are no longer in the commit messages:

```
$ git log -2
commit 10a16d60cffca14d454a15c6164378f4082bc5b0
Author: Perforce staff <support@perforce.com>
Date:   Thu Aug 19 10:18:45 2004 -0800

    Drop 'rc3' moniker of jam-2.5.  Folded rc2 and rc3 RELNOTES into
    the main part of the document.  Built new tar/zip balls.
```

Only 16 months later.

```
commit 2b6c6db311dd76c34c66ec1c40a49405e6b527b2
Author: Richard Geiger <rmg@perforce.com>
Date:   Tue Apr 22 20:51:34 2003 -0800
```

Update derived jamgram.c

Your import is ready to push up to your new Git server.

A Custom Importer

If your system isn't Subversion or Perforce, you should look for an importer online—quality importers are available for CVS, Clear Case, Visual Source Safe, even a directory of archives. If none of these tools works for you, you have a rarer tool, or you otherwise need a more custom importing process, you should use git fast-import. This command reads simple instructions from stdin to write specific Git data. It's much easier to create Git objects this way than to run the raw Git commands or try to write the raw objects (see Chapter 9 for more information). This way, you can write an import script that reads the necessary information out of the system you're importing from and prints straightforward instructions to stdout. You can then run this program and pipe its output through git fast-import.

To quickly demonstrate, you'll write a simple importer. Suppose you work in current, you back up your project by occasionally copying the directory into a time-stamped back_YYYY_MM_DD backup directory, and you want to import this into Git. Your directory structure looks like this:

```
$ ls /opt/import_from
back_2009_01_02
back_2009_01_04
back_2009_01_14
back_2009_02_03
current
```

In order to import a Git directory, you need to review how Git stores its data. As you may remember, Git is fundamentally a linked list of commit objects that point to a snapshot of content. All you have to do is tell fast-import what the content snapshots are, what commit data points to them, and the order they go in. Your strategy will be to go through the snapshots one at a time and create commits with the contents of each directory, linking each commit back to the previous one.

As you did in the "An Example Git-Enforced Policy" section of Chapter 7, you'll write this in Ruby, because it's what I generally work with and it tends to be easy to read. You can write this example pretty easily in anything you're familiar with—it just needs to print the appropriate information to stdout.

To begin, you'll change into the target directory and identify every subdirectory, each of which is a snapshot that you want to import as a commit. You'll change into each subdirectory and print the commands necessary to export it. Your basic main loop looks like this:

```
last_mark = nil

# loop through the directories
Dir.chdir(ARGV[0]) do
  Dir.glob("*").each do |dir|
    next if File.file?(dir)

    # move into the target directory
    Dir.chdir(dir) do
      last_mark = print_export(dir, last_mark)
    end
  end
end
```

You run `print_export` inside each directory, which takes the manifest and mark of the previous snapshot and returns the manifest and mark of this one; that way, you can link them properly. *Mark* is the `fast-import` term for an identifier you give to a commit; as you create commits, you give each one a mark that you can use to link to it from other commits. So, the first thing to do in your `print_export` method is generate a mark from the directory name:

```
mark = convert_dir_to_mark(dir)
```

You'll do this by creating an array of directories and using the index value as the mark, because a mark must be an integer. Your method looks like this:

```
$marks = []
def convert_dir_to_mark(dir)
  if !$marks.include?(dir)
    $marks << dir
  end
  ($marks.index(dir) + 1).to_s
end
```

Now that you have an integer representation of your commit, you need a date for the commit metadata. Because the date is expressed in the name of the directory, you'll parse it out. The next line in your `print_export` file is

```
date = convert_dir_to_date(dir)
```

where `convert_dir_to_date` is defined as

```
def convert_dir_to_date(dir)
  if dir == 'current'
    return Time.now().to_i
  else
    dir = dir.gsub('back_', '')
    (year, month, day) = dir.split('_')
    return Time.local(year, month, day).to_i
  end
end
```

That returns an integer value for the date of each directory. The last piece of meta-information you need for each commit is the committer data, which you hardcode in a global variable:

```
$author = 'Scott Chacon <schacon@example.com>'
```

Now you're ready to begin printing out the commit data for your importer. The initial information states that you're defining a commit object and what branch it's on, followed by the mark you've generated, the committer information and commit message, and then the previous commit, if any. The code looks like this:

```
# print the import information
puts 'commit refs/heads/master'
puts 'mark :' + mark
puts "committer #{$author} #{date} -0700"
export_data('imported from ' + dir)
puts 'from :' + last_mark if last_mark
```

You hardcode the time zone (-0700) because doing so is easy. If you're importing from another system, you must specify the time zone as an offset.

The commit message must be expressed in a special format:

```
data (size)\n(contents)
```

The format consists of the word data, the size of the data to be read, a newline, and finally the data. Because you need to use the same format to specify the file contents later, you create a helper method, export_data:

```
def export_data(string)
  print "data #{string.size}\n#{string}"
end
```

All that's left is to specify the file contents for each snapshot. This is easy, because you have each one in a directory—you can print out the deleteall command followed by the contents of each file in the directory. Git will then record each snapshot appropriately:

```
puts 'deleteall'
Dir.glob("**/*").each do |file|
  next if !File.file?(file)
  inline_data(file)
end
```

───

■**Note** Because many systems think of their revisions as changes from one commit to another, fast-import can also take commands with each commit to specify which files have been added, removed, or modified and what the new contents are. You could calculate the differences between snapshots and provide only this data, but doing so is more complex—you may as well give Git all the data and let it figure it out. If this is better suited to your data, check the fast-import man page for details about how to provide your data in this manner.

───

The format for listing the new file contents or specifying a modified file with the new contents is as follows:

```
M 644 inline path/to/file
data (size)
(file contents)
```

Here, 644 is the mode (if you have executable files, you need to detect and specify 755 instead), and `inline` says you'll list the contents immediately after this line. Your `inline_data` method looks like this:

```
def inline_data(file, code = 'M', mode = '644')
  content = File.read(file)
  puts "#{code} #{mode} inline #{file}"
  export_data(content)
end
```

You reuse the `export_data` method you defined earlier, because it's the same as the way you specified your commit message data.

The last thing you need to do is to return the current mark so it can be passed to the next iteration:

```
return mark
```

That's it. If you run this script, you'll get content that looks something like this (you can download the full script from http://github.com/progit/book-examples):

```
$ ruby import.rb /opt/import_from
commit refs/heads/master
mark :1
committer Scott Chacon <schacon@geemail.com> 1230883200 -0700
data 29
imported from back_2009_01_02deleteall
M 644 inline file.rb
data 12
version two
commit refs/heads/master
mark :2
committer Scott Chacon <schacon@geemail.com> 1231056000 -0700
data 29
imported from back_2009_01_04from :1
deleteall
M 644 inline file.rb
data 14
version three
M 644 inline new.rb
data 16
new version one
(...)
```

To run the importer, pipe this output through `git fast-import` while in the Git directory you want to import into. You can create a new directory and then run `git init` in it for a starting point, and then run your script:

```
$ git init
Initialized empty Git repository in /opt/import_to/.git/
$ ruby import.rb /opt/import_from | git fast-import
git-fast-import statistics:
---------------------------------------------------------------------
Alloc'd objects:       5000
Total objects:           18 (         1 duplicates                  )
      blobs  :            7 (         1 duplicates        0 deltas)
      trees  :            6 (         0 duplicates        1 deltas)
      commits:            5 (         0 duplicates        0 deltas)
      tags   :            0 (         0 duplicates        0 deltas)
Total branches:           1 (         1 loads     )
      marks:           1024 (         5 unique     )
      atoms:              3
Memory total:          2255 KiB
       pools:          2098 KiB
     objects:           156 KiB
---------------------------------------------------------------------
pack_report: getpagesize()            =         4096
pack_report: core.packedGitWindowSize =     33554432
pack_report: core.packedGitLimit      =    268435456
pack_report: pack_used_ctr            =            9
pack_report: pack_mmap_calls          =            5
pack_report: pack_open_windows        =            1 /            1
pack_report: pack_mapped              =         1356 /         1356
---------------------------------------------------------------------
```

As you can see, when it completes successfully, it gives you a bunch of statistics about what it accomplished. In this case, you imported 18 objects total for 5 commits into 1 branch. Now, you can run `git log` to see your new history:

```
$ git log -2
commit 10bfe7d22ce15ee25b60a824c8982157ca593d41
Author: Scott Chacon <schacon@example.com>
Date:   Sun May 3 12:57:39 2009 -0700

    imported from current

commit 7e519590de754d079dd73b44d695a42c9d2df452
Author: Scott Chacon <schacon@example.com>
Date:   Tue Feb 3 01:00:00 2009 -0700

    imported from back_2009_02_03
```

There you go—a nice, clean Git repository. It's important to note that nothing is checked out—you don't have any files in your working directory at first. To get them, you must reset your branch to where `master` is now:

```
$ ls
$ git reset --hard master
HEAD is now at 10bfe7d imported from current
$ ls
file.rb  lib
```

You can do a lot more with the `fast-import` tool—handle different modes, binary data, multiple branches and merging, tags, progress indicators, and more. A number of examples of more complex scenarios are available in the `contrib/fast-import` directory of the Git source code; one of the better ones is the `git-p4` script I just covered.

Summary

You should feel comfortable using Git with Subversion or importing nearly any existing repository into a new Git one without losing data. The next chapter will cover the raw internals of Git so you can craft every single byte, if need be.

CHAPTER 9

■■■

Git Internals

You may have skipped to this chapter from a previous chapter, or you may have gotten here after reading the rest of the book—in either case, this is where you'll go over the inner workings and implementation of Git. I found that learning this information was fundamentally important to understanding how useful and powerful Git is, but others have argued to me that it can be confusing and unnecessarily complex for beginners. Thus, I've made this discussion the last chapter in the book so you could read it early or later in your learning process. I leave it up to you to decide.

Now that you're here, let's get started. First, if it isn't yet clear, Git is fundamentally a content-addressable filesystem with a VCS user interface written on top of it. You'll learn more about what this means in a bit.

In the early days of Git (mostly pre 1.5), the user interface was much more complex because it emphasized this filesystem rather than a polished VCS. In the last few years, the UI has been refined until it's as clean and easy to use as any system out there; but often, the stereotype lingers about the early Git UI that was complex and difficult to learn.

The content-addressable filesystem layer is amazingly cool, so I'll cover that first in this chapter; then, you'll learn about the transport mechanisms and the repository maintenance tasks that you may eventually have to deal with.

Plumbing and Porcelain

This book covers how to use Git with 30 or so verbs such as `checkout`, `branch`, `remote`, and so on. But because Git was initially a toolkit for a VCS rather than a full user-friendly VCS, it has a bunch of verbs that do low-level work and were designed to be chained together UNIX style or called from scripts. These commands are generally referred to as *plumbing commands*, and the more user-friendly commands are called *porcelain commands*.

The book's first eight chapters deal almost exclusively with porcelain commands. But in this chapter, you'll be dealing mostly with the lower-level plumbing commands, because they give you access to the inner workings of Git and help demonstrate how and why Git does what it does. These commands aren't meant to be used manually on the command line, but rather to be used as building blocks for new tools and custom scripts.

When you run `git init` in a new or existing directory, Git creates the `.git` directory, which is where almost everything that Git stores and manipulates is located. If you want to back up or clone your repository, copying this single directory elsewhere gives you nearly everything you need. This entire chapter basically deals with the stuff in this directory. Here's what it looks like:

```
$ ls
HEAD
branches/
config
description
hooks/
index
info/
objects/
refs/
```

You may see some other files in there, but this is a fresh `git init` repository—it's what you see by default. The `branches` directory isn't used by newer Git versions, and the `description` file is only used by the GitWeb program, so don't worry about those. The `config` file contains your project-specific configuration options, and the `info` directory keeps a global exclude file for ignored patterns that you don't want to track in a `.gitignore` file. The `hooks` directory contains your client- or server-side hook scripts, which are discussed in detail in Chapter 6.

This leaves four important entries: the `HEAD` and `index` files and the `objects` and `refs` directories. These are the core parts of Git. The `objects` directory stores all the content for your database, the `refs` directory stores pointers into commit objects in that data (branches), the `HEAD` file points to the branch you currently have checked out, and the `index` file is where Git stores your staging area information. You'll now look at each of these sections in detail to see how Git operates.

Git Objects

Git is a content-addressable filesystem. Great. What does that mean?

It means that at the core of Git is a simple key-value data store. You can insert any kind of content into it, and it will give you back a key that you can use to retrieve the content again at any time. To demonstrate, you can use the plumbing command `hash-object`, which takes some data, stores it in your `.git` directory, and gives you back the key the data is stored as. First, you initialize a new Git repository and verify that there is nothing in the `objects` directory:

```
$ mkdir test
$ cd test
$ git init
Initialized empty Git repository in /tmp/test/.git/
$ find .git/objects
.git/objects
.git/objects/info
.git/objects/pack
$ find .git/objects -type f
$
```

Git has initialized the `objects` directory and created `pack` and `info` subdirectories in it, but there are no regular files. Now, store some text in your Git database:

```
$ echo 'test content' | git hash-object -w --stdin
d670460b4b4aece5915caf5c68d12f560a9fe3e4
```

The `-w` tells `hash-object` to store the object; otherwise, the command simply tells you what the key would be. `--stdin` tells the command to read the content from stdin; if you don't specify this, `hash-object` expects the path to a file. The output from the command is a 40-character checksum hash. This is the SHA-1 hash—a checksum of the content you're storing plus a header, which you'll learn about in a bit. Now you can see how Git has stored your data:

```
$ find .git/objects -type f
.git/objects/d6/70460b4b4aece5915caf5c68d12f560a9fe3e4
```

You can see a file in the `objects` directory. This is how Git stores the content initially—as a single file per piece of content, named with the SHA-1 checksum of the content and its header. The subdirectory is named with the first 2 characters of the SHA, and the filename is the remaining 38 characters.

You can pull the content back out of Git with the `cat-file` command. This command is sort of a Swiss army knife for inspecting Git objects. Passing -p to it instructs the `cat-file` command to figure out the type of content and display it nicely for you:

```
$ git cat-file -p d670460b4b4aece5915caf5c68d12f560a9fe3e4
test content
```

Now, you can add content to Git and pull it back out again. You can also do this with content in files. For example, you can do some simple version control on a file. First, create a new file and save its contents in your database:

```
$ echo 'version 1' > test.txt
$ git hash-object -w test.txt
83baae61804e65cc73a7201a7252750c76066a30
```

Then, write some new content to the file, and save it again:

```
$ echo 'version 2' > test.txt
$ git hash-object -w test.txt
1f7a7a472abf3dd9643fd615f6da379c4acb3e3a
```

Your database contains the two new versions of the file as well as the first content you stored there:

```
$ find .git/objects -type f
.git/objects/1f/7a7a472abf3dd9643fd615f6da379c4acb3e3a
.git/objects/83/baae61804e65cc73a7201a7252750c76066a30
.git/objects/d6/70460b4b4aece5915caf5c68d12f560a9fe3e4
```

Now you can revert the file back to the first version:

```
$ git cat-file -p 83baae61804e65cc73a7201a7252750c76066a30 > test.txt
$ cat test.txt
version 1
```

or the second version:

```
$ git cat-file -p 1f7a7a472abf3dd9643fd615f6da379c4acb3e3a > test.txt
$ cat test.txt
version 2
```

But remembering the SHA-1 key for each version of your file isn't practical; plus, you aren't storing the filename in your system—just the content. This object type is called a *blob*. You can have Git tell you the object type of any object in Git, given its SHA-1 key, with cat-file -t:

```
$ git cat-file -t 1f7a7a472abf3dd9643fd615f6da379c4acb3e3a
blob
```

Tree Objects

The next type you'll look at is the tree object, which solves the problem of storing the filename and also allows you to store a group of files together. Git stores content in a manner similar to a UNIX filesystem, but a bit simplified. All the content is stored as tree and blob objects, with trees corresponding to UNIX directory entries and blobs corresponding more or less to inodes or file contents. A single tree object contains one or more tree entries, each of which contains an SHA-1 pointer to a blob or subtree with its associated mode, type, and filename. For example, the most recent tree in the simplegit project may look something like this:

```
$ git cat-file -p master^{tree}
100644 blob a906cb2a4a904a152e80877d4088654daad0c859      README
100644 blob 8f94139338f9404f26296befa88755fc2598c289      Rakefile
040000 tree 99f1a6d12cb4b6f19c8655fca46c3ecf317074e0      lib
```

The master^{tree} syntax specifies the tree object that is pointed to by the last commit on your master branch. Notice that the lib subdirectory isn't a blob but a pointer to another tree:

```
$ git cat-file -p 99f1a6d12cb4b6f19c8655fca46c3ecf317074e0
100644 blob 47c6340d6459e05787f644c2447d2595f5d3a54b      simplegit.rb
```

Conceptually, the data that Git is storing is something like Figure 9-1.

You can create your own tree. Git normally creates a tree by taking the state of your staging area or index and writing a tree object from it. So, to create a tree object, you first have to set up an index by staging some files. To create an index with a single entry—the first version of your text.txt file—you can use the plumbing command update-index. You use this command to artificially add the earlier version of the test.txt file to a new staging area. You must pass it the --add option because the file doesn't yet exist in your staging area (you don't even have a staging area set up yet) and --cacheinfo because the file you're adding isn't in your directory but is in your database. Then, you specify the mode, SHA-1, and filename:

```
$ git update-index --add --cacheinfo 100644 \
  83baae61804e65cc73a7201a7252750c76066a30 test.txt
```

In this case, you're specifying a mode of 100644, which means it's a normal file. Other options are 100755, which means it's an executable file; and 120000, which specifies a symbolic link. The mode is taken from normal UNIX modes but is much less flexible—these three modes are the only ones that are valid for files in Git (although other modes are used for directories and submodules).

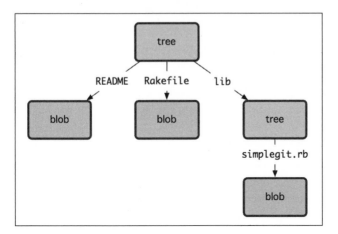

Figure 9-1. *Simple version of the Git data model*

Now, you can use the `write-tree` command to write the staging area out to a tree object. No -w option is needed—calling `write-tree` automatically creates a tree object from the state of the index if that tree doesn't yet exist:

```
$ git write-tree
d8329fc1cc938780ffdd9f94e0d364e0ea74f579
$ git cat-file -p d8329fc1cc938780ffdd9f94e0d364e0ea74f579
100644 blob 83baae61804e65cc73a7201a7252750c76066a30      test.txt
```

You can also verify that this is a tree object:

```
$ git cat-file -t d8329fc1cc938780ffdd9f94e0d364e0ea74f579
tree
```

You'll now create a new tree with the second version of test.txt and a new file as well:

```
$ echo 'new file' > new.txt
$ git update-index test.txt
$ git update-index --add new.txt
```

Your staging area now has the new version of test.txt as well as the new file new.txt. Write out that tree (recording the state of the staging area or index to a tree object) and see what it looks like:

```
$ git write-tree
0155eb4229851634a0f03eb265b69f5a2d56f341
$ git cat-file -p 0155eb4229851634a0f03eb265b69f5a2d56f341
100644 blob fa49b077972391ad58037050f2a75f74e3671e92      new.txt
100644 blob 1f7a7a472abf3dd9643fd615f6da379c4acb3e3a      test.txt
```

Notice that this tree has both file entries and also that the `test.txt` SHA is the version 2 SHA from earlier (1f7a7a). Just for fun, you'll add the first tree as a subdirectory into this one. You can read trees into your staging area by calling `read-tree`. In this case, you can read an existing tree into your staging area as a subtree by using the `--prefix` option to `read-tree`:

```
$ git read-tree --prefix=bak d8329fc1cc938780ffdd9f94e0d364e0ea74f579
$ git write-tree
3c4e9cd789d88d8d89c1073707c3585e41b0e614
$ git cat-file -p 3c4e9cd789d88d8d89c1073707c3585e41b0e614
040000 tree d8329fc1cc938780ffdd9f94e0d364e0ea74f579      bak
100644 blob fa49b077972391ad58037050f2a75f74e3671e92      new.txt
100644 blob 1f7a7a472abf3dd9643fd615f6da379c4acb3e3a      test.txt
```

If you created a working directory from the new tree you just wrote, you would get the two files in the top level of the working directory and a subdirectory named bak that contained the first version of the `test.txt` file. You can think of the data that Git contains for these structures as being like Figure 9-2.

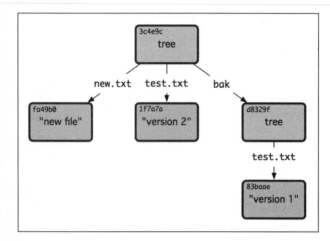

Figure 9-2. *The content structure of your current Git data*

Commit Objects

You have three trees that specify the different snapshots of your project that you want to track, but the earlier problem remains: you must remember all three SHA-1 values in order to recall the snapshots. You also don't have any information about who saved the snapshots, when they were saved, or why they were saved. This is the basic information that the commit object stores for you.

To create a commit object, you call `commit-tree` and specify a single tree SHA-1 and which commit objects, if any, directly preceded it. Start with the first tree you wrote:

```
$ echo 'first commit' | git commit-tree d8329f
fdf4fc3344e67ab068f836878b6c4951e3b15f3d
```

Now you can look at your new commit object with `cat-file`:

```
$ git cat-file -p fdf4fc3
tree d8329fc1cc938780ffdd9f94e0d364e0ea74f579
author Scott Chacon <schacon@gmail.com> 1243040974 -0700
committer Scott Chacon <schacon@gmail.com> 1243040974 -0700

first commit
```

The format for a commit object is simple: it specifies the top-level tree for the snapshot of the project at that point; the author/committer information pulled from your `user.name` and `user.email` configuration settings, with the current timestamp; a blank line, and then the commit message.

Next, you'll write the other two commit objects, each referencing the commit that came directly before it:

```
$ echo 'second commit' | git commit-tree 0155eb -p fdf4fc3
cac0cab538b970a37ea1e769cbbde608743bc96d
$ echo 'third commit'  | git commit-tree 3c4e9c -p cac0cab
1a410efbd13591db07496601ebc7a059dd55cfe9
```

Each of the three commit objects points to one of the three snapshot trees you created. Oddly enough, you have a real Git history now that you can view with the `git log` command, if you run it on the last commit SHA-1:

```
$ git log --stat 1a410e
commit 1a410efbd13591db07496601ebc7a059dd55cfe9
Author: Scott Chacon <schacon@gmail.com>
Date:   Fri May 22 18:15:24 2009 -0700

    third commit

 bak/test.txt |    1 +
 1 files changed, 1 insertions(+), 0 deletions(-)

commit cac0cab538b970a37ea1e769cbbde608743bc96d
Author: Scott Chacon <schacon@gmail.com>
Date:   Fri May 22 18:14:29 2009 -0700

    second commit

 new.txt  |    1 +
 test.txt |    2 +-
 2 files changed, 2 insertions(+), 1 deletions(-)

commit fdf4fc3344e67ab068f836878b6c4951e3b15f3d
Author: Scott Chacon <schacon@gmail.com>
Date:   Fri May 22 18:09:34 2009 -0700
```

```
    first commit

test.txt |    1 +
1 files changed, 1 insertions(+), 0 deletions(-)
```

Amazing. You've just done the low-level operations to build up a Git history without using any of the front ends. This is essentially what Git does when you run the `git add` and `git commit` commands—it stores blobs for the files that have changed, updates the index, writes out trees, and writes commit objects that reference the top-level trees and the commits that came immediately before them. These three main Git objects—the blob, the tree, and the commit— are initially stored as separate files in your `.git/objects` directory. Here are all the objects in the example directory now, commented with what they store:

```
$ find .git/objects -type f
.git/objects/01/55eb4229851634a0f03eb265b69f5a2d56f341 # tree 2
.git/objects/1a/410efbd13591db07496601ebc7a059dd55cfe9 # commit 3
.git/objects/1f/7a7a472abf3dd9643fd615f6da379c4acb3e3a # test.txt v2
.git/objects/3c/4e9cd789d88d8d89c1073707c3585e41b0e614 # tree 3
.git/objects/83/baae61804e65cc73a7201a7252750c76066a30 # test.txt v1
.git/objects/ca/c0cab538b970a37ea1e769cbbde608743bc96d # commit 2
.git/objects/d6/70460b4b4aece5915caf5c68d12f560a9fe3e4 # 'test content'
.git/objects/d8/329fc1cc938780ffdd9f94e0d364e0ea74f579 # tree 1
.git/objects/fa/49b077972391ad58037050f2a75f74e3671e92 # new.txt
.git/objects/fd/f4fc3344e67ab068f836878b6c4951e3b15f3d # commit 1
```

If you follow all the internal pointers, you get an object graph something like Figure 9-3.

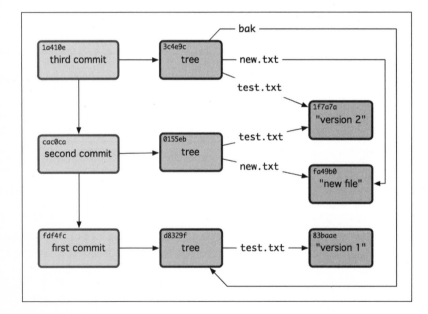

Figure 9-3. *All the objects in your Git directory*

Object Storage

I mentioned earlier that a header is stored with the content. Let's take a minute to look at how Git stores its objects. You'll see how to store a blob object—in this case, the string "what is up, doc?"—interactively in the Ruby scripting language. You can start up interactive Ruby mode with the `irb` command:

```
$ irb
>> content = "what is up, doc?"
=> "what is up, doc?"
```

Git constructs a header that starts with the type of the object, in this case a blob. Then, it adds a space followed by the size of the content and finally a null byte:

```
>> header = "blob #{content.length}\0"
=> "blob 16\000"
```

Git concatenates the header and the original content and then calculates the SHA-1 checksum of that new content. You can calculate the SHA-1 value of a string in Ruby by including the SHA1 digest library with the `require` command and then calling `Digest::SHA1.hexdigest()` with the string:

```
>> store = header + content
=> "blob 16\000what is up, doc?"
>> require 'digest/sha1'
=> true
>> sha1 = Digest::SHA1.hexdigest(store)
=> "bd9dbf5aae1a3862dd1526723246b20206e5fc37"
```

Git compresses the new content with zlib, which you can do in Ruby with the `zlib` library. First, you need to `require` the library and then run `Zlib::Deflate.deflate()` on the content:

```
>> require 'zlib'
=> true
>> zlib_content = Zlib::Deflate.deflate(store)
=> "x\234K\312\311OR04c(\317H,Q\310,V(-\320QH\3110\266\a\000 \034\a\235"
```

Finally, you'll write your zlib-deflated content to an object on disk. You'll determine the path of the object you want to write out (the first two characters of the SHA-1 value being the subdirectory name, and the last 38 characters being the filename within that directory). In Ruby, you can use the `FileUtils.mkdir_p()` function to create the subdirectory if it doesn't exist. Then, open the file with `File.open()` and write out the previously zlib-compressed content to the file with a `write()` call on the resulting file handle:

```
>> path = '.git/objects/' + sha1[0,2] + '/' + sha1[2,38]
=> ".git/objects/bd/9dbf5aae1a3862dd1526723246b20206e5fc37"
>> require 'fileutils'
=> true
>> FileUtils.mkdir_p(File.dirname(path))
=> ".git/objects/bd"
>> File.open(path, 'w') { |f| f.write zlib_content }
=> 32
```

That's it—you've created a valid Git blob object. All Git objects are stored the same way, just with different types—instead of the string blob, the header will begin with commit or tree. Also, although the blob content can be nearly anything, the commit and tree content are very specifically formatted.

Git References

You can run something like git log 1a410e to look through your whole history, but you still have to remember that 1a410e is the last commit in order to walk that history to find all those objects. You need a file in which you can store the SHA-1 value under a simple name so you can use that pointer rather than the raw SHA-1 value.

In Git, these are called *references* or *refs*; you can find the files that contain the SHA-1 values in the .git/refs directory. In the current project, this directory contains no files, but it does contain a simple structure:

```
$ find .git/refs
.git/refs
.git/refs/heads
.git/refs/tags
$ find .git/refs -type f
$
```

To create a new reference that will help you remember where your latest commit is, you can technically do something as simple as this:

```
$ echo "1a410efbd13591db07496601ebc7a059dd55cfe9" > .git/refs/heads/master
```

Now, you can use the head reference you just created instead of the SHA-1 value in your Git commands:

```
$ git log --pretty=oneline  master
1a410efbd13591db07496601ebc7a059dd55cfe9 third commit
cac0cab538b970a37ea1e769cbbde608743bc96d second commit
fdf4fc3344e67ab068f836878b6c4951e3b15f3d first commit
```

You aren't encouraged to directly edit the reference files. Git provides a safer command to do this if you want to update a reference called update-ref:

```
$ git update-ref refs/heads/master 1a410efbd13591db07496601ebc7a059dd55cfe9
```

That's basically what a branch in Git is: a simple pointer or reference to the head of a line of work. To create a branch back at the second commit, you can do this:

```
$ git update-ref refs/heads/test cac0ca
```

Your branch will contain only work from that commit down:

```
$ git log --pretty=oneline test
cac0cab538b970a37ea1e769cbbde608743bc96d second commit
fdf4fc3344e67ab068f836878b6c4951e3b15f3d first commit
```

Now, your Git database conceptually looks something like Figure 9-4.

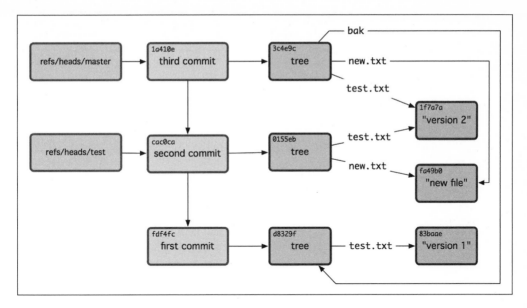

Figure 9-4. *Git directory objects with branch head references included*

When you run commands like git branch (*branchname*), Git basically runs that update-ref command to add the SHA-1 of the last commit of the branch you're on into whatever new reference you want to create.

The HEAD

The question now is, when you run git branch (*branchname*), how does Git know the SHA-1 of the last commit? The answer is the HEAD file. The HEAD file is a symbolic reference to the branch you're currently on. By *symbolic reference*, I mean that unlike a normal reference, it doesn't generally contain a SHA-1 value but rather a pointer to another reference. If you look at the file, you'll normally see something like this:

```
$ cat .git/HEAD
ref: refs/heads/master
```

If you run git checkout test, Git updates the file to look like this:

```
$ cat .git/HEAD
ref: refs/heads/test
```

When you run git commit, it creates the commit object, specifying the parent of that commit object to be whatever SHA-1 value the reference in HEAD points to.

You can also manually edit this file, but again a safer command exists to do so: symbolic-ref. You can read the value of your HEAD via this command:

```
$ git symbolic-ref HEAD
refs/heads/master
```

You can also set the value of HEAD:

```
$ git symbolic-ref HEAD refs/heads/test
$ cat .git/HEAD
ref: refs/heads/test
```

You can't set a symbolic reference outside of the refs style:

```
$ git symbolic-ref HEAD test
fatal: Refusing to point HEAD outside of refs/
```

Tags

You've just gone over Git's three main object types, but there is a fourth. The tag object is very much like a commit object—it contains a tagger, a date, a message, and a pointer. The main difference is that a tag object points to a commit rather than a tree. It's like a branch reference, but it never moves—it always points to the same commit but gives it a friendlier name.

As discussed in Chapter 2, there are two types of tags: annotated and lightweight. You can make a lightweight tag by running something like this:

```
$ git update-ref refs/tags/v1.0 cac0cab538b970a37ea1e769cbbde608743bc96d
```

That is all a lightweight tag is—a branch that never moves. An annotated tag is more complex, however. If you create an annotated tag, Git creates a tag object and then writes a reference to point to it rather than directly to the commit. You can see this by creating an annotated tag (-a specifies that it's an annotated tag):

```
$ git tag -a v1.1 1a410efbd13591db07496601ebc7a059dd55cfe9 -m 'test tag'
```

Here's the object SHA-1 value it created:

```
$ cat .git/refs/tags/v1.1
9585191f37f7b0fb9444f35a9bf50de191beadc2
```

Now, run the cat-file command on that SHA-1 value:

```
$ git cat-file -p 9585191f37f7b0fb9444f35a9bf50de191beadc2
object 1a410efbd13591db07496601ebc7a059dd55cfe9
type commit
tag v1.1
tagger Scott Chacon <schacon@gmail.com> Sat May 23 16:48:58 2009 -0700

test tag
```

Notice that the object entry points to the commit SHA-1 value that you tagged. Also notice that it doesn't need to point to a commit; you can tag any Git object. In the Git source code, for example, the maintainer has added their GPG public key as a blob object and then tagged it. You can view the public key by running

```
$ git cat-file blob junio-gpg-pub
```

in the Git source code. The Linux kernel also has a non-commit-pointing tag object—the first tag created points to the initial tree of the import of the source code.

Remotes

The third type of reference that you'll see is a remote reference. If you add a remote and push to it, Git stores the value you last pushed to that remote for each branch in the refs/remotes directory. For instance, you can add a remote called origin and push your master branch to it:

```
$ git remote add origin git@github.com:schacon/simplegit-progit.git
$ git push origin master
Counting objects: 11, done.
Compressing objects: 100% (5/5), done.
Writing objects: 100% (7/7), 716 bytes, done.
Total 7 (delta 2), reused 4 (delta 1)
To git@github.com:schacon/simplegit-progit.git
   a11bef0..ca82a6d  master -> master
```

Then, you can see what the master branch on the origin remote was the last time you communicated with the server, by checking the refs/remotes/origin/master file:

```
$ cat .git/refs/remotes/origin/master
ca82a6dff817ec66f44342007202690a93763949
```

Remote references differ from branches (refs/heads references) mainly in that they can't be checked out. Git moves them around as bookmarks to the last known state of where those branches were on those servers.

Packfiles

Let's go back to the objects database for your test Git repository. At this point, you have 11 objects—4 blobs, 3 trees, 3 commits, and 1 tag:

```
$ find .git/objects -type f
.git/objects/01/55eb4229851634a0f03eb265b69f5a2d56f341 # tree 2
.git/objects/1a/410efbd13591db07496601ebc7a059dd55cfe9 # commit 3
.git/objects/1f/7a7a472abf3dd9643fd615f6da379c4acb3e3a # test.txt v2
.git/objects/3c/4e9cd789d88d8d89c1073707c3585e41b0e614 # tree 3
.git/objects/83/baae61804e65cc73a7201a7252750c76066a30 # test.txt v1
.git/objects/95/85191f37f7b0fb9444f35a9bf50de191beadc2 # tag
.git/objects/ca/c0cab538b970a37ea1e769cbbde608743bc96d # commit 2
.git/objects/d6/70460b4b4aece5915caf5c68d12f560a9fe3e4 # 'test content'
.git/objects/d8/329fc1cc938780ffdd9f94e0d364e0ea74f579 # tree 1
.git/objects/fa/49b077972391ad58037050f2a75f74e3671e92 # new.txt
.git/objects/fd/f4fc3344e67ab068f836878b6c4951e3b15f3d # commit 1
```

Git compresses the contents of these files with zlib, and you're not storing much, so all these files collectively take up only 925 bytes. You'll add some larger content to the repository to demonstrate an interesting feature of Git. Add the repo.rb file from the Grit library you worked with earlier—this is about a 12K source code file:

```
$ curl http://github.com/mojombo/grit/raw/master/lib/grit/repo.rb > repo.rb
$ git add repo.rb
$ git commit -m 'added repo.rb'
[master 484a592] added repo.rb
 3 files changed, 459 insertions(+), 2 deletions(-)
 delete mode 100644 bak/test.txt
 create mode 100644 repo.rb
 rewrite test.txt (100%)
```

If you look at the resulting tree, you can see the SHA-1 value your repo.rb file got for the blob object:

```
$ git cat-file -p master^{tree}
100644 blob fa49b077972391ad58037050f2a75f74e3671e92      new.txt
100644 blob 9bc1dc421dcd51b4ac296e3e5b6e2a99cf44391e      repo.rb
100644 blob e3f094f522629ae358806b17daf78246c27c007b      test.txt
```

You can then use git cat-file to see how big that object is:

```
$ git cat-file -s 9bc1dc421dcd51b4ac296e3e5b6e2a99cf44391e
12898
```

Now, modify that file a little, and see what happens:

```
$ echo '# testing' >> repo.rb
$ git commit -am 'modified repo a bit'
[master ab1afef] modified repo a bit
 1 files changed, 1 insertions(+), 0 deletions(-)
```

Check the tree created by that commit, and you see something interesting:

```
$ git cat-file -p master^{tree}
100644 blob fa49b077972391ad58037050f2a75f74e3671e92      new.txt
100644 blob 05408d195263d853f09dca71d55116663690c27c      repo.rb
100644 blob e3f094f522629ae358806b17daf78246c27c007b      test.txt
```

The blob is now a different blob, which means that although you added only a single line to the end of a 400-line file, Git stored that new content as a completely new object:

```
$ git cat-file -s 05408d195263d853f09dca71d55116663690c27c
12908
```

You have two nearly identical 12K objects on your disk. Wouldn't it be nice if Git could store one of them in full but then store the second object only as the delta between it and the first?

It turns out that it can. The initial format in which Git saves objects on disk is called a *loose object format*. However, occasionally Git packs up several of these objects into a single binary file called a *packfile* in order to save space and be more efficient. Git does this if you have too many loose objects around, if you run the `git gc` command manually, or if you push to a remote server. To see what happens, you can manually ask Git to pack up the objects by calling the `git gc` command:

```
$ git gc
Counting objects: 17, done.
Delta compression using 2 threads.
Compressing objects: 100% (13/13), done.
Writing objects: 100% (17/17), done.
Total 17 (delta 1), reused 10 (delta 0)
```

If you look in your `objects` directory, you'll find that most of your objects are gone, and a new pair of files has appeared:

```
$ find .git/objects -type f
.git/objects/71/08f7ecb345ee9d0084193f147cdad4d2998293
.git/objects/d6/70460b4b4aece5915caf5c68d12f560a9fe3e4
.git/objects/info/packs
.git/objects/pack/pack-7a16e4488ae40c7d2bc56ea2bd43e25212a66c45.idx
.git/objects/pack/pack-7a16e4488ae40c7d2bc56ea2bd43e25212a66c45.pack
```

The objects that remain are the blobs that aren't pointed to by any commit—in this case, the "what is up, doc?" example and the "test content" example blobs you created earlier. Because you never added them to any commits, they're considered dangling and aren't packed up in your new packfile.

The other files are your new packfile and an index. The packfile is a single file containing the contents of all the objects that were removed from your filesystem. The index is a file that contains offsets into that packfile so you can quickly seek to a specific object. What is cool is that although the objects on disk before you ran the gc were collectively about 12K in size, the new packfile is only 6K. You've halved your disk usage by packing your objects.

How does Git do this? When Git packs objects, it looks for files that are named and sized similarly, and stores just the deltas from one version of the file to the next. You can look into the packfile and see what Git did to save space. The `git verify-pack` plumbing command allows you to see what was packed up:

```
$ git verify-pack -v pack-7a16e4488ae40c7d2bc56ea2bd43e25212a66c45.idx
0155eb4229851634a0f03eb265b69f5a2d56f341 tree    71 76 5400
05408d195263d853f09dca71d55116663690c27c blob    12908 3478 874
09f01cea547666f58d6a8d809583841a7c6f0130 tree    106 107 5086
1a410efbd13591db07496601ebc7a059dd55cfe9 commit 225 151 322
1f7a7a472abf3dd9643fd615f6da379c4acb3e3a blob    10 19 5381
3c4e9cd789d88d8d89c1073707c3585e41b0e614 tree    101 105 5211
484a59275031909e19aadb7c92262719cfcdf19a commit 226 153 169
83baae61804e65cc73a7201a7252750c76066a30 blob    10 19 5362
9585191f37f7b0fb9444f35a9bf50de191beadc2 tag     136 127 5476
9bc1dc421dcd51b4ac296e3e5b6e2a99cf44391e blob    7 18 5193 1➡
05408d195263d853f09dca71d55116663690c27c
ab1afef80fac8e34258ff41fc1b867c702daa24b commit 232 157 12
cac0cab538b970a37ea1e769cbbde608743bc96d commit 226 154 473
```

```
d8329fc1cc938780ffdd9f94e0d364e0ea74f579 tree    36 46 5316
e3f094f522629ae358806b17daf78246c27c007b blob    1486 734 4352
f8f51d7d8a1760462eca26eebafde32087499533 tree    106 107 749
fa49b077972391ad58037050f2a75f74e3671e92 blob    9 18 856
fdf4fc3344e67ab068f836878b6c4951e3b15f3d commit 177 122 627
chain length = 1: 1 object
pack-7a16e4488ae40c7d2bc56ea2bd43e25212a66c45.pack: ok
```

Here, the 9bc1d blob, which if you remember was the first version of your repo.rb file, is referencing the 05408 blob, which was the second version of the file. The third column in the output is the size of the object in the pack, so you can see that 05408 takes up 12K of the file but that 9bc1d only takes up 7 bytes. What is also interesting is that the second version of the file is the one that is stored intact, whereas the original version is stored as a delta—this is because you're most likely to need faster access to the most recent version of the file.

The really nice thing about this is that it can be repacked at any time. Git will occasionally repack your database automatically, always trying to save more space. You can also manually repack at any time by running git gc by hand.

The Refspec

Throughout this book, you've used simple mappings from remote branches to local references; but they can be more complex.

Suppose you add a remote like this:

```
$ git remote add origin git@github.com:schacon/simplegit-progit.git
```

It adds a section to your .git/config file, specifying the name of the remote (origin), the URL of the remote repository, and the refspec for fetching:

```
[remote "origin"]
        url = git@github.com:schacon/simplegit-progit.git
        fetch = +refs/heads/*:refs/remotes/origin/*
```

The format of the refspec is an optional +, followed by <src>:<dst>, where <src> is the pattern for references on the remote side and <dst> is where those references will be written locally. The + tells Git to update the reference even if it isn't a fast-forward.

In the default case that is automatically written by a git remote add command, Git fetches all the references under refs/heads/ on the server and writes them to refs/remotes/origin/ locally. So, if there is a master branch on the server, you can access the log of that branch locally via

```
$ git log origin/master
$ git log remotes/origin/master
$ git log refs/remotes/origin/master
```

They're all equivalent, because Git expands each of them to refs/remotes/origin/master.

If you want Git instead to pull down only the master branch each time, and not every other branch on the remote server, you can change the fetch line to

```
fetch = +refs/heads/master:refs/remotes/origin/master
```

This is just the default refspec for `git fetch` for that remote. If you want to do something one time, you can specify the refspec on the command line, too. To pull the `master` branch on the remote down to `origin/mymaster` locally, you can run

```
$ git fetch origin master:refs/remotes/origin/mymaster
```

You can also specify multiple refspecs. On the command line, you can pull down several branches like so:

```
$ git fetch origin master:refs/remotes/origin/mymaster \
   topic:refs/remotes/origin/topic
From git@github.com:schacon/simplegit
 ! [rejected]        master     -> origin/mymaster  (non fast forward)
 * [new branch]      topic      -> origin/topic
```

In this case, the `master` branch pull was rejected because it wasn't a fast-forward reference. You can override that by specifying the + in front of the refspec.

You can also specify multiple refspecs for fetching in your configuration file. If you want to always fetch the `master` and `experiment` branches, add two lines:

```
[remote "origin"]
       url = git@github.com:schacon/simplegit-progit.git
       fetch = +refs/heads/master:refs/remotes/origin/master
       fetch = +refs/heads/experiment:refs/remotes/origin/experiment
```

You can't use partial globs in the pattern, so this would be invalid:

```
fetch = +refs/heads/qa*:refs/remotes/origin/qa*
```

However, you can use namespacing to accomplish something like that. If you have a QA team that pushes a series of branches, and you want to get the `master` branch and any of the QA team's branches but nothing else, you can use a config section like this:

```
[remote "origin"]
       url = git@github.com:schacon/simplegit-progit.git
       fetch = +refs/heads/master:refs/remotes/origin/master
       fetch = +refs/heads/qa/*:refs/remotes/origin/qa/*
```

If you have a complex workflow process that has a QA team pushing branches, developers pushing branches, and integration teams pushing and collaborating on remote branches, you can namespace them easily this way.

Pushing Refspecs

It's nice that you can fetch namespaced references that way, but how does the QA team get their branches into a `qa/` namespace in the first place? You accomplish that by using refspecs to push.

If the QA team wants to push their `master` branch to `qa/master` on the remote server, they can run

```
$ git push origin master:refs/heads/qa/master
```

If they want Git to do that automatically each time they run `git push origin`, they can add a push value to their config file:

```
[remote "origin"]
        url = git@github.com:schacon/simplegit-progit.git
        fetch = +refs/heads/*:refs/remotes/origin/*
        push = refs/heads/master:refs/heads/qa/master
```

Again, this will cause a `git push origin` to push the local `master` branch to the remote qa/master branch by default.

Deleting References

You can also use the refspec to delete references from the remote server by running something like this:

```
$ git push origin :topic
```

Because the refspec is `<src>:<dst>`, by leaving off the `<src>` part, this basically says to make the topic branch on the remote nothing, which deletes it.

Transfer Protocols

Git can transfer data between two repositories in two major ways: over HTTP and via the so-called smart protocols used in the `file://`, `ssh://`, and `git://` transports. This section will quickly cover how these two main protocols operate.

The Dumb Protocol

Git transport over HTTP is often referred to as the *dumb protocol* because it requires no Git-specific code on the server side during the transport process. The fetch process is a series of `GET` requests, where the client can assume the layout of the Git repository on the server. Let's follow the `http-fetch` process for the `simplegit` library:

```
$ git clone http://github.com/schacon/simplegit-progit.git
```

The first thing this command does is pull down the `info/refs` file. This file is written by the `update-server-info` command, which is why you need to enable that as a post-receive hook in order for the HTTP transport to work properly:

```
=> GET info/refs
ca82a6dff817ec66f44342007202690a93763949        refs/heads/master
```

Now you have a list of the remote references and SHAs. Next, you look for what the `HEAD` reference is so you know what to check out when you're finished:

```
=> GET HEAD
ref: refs/heads/master
```

You need to check out the `master` branch when you've completed the process.

At this point, you're ready to start the walking process. Because your starting point is the ca82a6 commit object you saw in the info/refs file, you start by fetching that:

```
=> GET objects/ca/82a6dff817ec66f44342007202690a93763949
(179 bytes of binary data)
```

You get an object back—that object is in loose format on the server, and you fetched it over a static HTTP GET request. You can zlib-uncompress it, strip off the header, and look at the commit content:

```
$ git cat-file -p ca82a6dff817ec66f44342007202690a93763949
tree cfda3bf379e4f8dba8717dee55aab78aef7f4daf
parent 085bb3bcb608e1e8451d4b2432f8ecbe6306e7e7
author Scott Chacon <schacon@gmail.com> 1205815931 -0700
committer Scott Chacon <schacon@gmail.com> 1240030591 -0700

changed the version number
```

Next, you have two more objects to retrieve—cfda3b, which is the tree of content that the commit you just retrieved points to, and 085bb3, which is the parent commit:

```
=> GET objects/08/5bb3bcb608e1e8451d4b2432f8ecbe6306e7e7
(179 bytes of data)
```

That gives you your next commit object. Grab the tree object:

```
=> GET objects/cf/da3bf379e4f8dba8717dee55aab78aef7f4daf
(404 - Not Found)
```

Oops—it looks like that tree object isn't in loose format on the server, so you get a 404 response back. There are a couple of reasons for this—the object could be in an alternate repository, or it could be in a packfile in this repository. Git checks for any listed alternates first:

```
=> GET objects/info/http-alternates
(empty file)
```

If this comes back with a list of alternate URLs, Git checks for loose files and packfiles there—this is a nice mechanism for projects that are forks of one another to share objects on disk. However, because no alternates are listed in this case, your object must be in a packfile. To see what packfiles are available on this server, you need to get the objects/info/packs file, which contains a listing of them (also generated by update-server-info):

```
=> GET objects/info/packs
P pack-816a9b2334da9953e530f27bcac22082a9f5b835.pack
```

There is only one packfile on the server, so your object is obviously in there, but you'll check the index file to make sure. This is also useful if you have multiple packfiles on the server, so you can see which packfile contains the object you need:

```
=> GET objects/pack/pack-816a9b2334da9953e530f27bcac22082a9f5b835.idx
(4k of binary data)
```

Now that you have the packfile index, you can see if your object is in it—because the index lists the SHAs of the objects contained in the packfile and the offsets to those objects. Your object is there, so go ahead and get the whole packfile:

```
=> GET objects/pack/pack-816a9b2334da9953e530f27bcac22082a9f5b835.pack
(13k of binary data)
```

You have your tree object, so you continue walking your commits. They're all also within the packfile you just downloaded, so you don't have to do any more requests to your server. Git checks out a working copy of the master branch that was pointed to by the HEAD reference you downloaded at the beginning.

The entire output of this process looks like this:

```
$ git clone http://github.com/schacon/simplegit-progit.git
Initialized empty Git repository in /private/tmp/simplegit-progit/.git/
got ca82a6dff817ec66f44342007202690a93763949
walk ca82a6dff817ec66f44342007202690a93763949
got 085bb3bcb608e1e8451d4b2432f8ecbe6306e7e7
Getting alternates list for http://github.com/schacon/simplegit-progit.git
Getting pack list for http://github.com/schacon/simplegit-progit.git
Getting index for pack 816a9b2334da9953e530f27bcac22082a9f5b835
Getting pack 816a9b2334da9953e530f27bcac22082a9f5b835
 which contains cfda3bf379e4f8dba8717dee55aab78aef7f4daf
walk 085bb3bcb608e1e8451d4b2432f8ecbe6306e7e7
walk a11bef06a3f659402fe7563abf99ad00de2209e6
```

The Smart Protocol

The HTTP method is simple but a bit inefficient. Using smart protocols is a more common method of transferring data. These protocols have a process on the remote end that is intelligent about Git—it can read local data and figure out what the client has or needs and generate custom data for it. There are two sets of processes for transferring data: a pair for uploading data and a pair for downloading data.

Uploading Data

To upload data to a remote process, Git uses the send-pack and receive-pack processes. The send-pack process runs on the client and connects to a receive-pack process on the remote side.

For example, say you run git push origin master in your project, and origin is defined as a URL that uses the SSH protocol. Git fires up the send-pack process, which initiates a connection over SSH to your server. It tries to run a command on the remote server via an SSH call that looks something like this:

```
$ ssh -x git@github.com "git-receive-pack 'schacon/simplegit-progit.git'"
005bca82a6dff817ec66f4437202690a93763949 refs/heads/master report-status delete-refs
003e085bb3bcb608e1e84b2432f8ecbe6306e7e7 refs/heads/topic
0000
```

The `git-receive-pack` command immediately responds with one line for each reference it currently has—in this case, just the `master` branch and its SHA. The first line also has a list of the server's capabilities (here, `report-status` and `delete-refs`).

Each line starts with a 4-byte hex value specifying how long the rest of the line is. Your first line starts with 005b, which is 91 in hex, meaning that 91 bytes remain on that line. The next line starts with 003e, which is 62, so you read the remaining 62 bytes. The next line is 0000, meaning the server is done with its references listing.

Now that it knows the server's state, your `send-pack` process determines what commits it has that the server doesn't. For each reference that this push will update, the `send-pack` process tells the `receive-pack` process that information. For instance, if you're updating the `master` branch and adding an `experiment` branch, the `send-pack` response may look something like this:

```
0085ca82a6dff817ec66f44342007202690a93763949 \
  15027957951b64cf874c3557a0f3547bd83b3ff6 refs/heads/master report-status
0067000000000000000000000000000000000000000000 \
  cdfdb42577e2506715f8cfeacdbabc092bf63e8d refs/heads/experiment
0000
```

The SHA-1 value of all 0s means that nothing was there before—because you're adding the `experiment` reference. If you were deleting a reference, you would see the opposite: all 0s on the right side.

Git sends a line for each reference you're updating with the old SHA, the new SHA, and the reference that is being updated. The first line also has the client's capabilities. Next, the client uploads a packfile of all the objects the server doesn't have yet. Finally, the server responds with a success (or failure) indication:

```
000Aunpack ok
```

Downloading Data

When you download data, the `fetch-pack` and `upload-pack` processes are involved. The client initiates a `fetch-pack` process that connects to an `upload-pack` process on the remote side to negotiate what data will be transferred down.

There are different ways to initiate the `upload-pack` process on the remote repository. You can run via SSH in the same manner as the `receive-pack` process. You can also initiate the process via the Git daemon, which listens on a server on port 9418 by default. The `fetch-pack` process sends data that looks like this to the daemon after connecting:

```
003fgit-upload-pack schacon/simplegit-progit.git\0host=myserver.com\0
```

It starts with the 4 bytes specifying how much data is following, then the command to run followed by a null byte, and then the server's hostname followed by a final null byte. The Git daemon checks that the command can be run and that the repository exists and has public permissions. If everything is cool, it fires up the `upload-pack` process and hands off the request to it.

If you're doing the fetch over SSH, `fetch-pack` instead runs something like this:

```
$ ssh -x git@github.com "git-upload-pack 'schacon/simplegit-progit.git'"
```

In either case, after `fetch-pack` connects, `upload-pack` sends back something like this:

```
0088ca82a6dff817ec66f44342007202690a93763949 HEAD\0multi_ack thin-pack \
  side-band side-band-64k ofs-delta shallow no-progress include-tag
003fca82a6dff817ec66f44342007202690a93763949 refs/heads/master
003e085bb3bcb608e1e8451d4b2432f8ecbe6306e7e7 refs/heads/topic
0000
```

This is very similar to what `receive-pack` responds with, but the capabilities are different. In addition, it sends back the HEAD reference so the client knows what to check out if this is a clone.

At this point, the `fetch-pack` process looks at what objects it has and responds with the objects that it needs by sending "want" and then the SHA it wants. It sends all the objects it already has with "have" and then the SHA. At the end of this list, it writes "done" to initiate the `upload-pack` process to begin sending the packfile of the data it needs:

```
0054want ca82a6dff817ec66f44342007202690a93763949 ofs-delta
0032have 085bb3bcb608e1e8451d4b2432f8ecbe6306e7e7
0000
0009done
```

That is a very basic case of the transfer protocols. In more complex cases, the client supports `multi_ack` or `side-band` capabilities; but this example shows you the basic back and forth used by the smart protocol processes.

Maintenance and Data Recovery

Occasionally, you may have to do some cleanup—make a repository more compact, clean up an imported repository, or recover lost work. This section will cover some of these scenarios.

Maintenance

Occasionally, Git automatically runs a command called `auto gc`. Most of the time, this command does nothing. However, if there are too many loose objects (objects not in a packfile) or too many packfiles, Git launches a full-fledged `git gc` command. The gc stands for *garbage collect*, and the command does a number of things: it gathers up all the loose objects and places them in packfiles, it consolidates packfiles into one big packfile, and it removes objects that aren't reachable from any commit and are a few months old.

You can run `auto gc` manually as follows:

```
$ git gc --auto
```

Again, this generally does nothing. You must have around 7,000 loose objects or more than 50 packfiles for Git to fire up a real gc command. You can modify these limits with the `gc.auto` and `gc.autopacklimit` config settings, respectively.

The other thing gc will do is pack up your references into a single file. Suppose your repository contains the following branches and tags:

```
$ find .git/refs -type f
.git/refs/heads/experiment
```

```
.git/refs/heads/master
.git/refs/tags/v1.0
.git/refs/tags/v1.1
```

If you run git gc, you'll no longer have these files in the refs directory. Git will move them for the sake of efficiency into a file named .git/packed-refs that looks like this:

```
$ cat .git/packed-refs
# pack-refs with: peeled
cac0cab538b970a37ea1e769cbbde608743bc96d refs/heads/experiment
ab1afef80fac8e34258ff41fc1b867c702daa24b refs/heads/master
cac0cab538b970a37ea1e769cbbde608743bc96d refs/tags/v1.0
9585191f37f7b0fb9444f35a9bf50de191beadc2 refs/tags/v1.1
^1a410efbd13591db07496601ebc7a059dd55cfe9
```

If you update a reference, Git doesn't edit this file but instead writes a new file to refs/heads. To get the appropriate SHA for a given reference, Git checks for that reference in the refs directory and then checks the packed-refs file as a fallback. However, if you can't find a reference in the refs directory, it's probably in your packed-refs file.

Notice the last line of the file, which begins with a ^. This means the tag directly above is an annotated tag and that line is the commit that the annotated tag points to.

Data Recovery

At some point in your Git journey, you may accidentally lose a commit. Generally, this happens because you force-delete a branch that had work on it, and it turns out you wanted the branch after all; or you hard-reset a branch, thus abandoning commits that you wanted something from. Assuming this happens, how can you get your commits back?

Here's an example that hard-resets the master branch in your test repository to an older commit and then recovers the lost commits. First, let's review where your repository is at this point:

```
$ git log --pretty=oneline
ab1afef80fac8e34258ff41fc1b867c702daa24b modified repo a bit
484a59275031909e19aadb7c92262719cfcdf19a added repo.rb
1a410efbd13591db07496601ebc7a059dd55cfe9 third commit
cac0cab538b970a37ea1e769cbbde608743bc96d second commit
fdf4fc3344e67ab068f836878b6c4951e3b15f3d first commit
```

Now, move the master branch back to the middle commit:

```
$ git reset --hard 1a410efbd13591db07496601ebc7a059dd55cfe9
HEAD is now at 1a410ef third commit
$ git log --pretty=oneline
1a410efbd13591db07496601ebc7a059dd55cfe9 third commit
cac0cab538b970a37ea1e769cbbde608743bc96d second commit
fdf4fc3344e67ab068f836878b6c4951e3b15f3d first commit
```

You've effectively lost the top two commits—you have no branch from which those commits are reachable. You need to find the latest commit SHA and then add a branch that points to it. The trick is finding that latest commit SHA—it's not like you've memorized it, right?

Often, the quickest way is to use a tool called `git reflog`. As you're working, Git silently records what your `HEAD` is every time you change it. Each time you commit or change branches, the reflog is updated. The reflog is also updated by the `git update-ref` command, which is another reason to use it instead of just writing the SHA value to your ref files, as you learned in the "Git References" section of this chapter. You can see where you've been at any time by running `git reflog`:

```
$ git reflog
1a410ef HEAD@{0}: 1a410efbd13591db07496601ebc7a059dd55cfe9: updating HEAD
ab1afef HEAD@{1}: ab1afef80fac8e34258ff41fc1b867c702daa24b: updating HEAD
```

Here you can see the two commits you checked out, but there isn't much information. To see the same information in a much more useful way, you can run `git log -g`, which provides normal `log` output for your reflog:

```
$ git log -g
commit 1a410efbd13591db07496601ebc7a059dd55cfe9
Reflog: HEAD@{0} (Scott Chacon <schacon@gmail.com>)
Reflog message: updating HEAD
Author: Scott Chacon <schacon@gmail.com>
Date:   Fri May 22 18:22:37 2009 -0700

    third commit

commit ab1afef80fac8e34258ff41fc1b867c702daa24b
Reflog: HEAD@{1} (Scott Chacon <schacon@gmail.com>)
Reflog message: updating HEAD
Author: Scott Chacon <schacon@gmail.com>
Date:   Fri May 22 18:15:24 2009 -0700

    modified repo a bit
```

It looks like the bottom commit is the one you lost, so you can recover it by creating a new branch at that commit. For example, you can start a branch named `recover-branch` at that commit (ab1afef):

```
$ git branch recover-branch ab1afef
$ git log --pretty=oneline recover-branch
ab1afef80fac8e34258ff41fc1b867c702daa24b modified repo a bit
484a59275031909e19aadb7c92262719cfcdf19a added repo.rb
1a410efbd13591db07496601ebc7a059dd55cfe9 third commit
cac0cab538b970a37ea1e769cbbde608743bc96d second commit
fdf4fc3344e67ab068f836878b6c4951e3b15f3d first commit
```

Cool—now you have a branch named `recover-branch` that is where your `master` branch used to be, making the first two commits reachable again.

Next, suppose your loss was for some reason not in the reflog—you can simulate that by removing recover-branch and deleting the reflog. Now the first two commits aren't reachable by anything:

```
$ git branch -D recover-branch
$ rm -Rf .git/logs/
```

Because the reflog data is kept in the .git/logs/ directory, you effectively have no reflog. How can you recover that commit at this point? One way is to use the git fsck utility, which checks your database for integrity. If you run it with the --full option, it shows you all objects that aren't pointed to by another object:

```
$ git fsck --full
dangling blob d670460b4b4aece5915caf5c68d12f560a9fe3e4
dangling commit ab1afef80fac8e34258ff41fc1b867c702daa24b
dangling tree aea790b9a58f6cf6f2804eeac9f0abbe9631e4c9
dangling blob 7108f7ecb345ee9d0084193f147cdad4d2998293
```

In this case, you can see your missing commit after the dangling commit. You can recover it the same way, by adding a branch that points to that SHA.

Removing Objects

There are a lot of great things about Git, but one feature that can cause issues is the fact that a Git clone downloads the entire history of the project, including every version of every file. This is fine if the whole thing is source code, because Git is highly optimized to compress that data efficiently. However, if someone at any point in the history of your project added a single huge file, every clone for all time will be forced to download that large file, even if it was removed from the project in the very next commit. Because it's reachable from the history, it will always be there.

This can be a huge problem when you're converting Subversion or Perforce repositories into Git. Because you don't download the whole history in those systems, this type of addition carries few consequences. If you did an import from another system or otherwise find that your repository is much larger than it should be, here is how you can find and remove large objects.

Be warned: this technique is destructive to your commit history. It rewrites every commit object downstream from the earliest tree you have to modify to remove a large file reference. If you do this immediately after an import, before anyone has started to base work on the commit, you're fine—otherwise, you have to notify all contributors that they must rebase their work onto your new commits.

To demonstrate, you'll add a large file into your test repository, remove it in the next commit, find it, and remove it permanently from the repository. First, add a large object to your history:

```
$ curl http://kernel.org/pub/software/scm/git/git-1.6.3.1.tar.bz2 > git.tbz2
$ git add git.tbz2
$ git commit -am 'added git tarball'
[master 6df7640] added git tarball
 1 files changed, 0 insertions(+), 0 deletions(-)
 create mode 100644 git.tbz2
```

Oops—you didn't want to add a huge tarball to your project. Better get rid of it:

```
$ git rm git.tbz2
rm 'git.tbz2'
$ git commit -m 'oops - removed large tarball'
[master da3f30d] oops - removed large tarball
 1 files changed, 0 insertions(+), 0 deletions(-)
 delete mode 100644 git.tbz2
```

Now, gc your database and see how much space you're using:

```
$ git gc
Counting objects: 21, done.
Delta compression using 2 threads.
Compressing objects: 100% (16/16), done.
Writing objects: 100% (21/21), done.
Total 21 (delta 3), reused 15 (delta 1)
```

You can run the count-objects command to quickly see how much space you're using:

```
$ git count-objects -v
count: 4
size: 16
in-pack: 21
packs: 1
size-pack: 2016
prune-packable: 0
garbage: 0
```

The size-pack entry is the size of your packfiles in kilobytes, so you're using 2MB. Before the last commit, you were using closer to 2K—clearly, removing the file from the previous commit didn't remove it from your history. Every time anyone clones this repository, they will have to clone all 2MB just to get this tiny project, because you accidentally added a big file. Let's get rid of it.

First you have to find it. In this case, you already know what file it is. But suppose you didn't; how would you identify what file or files were taking up so much space? If you run git gc, all the objects are in a packfile; you can identify the big objects by running another plumbing command called git verify-pack and sorting on the third field in the output, which is file size. You can also pipe it through the tail command because you're only interested in the last few largest files:

```
$ git verify-pack -v .git/objects/pack/pack-3f8c0...bb.idx | sort -k 3 -n | tail -3
e3f094f522629ae358806b17daf78246c27c007b blob   1486 734 4667
05408d195263d853f09dca71d55116663690c27c blob   12908 3478 1189
7a9eb2fba2b1811321254ac360970fc169ba2330 blob   2056716 2056872 5401
```

The big object is at the bottom: 2MB. To find out what file it is, you'll use the rev-list command, which you used briefly in Chapter 7. If you pass --objects to rev-list, it lists all the commit SHAs and also the blob SHAs with the file paths associated with them. You can use this to find your blob's name:

```
$ git rev-list --objects --all | grep 7a9eb2fb
7a9eb2fba2b1811321254ac360970fc169ba2330 git.tbz2
```

Now, you need to remove this file from all trees in your past. You can easily see what commits modified this file:

```
$ git log --pretty=oneline -- git.tbz2
da3f30d019005479c99eb4c3406225613985a1db oops - removed large tarball
6df764092f3e7c8f5f94cbe08ee5cf42e92a0289 added git tarball
```

You must rewrite all the commits downstream from 6df76 to fully remove this file from your Git history. To do so, you use filter-branch, which you used in Chapter 6:

```
$ git filter-branch --index-filter \
   'git rm --cached --ignore-unmatch git.tbz2' -- 6df7640^..
Rewrite 6df764092f3e7c8f5f94cbe08ee5cf42e92a0289 (1/2)rm 'git.tbz2'
Rewrite da3f30d019005479c99eb4c3406225613985a1db (2/2)
Ref 'refs/heads/master' was rewritten
```

The --index-filter option is similar to the --tree-filter option used in Chapter 6, except that instead of passing a command that modifies files checked out on disk, you're modifying your staging area or index each time. Rather than remove a specific file with something like rm file, you have to remove it with git rm --cached—you must remove it from the index, not from disk. The reason to do it this way is speed—because Git doesn't have to check out each revision to disk before running your filter, the process can be much, much faster. You can accomplish the same task with --tree-filter if you want. The --ignore-unmatch option to git rm tells it not to error out if the pattern you're trying to remove isn't there. Finally, you ask filter-branch to rewrite your history only from the 6df7640 commit up, because you know that is where this problem started. Otherwise, it will start from the beginning and will unnecessarily take longer.

Your history no longer contains a reference to that file. However, your reflog and a new set of refs that Git added when you did the filter-branch under .git/refs/original still do, so you have to remove them and then repack the database. You need to get rid of anything that has a pointer to those old commits before you repack:

```
$ rm -Rf .git/refs/original
$ rm -Rf .git/logs/
$ git gc
Counting objects: 19, done.
Delta compression using 2 threads.
Compressing objects: 100% (14/14), done.
Writing objects: 100% (19/19), done.
Total 19 (delta 3), reused 16 (delta 1)
```

Let's see how much space you saved:

```
$ git count-objects -v
count: 8
size: 2040
in-pack: 19
packs: 1
```

```
size-pack: 7
prune-packable: 0
garbage: 0
```

The packed repository size is down to 7K, which is much better than 2MB. You can see from the size value that the big object is still in your loose objects, so it's not gone; but it won't be transferred on a push or subsequent clone, which is what's important. If you really wanted to, you could remove the object completely by running git prune --expire.

Summary

You should have a pretty good understanding of what Git does in the background and, to some degree, how it's implemented. This chapter has covered a number of plumbing commands—commands that are lower level and simpler than the porcelain commands you've learned about in the rest of the book. Understanding how Git works at a lower level should make it easier to understand why it's doing what it's doing and also to write your own tools and helping scripts to make your specific workflow work for you.

Git as a content-addressable filesystem is a very powerful tool that you can easily use as more than just a VCS. I hope you can use your newfound knowledge of Git internals to implement your own cool application of this technology and feel more comfortable using Git in more advanced ways.

■ ■ ■

Creative Commons Legal Code

Attribution-NonCommercial-ShareAlike 3.0 Unported

Reprinted from http://creativecommons.org/licenses/by-nc-sa/3.0/legalcode

License

THE WORK (AS DEFINED BELOW) IS PROVIDED UNDER THE TERMS OF THIS CREATIVE COMMONS PUBLIC LICENSE ("CCPL" OR "LICENSE"). THE WORK IS PROTECTED BY COPYRIGHT AND/OR OTHER APPLICABLE LAW. ANY USE OF THE WORK OTHER THAN AS AUTHORIZED UNDER THIS LICENSE OR COPYRIGHT LAW IS PROHIBITED.

BY EXERCISING ANY RIGHTS TO THE WORK PROVIDED HERE, YOU ACCEPT AND AGREE TO BE BOUND BY THE TERMS OF THIS LICENSE. TO THE EXTENT THIS LICENSE MAY BE CONSIDERED TO BE A CONTRACT, THE LICENSOR GRANTS YOU THE RIGHTS CONTAINED HERE IN CONSIDERATION OF YOUR ACCEPTANCE OF SUCH TERMS AND CONDITIONS.

1. **Definitions**

    a. **"Adaptation"** means a work based upon the Work, or upon the Work and other pre-existing works, such as a translation, adaptation, derivative work, arrangement of music or other alterations of a literary or artistic work, or phonogram or performance and includes cinematographic adaptations or any other form in which the Work may be recast, transformed, or adapted including in any form recognizably derived from the original, except that a work that constitutes a Collection will not be considered an Adaptation for the purpose of this License. For the avoidance of doubt, where the Work is a musical work, performance or phonogram, the synchronization of the Work in timed-relation with a moving image ("synching") will be considered an Adaptation for the purpose of this License.

b. **"Collection"** means a collection of literary or artistic works, such as encyclopedias and anthologies, or performances, phonograms or broadcasts, or other works or subject matter other than works listed in Section 1(g) below, which, by reason of the selection and arrangement of their contents, constitute intellectual creations, in which the Work is included in its entirety in unmodified form along with one or more other contributions, each constituting separate and independent works in themselves, which together are assembled into a collective whole. A work that constitutes a Collection will not be considered an Adaptation (as defined above) for the purposes of this License.

c. **"Distribute"** means to make available to the public the original and copies of the Work or Adaptation, as appropriate, through sale or other transfer of ownership.

d. **"License Elements"** means the following high-level license attributes as selected by Licensor and indicated in the title of this License: Attribution, Noncommercial, ShareAlike.

e. **"Licensor"** means the individual, individuals, entity or entities that offer(s) the Work under the terms of this License.

f. **"Original Author"** means, in the case of a literary or artistic work, the individual, individuals, entity or entities who created the Work or if no individual or entity can be identified, the publisher; and in addition (i) in the case of a performance the actors, singers, musicians, dancers, and other persons who act, sing, deliver, declaim, play in, interpret or otherwise perform literary or artistic works or expressions of folklore; (ii) in the case of a phonogram the producer being the person or legal entity who first fixes the sounds of a performance or other sounds; and, (iii) in the case of broadcasts, the organization that transmits the broadcast.

g. **"Work"** means the literary and/or artistic work offered under the terms of this License including without limitation any production in the literary, scientific and artistic domain, whatever may be the mode or form of its expression including digital form, such as a book, pamphlet and other writing; a lecture, address, sermon or other work of the same nature; a dramatic or dramatico-musical work; a choreographic work or entertainment in dumb show; a musical composition with or without words; a cinematographic work to which are assimilated works expressed by a process analogous to cinematography; a work of drawing, painting, architecture, sculpture, engraving or lithography; a photographic work to which are assimilated works expressed by a process analogous to photography; a work of applied art; an illustration, map, plan, sketch or three-dimensional work relative to geography, topography, architecture or science; a performance; a broadcast; a phonogram; a compilation of data to the extent it is protected as a copyrightable work; or a work performed by a variety or circus performer to the extent it is not otherwise considered a literary or artistic work.

h. **"You"** means an individual or entity exercising rights under this License who has not previously violated the terms of this License with respect to the Work, or who has received express permission from the Licensor to exercise rights under this License despite a previous violation.

i. **"Publicly Perform"** means to perform public recitations of the Work and to communicate to the public those public recitations, by any means or process, including by wire or wireless means or public digital performances; to make available to the public Works in such a way that members of the public may access these Works from a place and at a place individually chosen by them; to perform the Work to the public by any means or process and the communication to the public of the performances of the Work, including by public digital performance; to broadcast and rebroadcast the Work by any means including signs, sounds or images.

j. **"Reproduce"** means to make copies of the Work by any means including without limitation by sound or visual recordings and the right of fixation and reproducing fixations of the Work, including storage of a protected performance or phonogram in digital form or other electronic medium.

2. **Fair Dealing Rights.** Nothing in this License is intended to reduce, limit, or restrict any uses free from copyright or rights arising from limitations or exceptions that are provided for in connection with the copyright protection under copyright law or other applicable laws.

3. **License Grant.** Subject to the terms and conditions of this License, Licensor hereby grants You a worldwide, royalty-free, non-exclusive, perpetual (for the duration of the applicable copyright) license to exercise the rights in the Work as stated below:

   a. to Reproduce the Work, to incorporate the Work into one or more Collections, and to Reproduce the Work as incorporated in the Collections;

   b. to create and Reproduce Adaptations provided that any such Adaptation, including any translation in any medium, takes reasonable steps to clearly label, demarcate or otherwise identify that changes were made to the original Work. For example, a translation could be marked "The original work was translated from English to Spanish," or a modification could indicate "The original work has been modified.";

   c. to Distribute and Publicly Perform the Work including as incorporated in Collections; and,

   d. to Distribute and Publicly Perform Adaptations.

The above rights may be exercised in all media and formats whether now known or hereafter devised. The above rights include the right to make such modifications as are technically necessary to exercise the rights in other media and formats. Subject to Section 8(f), all rights not expressly granted by Licensor are hereby reserved, including but not limited to the rights described in Section 4(e).

4. **Restrictions.** The license granted in Section 3 above is expressly made subject to and limited by the following restrictions:

a. You may Distribute or Publicly Perform the Work only under the terms of this License. You must include a copy of, or the Uniform Resource Identifier (URI) for, this License with every copy of the Work You Distribute or Publicly Perform. You may not offer or impose any terms on the Work that restrict the terms of this License or the ability of the recipient of the Work to exercise the rights granted to that recipient under the terms of the License. You may not sublicense the Work. You must keep intact all notices that refer to this License and to the disclaimer of warranties with every copy of the Work You Distribute or Publicly Perform. When You Distribute or Publicly Perform the Work, You may not impose any effective technological measures on the Work that restrict the ability of a recipient of the Work from You to exercise the rights granted to that recipient under the terms of the License. This Section 4(a) applies to the Work as incorporated in a Collection, but this does not require the Collection apart from the Work itself to be made subject to the terms of this License. If You create a Collection, upon notice from any Licensor You must, to the extent practicable, remove from the Collection any credit as required by Section 4(d), as requested. If You create an Adaptation, upon notice from any Licensor You must, to the extent practicable, remove from the Adaptation any credit as required by Section 4(d), as requested.

b. You may Distribute or Publicly Perform an Adaptation only under: (i) the terms of this License; (ii) a later version of this License with the same License Elements as this License; (iii) a Creative Commons jurisdiction license (either this or a later license version) that contains the same License Elements as this License (e.g., Attribution-NonCommercial-ShareAlike 3.0 US) ("Applicable License"). You must include a copy of, or the URI, for Applicable License with every copy of each Adaptation You Distribute or Publicly Perform. You may not offer or impose any terms on the Adaptation that restrict the terms of the Applicable License or the ability of the recipient of the Adaptation to exercise the rights granted to that recipient under the terms of the Applicable License. You must keep intact all notices that refer to the Applicable License and to the disclaimer of warranties with every copy of the Work as included in the Adaptation You Distribute or Publicly Perform. When You Distribute or Publicly Perform the Adaptation, You may not impose any effective technological measures on the Adaptation that restrict the ability of a recipient of the Adaptation from You to exercise the rights granted to that recipient under the terms of the Applicable License. This Section 4(b) applies to the Adaptation as incorporated in a Collection, but this does not require the Collection apart from the Adaptation itself to be made subject to the terms of the Applicable License.

c. You may not exercise any of the rights granted to You in Section 3 above in any manner that is primarily intended for or directed toward commercial advantage or private monetary compensation. The exchange of the Work for other copyrighted works by means of digital file-sharing or otherwise shall not be considered to be intended for or directed toward commercial advantage or private monetary compensation, provided there is no payment of any monetary compensation in connection with the exchange of copyrighted works.

d. If You Distribute, or Publicly Perform the Work or any Adaptations or Collections, You must, unless a request has been made pursuant to Section 4(a), keep intact all copyright notices for the Work and provide, reasonable to the medium or means You are utilizing: (i) the name of the Original Author (or pseudonym, if applicable) if supplied, and/or if the Original Author and/or Licensor designate another party or parties (e.g., a sponsor institute, publishing entity, journal) for attribution ("Attribution Parties") in Licensor's copyright notice, terms of service or by other reasonable means, the name of such party or parties; (ii) the title of the Work if supplied; (iii) to the extent reasonably practicable, the URI, if any, that Licensor specifies to be associated with the Work, unless such URI does not refer to the copyright notice or licensing information for the Work; and, (iv) consistent with Section 3(b), in the case of an Adaptation, a credit identifying the use of the Work in the Adaptation (e.g., "French translation of the Work by Original Author," or "Screenplay based on original Work by Original Author"). The credit required by this Section 4(d) may be implemented in any reasonable manner; provided, however, that in the case of a Adaptation or Collection, at a minimum such credit will appear, if a credit for all contributing authors of the Adaptation or Collection appears, then as part of these credits and in a manner at least as prominent as the credits for the other contributing authors. For the avoidance of doubt, You may only use the credit required by this Section for the purpose of attribution in the manner set out above and, by exercising Your rights under this License, You may not implicitly or explicitly assert or imply any connection with, sponsorship or endorsement by the Original Author, Licensor and/or Attribution Parties, as appropriate, of You or Your use of the Work, without the separate, express prior written permission of the Original Author, Licensor and/or Attribution Parties.

e. For the avoidance of doubt:

  i. **Non-waivable Compulsory License Schemes.** In those jurisdictions in which the right to collect royalties through any statutory or compulsory licensing scheme cannot be waived, the Licensor reserves the exclusive right to collect such royalties for any exercise by You of the rights granted under this License;

  ii. **Waivable Compulsory License Schemes.** In those jurisdictions in which the right to collect royalties through any statutory or compulsory licensing scheme can be waived, the Licensor reserves the exclusive right to collect such royalties for any exercise by You of the rights granted under this License if Your exercise of such rights is for a purpose or use which is otherwise than noncommercial as permitted under Section 4(c) and otherwise waives the right to collect royalties through any statutory or compulsory licensing scheme; and,

  iii. **Voluntary License Schemes.** The Licensor reserves the right to collect royalties, whether individually or, in the event that the Licensor is a member of a collecting society that administers voluntary licensing schemes, via that society, from any exercise by You of the rights granted under this License that is for a purpose or use which is otherwise than noncommercial as permitted under Section 4(c).

f. Except as otherwise agreed in writing by the Licensor or as may be otherwise permitted by applicable law, if You Reproduce, Distribute or Publicly Perform the Work either by itself or as part of any Adaptations or Collections, You must not distort, mutilate, modify or take other derogatory action in relation to the Work which would be prejudicial to the Original Author's honor or reputation. Licensor agrees that in those jurisdictions (e.g. Japan), in which any exercise of the right granted in Section 3(b) of this License (the right to make Adaptations) would be deemed to be a distortion, mutilation, modification or other derogatory action prejudicial to the Original Author's honor and reputation, the Licensor will waive or not assert, as appropriate, this Section, to the fullest extent permitted by the applicable national law, to enable You to reasonably exercise Your right under Section 3(b) of this License (right to make Adaptations) but not otherwise.

5. Representations, Warranties and Disclaimer

UNLESS OTHERWISE MUTUALLY AGREED TO BY THE PARTIES IN WRITING AND TO THE FULLEST EXTENT PERMITTED BY APPLICABLE LAW, LICENSOR OFFERS THE WORK AS-IS AND MAKES NO REPRESENTATIONS OR WARRANTIES OF ANY KIND CONCERNING THE WORK, EXPRESS, IMPLIED, STATUTORY OR OTHERWISE, INCLUDING, WITHOUT LIMITATION, WARRANTIES OF TITLE, MERCHANTABILITY, FITNESS FOR A PARTICULAR PURPOSE, NONINFRINGEMENT, OR THE ABSENCE OF LATENT OR OTHER DEFECTS, ACCURACY, OR THE PRESENCE OF ABSENCE OF ERRORS, WHETHER OR NOT DISCOVERABLE. SOME JURISDICTIONS DO NOT ALLOW THE EXCLUSION OF IMPLIED WARRANTIES, SO THIS EXCLUSION MAY NOT APPLY TO YOU.

6. Limitation on Liability. EXCEPT TO THE EXTENT REQUIRED BY APPLICABLE LAW, IN NO EVENT WILL LICENSOR BE LIABLE TO YOU ON ANY LEGAL THEORY FOR ANY SPECIAL, INCIDENTAL, CONSEQUENTIAL, PUNITIVE OR EXEMPLARY DAMAGES ARISING OUT OF THIS LICENSE OR THE USE OF THE WORK, EVEN IF LICENSOR HAS BEEN ADVISED OF THE POSSIBILITY OF SUCH DAMAGES.

7. Termination

a. This License and the rights granted hereunder will terminate automatically upon any breach by You of the terms of this License. Individuals or entities who have received Adaptations or Collections from You under this License, however, will not have their licenses terminated provided such individuals or entities remain in full compliance with those licenses. Sections 1, 2, 5, 6, 7, and 8 will survive any termination of this License.

b. Subject to the above terms and conditions, the license granted here is perpetual (for the duration of the applicable copyright in the Work). Notwithstanding the above, Licensor reserves the right to release the Work under different license terms or to stop distributing the Work at any time; provided, however that any such election will not serve to withdraw this License (or any other license that has been, or is required to be, granted under the terms of this License), and this License will continue in full force and effect unless terminated as stated above.

8. **Miscellaneous**

    a. Each time You Distribute or Publicly Perform the Work or a Collection, the Licensor offers to the recipient a license to the Work on the same terms and conditions as the license granted to You under this License.

    b. Each time You Distribute or Publicly Perform an Adaptation, Licensor offers to the recipient a license to the original Work on the same terms and conditions as the license granted to You under this License.

    c. If any provision of this License is invalid or unenforceable under applicable law, it shall not affect the validity or enforceability of the remainder of the terms of this License, and without further action by the parties to this agreement, such provision shall be reformed to the minimum extent necessary to make such provision valid and enforceable.

    d. No term or provision of this License shall be deemed waived and no breach consented to unless such waiver or consent shall be in writing and signed by the party to be charged with such waiver or consent.

    e. This License constitutes the entire agreement between the parties with respect to the Work licensed here. There are no understandings, agreements or representations with respect to the Work not specified here. Licensor shall not be bound by any additional provisions that may appear in any communication from You. This License may not be modified without the mutual written agreement of the Licensor and You.

    f. The rights granted under, and the subject matter referenced, in this License were drafted utilizing the terminology of the Berne Convention for the Protection of Literary and Artistic Works (as amended on September 28, 1979), the Rome Convention of 1961, the WIPO Copyright Treaty of 1996, the WIPO Performances and Phonograms Treaty of 1996 and the Universal Copyright Convention (as revised on July 24, 1971). These rights and subject matter take effect in the relevant jurisdiction in which the License terms are sought to be enforced according to the corresponding provisions of the implementation of those treaty provisions in the applicable national law. If the standard suite of rights granted under applicable copyright law includes additional rights not granted under this License, such additional rights are deemed to be included in the License; this License is not intended to restrict the license of any rights under applicable law.

Creative Commons Notice

Creative Commons is not a party to this License, and makes no warranty whatsoever in connection with the Work. Creative Commons will not be liable to You or any party on any legal theory for any damages whatsoever, including without limitation any general, special, incidental or consequential damages arising in connection to this license. Notwithstanding the foregoing two (2) sentences, if Creative Commons has expressly identified itself as the Licensor hereunder, it shall have all rights and obligations of Licensor.

Except for the limited purpose of indicating to the public that the Work is licensed under the CCPL, Creative Commons does not authorize the use by either party of the trademark "Creative Commons" or any related trademark or logo of Creative Commons without the prior written consent of Creative Commons. Any permitted use will be in compliance with Creative Commons' then-current trademark usage guidelines, as may be published on its website or otherwise made available upon request from time to time. For the avoidance of doubt, this trademark restriction does not form part of this License.

Creative Commons may be contacted at `http://creativecommons.org/`.

Index

Numbers and Symbols

[0-9], 20
-3 option, 132
* (asterisk), 20, 61
\ (backslash), 25
^ (caret), 147, 149
! (exclamation point), 45
| (pipe), 195
? (question mark), 20
~ (tilde), 20, 147

A

[abc], 20
access, read-only, unauthenticated, 95–96
access control, with Gitosis, 91–95
access control list (ACL), 195–197
access_path, 197
active contributor size, 110
add command, 18, 19, 150, 153, 230
--add option, 226
aliases, 44–45
am command, 131–133, 191
--amend option, 32–33
ancestry references, 147
annotated tags, 39, 141, 234
-a option, 24
apply command, 130
archive command, 141
asterisk (*), 20, 61
attributes, 184–190
  binary files, 184–186
  exporting repository, 189–190
  keyword expansion, 186–189
  merge strategies, 190
authentication, generating SSH public key, 85–86
author, 29
--author option, 30
authorization, 86–87
authorized_keys method, 86–87
auto-completion, 43–44
auto gc command, 244

B

backslash (\), 25
--bare option, 83
bare repository, 79, 84

--base-path option, 95
benevolent dictator, 109
binary files, 184–186
  diffing, 184–186
  identifying, 184
binary search, 163–164
bisect command, 163–164
bisect start command, 164
BitKeeper, 5
blame command, 162
blobs, 226
branch command, 48, 60, 233
branches/branching
  basic, 53–56
  checking out remote, 133
  creating, 48
  creating, from stash, 156
  deleting, 61
  hotfix, 55
  issues, 208–209
  long-running, 63
  management of, 60–61
  merge conflicts, 58–60
  merging, 57–70
  overview, 47–52
  proposed, 63
  rebasing, 70–76
  remote, 64–65, 68–69
  sharing, 68–69
  specifying multiple points, 149
  Subversion, 209–210
  switching, 50–52
  topic, 63–64, 130, 137, 139–140
  tracking, 69
  workflows, 61–64
branches directory, 224
branch references, 145
-b switch, git checkout command, 53
build numbers, generating, 141

C

--cached option, 25
--cacheinfo option, 226
cat-file command, 225
Centralized Version Control Systems (CVCSs), 3, 107
centralized workflows, 107–108

■D

■E

You Need the Companion eBook

Your purchase of this book entitles you to buy the companion PDF-version eBook for only $10. Take the weightless companion with you anywhere.

We believe this Apress title will prove so indispensable that you'll want to carry it with you everywhere, which is why we are offering the companion eBook (in PDF format) for $10 to customers who purchase this book now. Convenient and fully searchable, the PDF version of any content-rich, page-heavy Apress book makes a valuable addition to your programming library. You can easily find and copy code—or perform examples by quickly toggling between instructions and the application. Even simultaneously tackling a donut, diet soda, and complex code becomes simplified with hands-free eBooks!

Once you purchase your book, getting the $10 companion eBook is simple:

➊ Visit **www.apress.com/promo/tendollars/**.

➋ Complete a basic registration form to receive a randomly generated question about this title.

➌ Answer the question correctly in 60 seconds, and you will receive a promotional code to redeem for the $10.00 eBook.

THE EXPERT'S VOICE™

2855 TELEGRAPH AVENUE │ SUITE 600 │ BERKELEY, CA 94705

Offer valid through 2/10.